A Marxist Education

A Marxist Education

Learning to Change the World

Wayne Au

Haymarket Books
Chicago, Illinois

Published in 2018 by
Haymarket Books
P.O. Box 180165
Chicago, IL 60618
773-583-7884
www.haymarketbooks.org
info@haymarketbooks.org

ISBN: 978-1-60846-905-5

Trade distribution:
In the US, Consortium Book Sales and Distribution, www.cbsd.com
In Canada, Publishers Group Canada, www.pgcbooks.ca
In the UK, Turnaround Publisher Services, www.turnaround-uk.com
All other countries, Ingram Publisher Services International, IPS_Intlsales@ingramcontent.com

This book was published with the generous support of Lannan Foundation and Wallace Action Fund.

Cover design by Jana Vuković.

Printed in Canada by union labor.

Library of Congress Cataloging-in-Publication data is available.

10 9 8 7 6 5 4 3 2 1

Table of Contents

Chapter 1

I Am My Relations

Becoming a Marxist Educator

I have been scared to write this book, for a long time and for a lot of reasons. Part of my fear comes from my understanding of US history, and that here in the heart of the empire and in one of the centers of global neoliberalism, capitalist ideology and economics reign supreme. The powerful have worked hard through textbooks and the media to construct a commonsense understanding that capitalism is a normal, if not progressive, manifestation of natural human relations—an inevitable outcome of human evolution. For those of us living in the United States, this hegemonic, pro-capitalist common sense is built on a constructed historical memory that is at once anti-communist, anti-socialist, and anti-Marxist—a fictive national narrative that both individual freedom and societal equality can be attained through self-interested competition, while completely disregarding structural and material inequalities.

The 2016 election of Donald Trump as president of the United States has also heightened fears of right-wing attacks. The mass hysteria of the "Red Scare" and McCarthyism of the 1950s that once felt so far off is now suddenly and intimately close to us again as the new American proto-fascists rise to power, as we face leftist professor watch lists, death threats made against socialist professors, talk of imprisonment for flag burning, proposals for Muslim registries and incarceration camps, threats to immigrants, attacks on the rights of women and the LGBTQ community, and promises to dismantle the public sector in the name of the free market. The white nationalists in power and the ruling class that is supporting them are firmly drawing the definition of what is "American" and entrenching whiteness, maleness, Christianity, heterosexuality, and free market capitalism as the only acceptable currency of the land, all else be bankrupt or be damned.

My fears are also grounded in my own awareness of profound political misunderstandings of Marxism by those around me. I work a lot with liberal and progressive activists in education organizing, as well as in my professional capacity as an education professor. Together we have fought back against various free market educational reforms, from high-stakes testing and standards, to charter schools, to private school vouchers, to school closings, to corporate curriculum, to mayoral control of school districts, to public school (de) funding. There is an angst among these allies. They feel an alienation from a system of education that so clearly does not meet their children's or their communities' needs, and they feel the loss of power and of democratic governance that comes from neoliberal models of deregulation and market competition.

However, because of the pervasiveness of anti-communist, anti-socialist, and anti-Marxist common sense in the United States, many of these allies are fearful of crossing a threshold of understanding that our critiques of these reforms are, fundamentally, deeply rooted critiques of capitalism and its shaping of our entire system of public education. It sometimes seems that, for these allies, even though they see and acknowledge all of the inequalities around us, critiquing capitalism is just too far beyond their horizons of "acceptable" or feasible options within the struggle for educational justice. This fear (and denial) then preempts any discussion of how, if we truly intend to create a system of education built on the fundaments of justice and equality, we must attack and overthrow the very system that our schools are built on, one that is predicated on and requires injustice and inequality. These liberal and progressive allies have not read, or even entertained reaching for, Marx and Marxist critiques of capitalism, leaving ample room for misunderstandings, misconstructions, and mistrust of Marxism.

As I discuss later in this chapter, I grew up with a communist father with connections to some cadre organizations.[1] This has meant that I am also fearfully aware of the Left's history and practice of cannibalizing itself, posturing about who is the most radical, and rupturing under harsh critique. While I strongly believe in struggle—and I mean difficult struggle over political differences and understandings (the kind of struggle I learned about from my father)—I have seen enough allies and comrades torn down to know that almost anything I write within the broad framework of "Marxist analysis" will inevitably come under attack from both the Right and the Left. For this reason there are a lot of topics that I purposefully don't expound upon or take up here. There are tomes written on various left ideological fights and political lines, and my strategy has always been to start with Marx and dialectical materialism, letting my analysis extend from that as a base, and staying above the fray.

My trepidation to write this book extends, in part, from my position in the academy. If Marxism is not particularly popular among US academics these days (although internationally, critical, Marxist perspectives do not earn the immediate shock and repulsion that they do in the United States), this is certainly the case within educational scholarship. Mostly, work explicitly announcing itself as Marxist isn't taken seriously and is seen as too fringe to be legitimate. I remember vividly how one of my faculty advisors at the University of Wisconsin–Madison tried to warn me against openly writing in the introduction to my book on high-stakes standardized testing, *Unequal by Design*, that my analysis was guided by Marxism.[2] I kept the radical confession in the text, and I think hardly anyone noticed; frankly, you would have to be willfully ignorant not to read Marx in that book. However, my disappointment in that particular faculty advisor—as well as some of my self-doubts about when, where, and how I should "come out" as a Marxist—clearly still linger. That was just one instance, but there are countless others where, in the academy, being a Marxist is too far out of the bounds of scholarly legitimacy for liberal and progressive professors (let alone the conservatives) to handle. So I've been very strategic about how I position myself within educational scholarship, in order to maintain my legitimacy as a "real" and "serious" educational scholar without sacrificing my political integrity. Conversely, I haven't purposefully hidden the Marxist foundations of my research, and anyone who is paying attention should know their importance to my politics, writing, and speaking.

But fear is not the only emotion I've encountered in writing this book. Importantly, I have also felt hope and uplift. As I write, Donald Trump has taken over as the president of the United States. White supremacist-nationalism is rising, with violent attacks and public hate speech increasing seemingly every day. Anti-LGBTQ laws are being pushed with new vigor in some states. The attacks on women's bodies and their right to choose have been ratcheted up. Trump has repeatedly tried to ban the entry of immigrants and refugees from countries that are predominantly Muslim. Talk of building a wall between the United States and Mexico has resurfaced with new vigor. Discussion of spreading conservative Christian values through public school vouchers are being taken more seriously in the halls of the White House. Trump has repealed the Deferred Action for Childhood Arrivals (DACA) program that protected so many of our immigrant students and their parents. Victories stalling the Dakota Access Pipeline have proven to be fleeting, as the new administration renews its commitment to supporting Big Oil. Laws are being proposed to make protesters liable for the costs of the anti-protest police forces and to make resisting arrest a hate crime against the police—all in direct response to mass actions taken by organizations like #DisruptJ20, the powerful 2017 Womxn's marches against the Trump presidency, the #NoDAPL resistance, and the #BlackLivesMatter protests of the last several years. These dire times have sparked an upsurge in activism and protest that is heartening and full of revolutionary potential, and I think a new generation of teachers could build upon this radical momentum by helping their students explore and consider Marxist and socialist ideas. This fact speaks to why I am writing a book on Marxism and educational theory right now.

Suffice it to say, these are intensely political times. Both the present and the future seem very uncertain, and while we face dread and despair on a day-to-day basis, we also reside in a moment of great possibility. For all the limitations of their liberal rhetoric and racial homogeneity, together the Womxn's marches represented the largest single protest in the history of the United States. For many, these marches—which may have totaled more than three million people—were their first-ever protest, and such first steps are critical to the development of critical consciousness and for building a mass movement.[3] Similarly, in response to several people being detained in airports due to Trump's executive order banning immigrants and refugees from certain countries, large protests—with thousands of people each—developed almost spontaneously at major airports around the United States where people affected by the ban were being detained. Likewise, more protests and marches happened around the country the following day, and tens of thousands in major cities came out in support of immigrant and refugee rights—and this is on top of the #BlackLivesMatter and Occupy protest movements that emerged under the Obama administration. One thing is clear: new people are being activated, and this is something we should all be celebrating.

The contradictions presented by this whole—tumult, violence, and uncertainty, along with the possibility bred by a growing resistance—are typical of times of great change, and in times like these I personally feel the need to turn to theory to help me better understand the material realities that people, myself included, are experiencing. I want to make sense of things, and Marxist theory, in conjunction with ongoing practice, helps me do this. Marxist theory and analysis always seemed to me to peel back outer appearances, while revealing relations, power, and mechanisms of change that were always lurking underneath. Marxist theory shaped who I was as a public high school teacher and burgeoning education activist, and it shaped who I became as a professor, public intellectual, and radical scholar-activist. Even if I don't always say it explicitly, Marxism is present in all my analysis of education politics, policy, and practice—whether in academic articles, books, blog posts, or editorials. So, in these breathtaking times, when it feels like there is a new atrocity committed and a new protest to attend almost every day, *A Marxist Education* is a part of my commitment to understanding the politics of education in this world: it is an argument that Marxist theory helps us understand not only the processes of teaching and learning, but also the politics of curriculum, the relationship between schools and capitalist production, and the building of critical consciousness toward resistance and social justice.

Marxist theory is particularly important in this historical moment. The ravages and contradictions of capitalism are all too clear. The capitalist class is extracting wealth from everywhere and everything possible, and in the process they are killing the planet and exploiting labor around the world. Capitalism is so clearly unsustainable, relative to humanity and nature, that we have to do something different, and urgently. And here is the thing: after all these years, Marx and Marxism still provide the sharpest analysis of how capitalism functions at its most fundamental levels of production, profit, and exploitation. No, Marxism is not perfect; and yes, there are critiques, complications, and extensions to be made (see chapter 2, "The Heart of Marxism"). However, we still have not seen an analysis of capitalism that moves, fundamentally, past the depth of what Marx produced. So, if we are interested in understanding capitalism with the intent of creating an economic and social system in the interests of all peoples and the world itself, then Marx and Marxism are good places to start. And, speaking honestly, the world can't wait.

My Own Marxist Education

This book is not just a book about Marxist educational theory. It is also an expression of my development as a Marxist, critical educator. What follows is a narrative introduction that traces some of my own personal development as a political being and as a Marxist. I start with this narrative not out of an ego-driven self-importance, but because it captures much of what this book aims to be: a discussion of the relationship between Marxism, schools, teaching, and learning. Indeed, my own journey and development as a Marxist educator in some ways reflects the journey of this book, and the ideas and concepts I have struggled with across my life thus far ended up as focuses for various chapters here. In this regard I think of this introductory chapter as beginning some conceptual spirals that are developed and explained in detail later in the book. For instance, in this introductory chapter, I will discuss some aspects of Marxist dialectical materialism, but I will do so only briefly in the context of the narrative. It is not until chapter 2 that I spend significant time delving into dialectical materialism. The same can be said of concepts like neo-Marxism or critical consciousness, which are discussed in depth in chapters 3 and 5, respectively.

This reflective narrative also serves to situate me as an author, writer, and thinker in a way that speaks to the positionality of my cultural and political identity. It is critical to lay these things bare because nothing we do is neutral or nonpartisan, and this is especially true when it comes to both educational research and Marxist theory. Indeed, I am a firm believer in what Marxist-feminist theorists Nancy Hartsock and Sandra Harding both refer to as "strong objectivity"—that at every turn, every knowledge project is power laden; that there is no neutral researcher, commentator, or observer, nor value-free production or consumption of knowledge.[4] Rather, for both Hartsock and Harding, if we are going to be honest, transparent, and materialist in our research about the world, we need to embrace our social locations, our positionality, and lay that bare for our audiences to see as part and parcel of our research and theorizing. What follows situates me and who I am within the context of *A Marxist Education.*

My Dad, the Communist

For as long as I can remember, my dad has been a communist. What did that mean for me? Well, it meant a childhood of conversations (and sometimes lectures) about women's oppression and my job as a male to fight against that oppression. It meant learning about US war and imperialism around the world and understanding that our government was basically bombing kids *just like me* somewhere in Asia or Africa or the Middle East. It meant learning about police brutality and, from a very early age, also learning that the police could not be trusted because, as agents of the state, they will come after you or your parents or someone you know, since that is their job. Having a communist father also meant a life of secrets because *you can't tell anyone* that you have a communist father—not your friends, not your neighbors, and certainly not your teachers. It also meant sticking out among classmates for not standing and reciting the Pledge of Allegiance to the American flag, and navigating life as an atheist in Christian America.

Having a communist father meant participating in many a May Day rally or march, both in Seattle and in the San Francisco Bay Area of my youth. One of those early memories includes a decision by marchers to swarm through the Nordstrom's clothing store in downtown Seattle. As we wove our way between the clothing racks and perfume counters, I distinctly remember looking around and wondering to myself, "You mean we can just do this and not get into trouble?" Quickly followed by the realization, "Wow. When people are together like this, we're hard to stop." One summer in the 1980s when I stayed with my father (my folks had divorced by then) was during the height of the anti–South African apartheid divestment movement at UC Berkeley. My teenage sister, who was also very politically involved at that point, had been organizing and agitating with student and community activists who had symbolically constructed a shantytown to occupy the campus square (facing police brutality in the process). Telegraph Avenue, a street that runs almost directly into the campus square, was also a site of protest, and as part of an anti-apartheid march and rally I recall gleefully tossing toilet paper rolls through the signs and trees along the street. Having a communist father meant that there were political meetings at our house and at the houses of others, and the "war stories" of fighting with the cops at a protest here, or fighting the fascists on the shipyard docks while trying to organize workers there. It also meant growing with a tension between being "political" and just being a kid, engaged in pop culture and still figuring himself out.

Having a communist father did not necessarily guarantee that I'd turn out to be the radical that I am (my older brother, for instance, took another path entirely after a radical youth), but it did introduce me to a new worldview and open some avenues of analysis. These became important in my path as a Marxist educator. Even though at the time I could not tie my childhood experiences to a specific intellectual or political tradition (I certainly didn't consciously have those traditions in mind as I tossed toilet paper along Telegraph Avenue), these experiences and stories oriented me toward justice, and they taught me that people got together to fight against that injustice. My early experiences in protests, in particular, allowed me to glimpse moments of what it meant to *feel free* in some sense. I may not have understood what exactly I was feeling free from, but I definitely felt it. And it was something I came to feel again multiple times at protests later in my life.

Additionally, despite what I see as a lack of self-interrogation of his own racial identity, my dad did contribute to my own identity development in some key ways. Whether through the simplicity of food, his tai chi practice, or stories about our family history (Chinese American via Hawai'i as early as the 1880s, as well as my Chinese grandfather's own communism), I was learning about what it meant to be mixed, to be a part of the Asian American and Chinese diaspora, and what differentiated me from the predominantly white family members and non-Asian communities among whom I was living during my formative pre- and early adolescent years.

Identity, Racism, and a Hip Hop Education

Some time after my parents divorced, my mother remarried and, along with my brother and sister, we moved to my mom's hometown of Vernon, Connecticut, to be closer to her aging parents. Vernon is a predominantly white suburb of Hartford, and moving there proved crucial to my political development in two ways. First, it was there in Vernon that I viscerally experienced blatant racism on a completely different scale than I had in my childhood in Seattle. Second, in part because I was pushing back against whiteness there, and in part due to our proximity to New York City, it was during this time in my life that I found hip hop.

Moving to Vernon in the fourth grade was a shock: I had gone from a very diverse, working-class urban community in West Seattle to a super-white, generally affluent suburban community in Connecticut. Living in Vernon shaped my racial-political identity in some very important ways. It taught me, for instance, that even though I was "mixed" Chinese and white, in lily-white Vernon my black hair and features were still a dead giveaway to my peers. The first day on the bus to elementary school, as soon as I got on, some of the older white kids in back remarked out loud, "Look at that chink." My racist aunt had a black cat she named Sambo. My racist uncle used to complain when I would bring my Black friends from school over to swim or hang out at their house. My white friend had a Puerto Rican cousin, and in his family this cousin was regularly called a "pecan" or a "Rican dude." There was plenty of benevolent whiteness there as well. For instance, I remember one conversation with my white grandfather, a very sweet man who was relatively wealthy, where he said he wanted me to join the Freemasons like he had. As soon as he suggested it, however, he paused for a moment—clearly thinking to himself—and followed up by saying, "I think they are an international organization now." At that moment it was clear to me that he was making a racial consideration about whether or not I could even be a Freemason (for the record, I am not). In these ways, Vernon, Connecticut, introduced me to a whole vernacular of racism I hadn't heard articulated before.

Various forms of racist "othering" also happened in Vernon as well. I was always used as an example by white teachers when it came to talking about family roots, since I had both Hawai'i and China in my mix. My name was constantly mispronounced by teachers too: I knew I was first or second on the class list on the first day of school when the teacher would look at their roster, pause, stumble a little, and then immediately say, "I know I'm going to mispronounce some of these . . . so please forgive me." I ate Chinese snacks my friends thought were "weird," and I knew how to make fried rice. I had a Chinese popo and a white grandmother. I had a two-part Chinese middle name of which no one could make sense—"Why do you have four initials in your name?" I was exotic, experiencing the kind of "racist love" reserved for "Orientals" and Asian Americans.[5] In these big and small ways, the whiteness of Vernon, Connecticut, taught me about aggressively hateful racism, *and* it taught me about the "kinder" racism reserved for the exoticized other. Both are violent, and both shaped my racial-political identity growing up. Thankfully, hip hop saved me.

In retrospect, my embrace of hip hop music and culture was in part a rejection of my new white suburban surroundings (and the overbearing whiteness that came with it) and in part a romantic clinging to the urban-ness of my old neighborhood back in West Seattle. In Connecticut I attended a large, comprehensive middle school that had two to three African American students out of several hundred students total, and, not counting myself or my siblings, typically had no Asian American students at all (and no Latinx or Native American kids either). It makes perfect sense to me now that I became close friends with several of the African American kids at school. They were more like the kids I knew back home in a diverse working-class neighborhood in West Seattle, and one of our shared loves was hip hop music and the growing b-boy (aka breakdance) and graffiti scenes, which at that moment had entered pop culture and were being mass-marketed for the first time.[6] In Connecticut I found out I could stay up late on the weekend nights fine-tuning my boom box radio to catch and record New York City deejays cutting up and mixing hip hop records of the early to mid-1980s. My identification with hip hop culture and Blackness became an important political and racial rudder as I navigated Vernon's cultural politics of overwhelming whiteness, especially since I could not find much of a Chinese American cultural home there.

After middle school, my mom and I moved back to Seattle where I attended Garfield High School—located in Seattle's historically (but now gentrified) African American community, once home of Quincy Jones, Jimi Hendrix, and the Seattle chapter of the Black Panther Party. Always negotiating a fluid and messy mix of whiteness, being Chinese American, identifying with hip hop culture (and by extension, some amount of Blackness), and attending Seattle's historically Black high school, I continued to make my own political-cultural way. This was a highly politicized moment in hip hop,[7] and the music of Public Enemy, Boogie Down Productions, N.W.A., and Queen Latifah offered an education for me—one that continued into my college years through emcees like Paris, the Poor Righteous Teachers, and Ice Cube.

At Garfield High School I engaged my friends and peers on issues of culture and race politics through hip hop music. I also was lucky enough to stumble upon two courses that took up an African and African American–centric orientation to curriculum: a course on the Harlem Renaissance and a world history course, both taught by Mr. Davis, who purposefully offered these classes with a mission to try and decolonize the thinking of his Black students and help them recover from the deleterious effects of institutional racism and white supremacy. Those classes were critical to my political and intellectual development. I was one of only two non–African American students in each class, and certainly the only Asian American. Through Mr. Davis's curriculum we entered into incredibly important conversations and arguments about history, culture, race, and racism, and through those conversations and arguments we also developed meaningful relationships with each other.[8]

Thinking back on that time, those courses served three important purposes for me. First, it was a time where I existed in an educational space that was decidedly Black, full of a wide range of African American students expressing diverse perspectives on Black experiences and Black culture in Seattle, in education, and in the world. Second, that space allowed me to hone and shape my own political analysis. I brought my own then-unnamed Marxism as well as my own scrambled identity, and we politically sharpened each other through conversation and argument. Third, by that time in high school I had already decided that I wanted to be a teacher, and Mr. Davis's class taught me about how a powerful curriculum can make a difference in the consciousness of students. There were, of course, other important influences during these formative years. My communist father was still in the mix, supporting my love for science and science fiction by giving me books by radical evolutionary biologist Stephen Jay Gould and political science fiction author Ursula K. Le Guin. However, when thinking about my high school experiences, Mr. Davis's classes loom large in my mind's eye.

College Politics

As I looked to attending college, I was drawn to more "alternative" universities that didn't rely on letter grades and instead focused on narrative evaluations for assessment. I ended up at the University of California, Santa Cruz, for the 1990–1991 academic year, eventually settling on an American Studies major, because I was drawn to the history courses and my first-year core course that focused on politics and culture in the United States. There, I had the chance to view the film *Who Killed Vincent Chin?*,[9] which explores the premeditated murder of Vincent Chin by two white auto workers in Detroit, who beat Chin to death with a baseball bat out of racist rage produced by the rise of Japanese car companies and the fall of the US automotive industry. Both of the killers were found not guilty, and this film left an indelible mark on my understanding of race, racism, and Asian Americans in the United States. In particular it gave me a visceral understanding of the ways that violent racism and white supremacy can be wielded against Asian Americans, especially because I left the film angry and thinking, "That could have been me that was killed." The first US war against Iraq began in January of 1991, which also coincided with my first year at UC Santa Cruz. There I joined other students in a large protest march of over ten thousand students that wound its way down the hill, through the city of Santa Cruz, and eventually shut down Highway 17 for a number of hours. Soon after, I traveled to my father's house in Oakland to take part in a massive rally and march of one hundred thousand protesters through the streets of San Francisco (not knowing that I would return about ten years later for an even larger protest of Gulf War II).

I eventually transferred to The Evergreen State College (TESC) in Olympia, Washington, just over an hour's drive south of my hometown, Seattle.[10] Sparked by my viewing of *Who Killed Vincent Chin?* as well the Asian American history I had learned at UC Santa Cruz, at Evergreen I found the space to work through much of my identity development as someone racially and culturally both Chinese and white, who identified with hip hop culture and radical politics.[11] TESC also gave me time to work on my political identity. I was able to take courses in Marxist theory, US and world history, and cultural politics. I was afforded the flexibility to study independently, both to prepare to become a social studies teacher and to spend time in Hawai'i living with my Chinese family. The Los Angeles rebellion after the 1993 LAPD beating of Rodney King took place while I was at TESC, as did the national uproar over Supreme Court Justice Clarence Thomas's sexual harassment of Anita Hill.

These national incidents and conversations only heightened my political awareness, feeding the development of my analysis of race, class, gender, and sexuality.

Being at TESC during this time also profoundly influenced my understanding of race and education, particularly relative to indigenous politics. The year 1992 was the five-hundred-year anniversary of Christopher Columbus's first genocidal contact with the indigenous peoples of the Americas. As such there was an explosion of art and political work being done around issues of Native sovereignty, colonization, and indigenous resistance. It was at this point that I had my first encounter with Rethinking Schools, specifically teacher, editor, and author Bill Bigelow, who was touring the country doing workshops on the portrayal of Columbus in kids' books and the rethinking of how this important history might be taught from a Native point of view.[12] My ongoing understanding of indigenous issues and sovereignty also continued to grow while I was in Hawai'i studying my family's history. My trip to the islands coincided with the one-hundred-year anniversary of the illegal overthrow of the Hawaiian kingdom by a cabal of European colonizers, and I was mentored by one of the leading Native Hawaiian sovereignty activists of the time, Haunani-Kay Trask.[13]

My undergraduate years at TESC were particularly critical to my intellectual development. This period, the early 1990s, was a pivotal time in the United States. It was the end of the Cold War, the time of the escalation of neoliberal capitalism as the be-all and end-all of human history, and a period that witnessed the rightward lurch of the Democrats. All of this set the stage for the growth of a virulent anti-Marxism in the academy, which was accompanied by the rise of postmodern identity politics—a set of politics that foregrounds the subject positions of our identities as central to our ways of knowing and understanding reality. These identity politics contributed very positively to my own development in making sense of my mixed-ness, being from a radical family, my identification with hip hop culture (and, to a lesser extent, Black culture—at this point I was a deejay on the college radio station, making mixtapes and developing ties to the hip hop community in Seattle), and understanding myself as Asian American and a part of the Asian diaspora. While all of this was important to me, I was simultaneously pushing back on postmodern identity politics as well. I was starting to identify more strongly as a Marxist, partly through my ongoing discussions with my communist father and partly through my own exploration of Marxism relative to the clearly systemic racial, gender, and class inequalities produced by capitalism, facilitated through courses in Marxist theory and political economy at Evergreen.

Between ongoing discussions with my father, campus activism, personal study, and coursework, I was developing an understanding of dialectical materialism, which I grew to know as the core of Marxist theory and practice; it was here that my concerns with postmodernism arose. I felt like I understood postmodernism's focus on the subjectivity of reality, particularly in response to the white, Western, capitalist patriarchy that, through historical control of the sciences and institutions of education, had laid claim to defining reality for so long. However, I also had concerns about how, even though in some ways the approach validated the perspectives and experiences of marginalized groups—particularly women and people of color—a reliance on the subjectivity of individual experience ultimately left us nowhere, because reality was up to the individual to define. On that basis, it was clear to me that postmodern subjectivity couldn't actually challenge the concrete, material realities that existed for the masses of the world, because for postmodernists there was no material reality, only each individual's perception of the world.[14] Marxist dialectical materialism allowed (and allows) me to split the difference, so to speak, because it enables me, on the one hand, to reject power-laden constructions of truth and objectivity that I saw supporting patriarchy, white supremacy, and capitalist exploitation, and on the other, to reject postmodern overreliance on an individual's perception and experience of constructed reality. As a materialist I believe that a world does indeed exist "objectively" outside of our immediate, individual perceptions and experiences, and that this world could be changed to improve our conditions. My dialectics also takes the world to consist of human relations such that we shape and are shaped by the objectively existing reality—implying that all of our identities are articulations of social relations and differences in power.

One book I picked up later during graduate school that helped me understand this period of the 1990s and the rise of subjective idealism better was Fredric Jameson's *Postmodernism, or, The Cultural Logic of Late Capitalism*.[15] Jameson's text helped me make a connection that I couldn't see and didn't understand while I was in the midst of this rise of postmodernist theory and philosophy. The 1980s and 1990s saw the ascent of neoliberalism as a major force in social and economic policy. Neoliberalism is constructed upon the idea of the invisible hand of the free market as the guide to everything social and economic. In this model deregulation is key, unions and taxation are anathema, the state should shrink and focus on the maintenance of property, law, and military, "public" is to be shunned in favor of "private," and people increasingly see themselves as individuals competing with each other in the marketplace of society.[16] In simpler terms, neoliberalism signaled the advent of a deeply individualistic "consumer society" in mainstream consciousness. What Jameson helped me understand is that postmodern subjective idealism is philosophically and epistemologically aligned with neoliberalism in a very fundamental way: in the same sense that postmodern subjectivity posits that the world is made up of individually competing realities (again, as a reasonable pushback against the racist, sexist, and colonial norms associated with positivism), neoliberalism posits an atomized worldview of individuals and individual products competing with each other to define marketplace reality. As Jameson essentially argues, the individual subjectivity of postmodernism is a logical and cultural parallel to the market subjectivity of late-stage capitalism.

Becoming a Radical Teacher

But I didn't come upon Jameson until I was working on my PhD. Back at The Evergreen State College, several years earlier as both an undergraduate and a master's student, I decided to work toward becoming a public school teacher. As an undergraduate I began working with the Upward Bound program, which provided support for students who were low income and the first generation in their families to attend college. Upward Bound at Evergreen taught me about the material reality of settler colonialism and Native culture, and it only reinforced my desire to teach. Through the program, I visited indigenous kids in their homes on various Native reservations around the South Puget Sound region. In the process, I saw levels of poverty that I didn't know could exist in the United States, and I learned about Pacific Northwest Native cultures in some very deep ways. I also worked with African American, Latinx, white, and Native students from urban schools and communities in Tacoma, Washington. Some of our students were on the edge of gang life. Some had experienced abuse in their homes. Some were dealing with drugs either personally or in their families. All of them were poor, and all of them were sharp as nails. I loved working with those students and their families and still miss them today. They gave me an education on the concrete realities for so many in this country, as well as one of the reasons it is mportant to teach and change lives—and change society by extension.

After graduating from Evergreen with my bachelor's degree, I immediately entered the Master in Teaching (MiT) program to work toward my social studies and language arts teaching credential. The Evergreen MiT program was also pivotal in my political and intellectual development. For one, the Evergreen MiT program was constructed around the same principles of interdisciplinarity, graduate seminars, and team teaching that guided its undergraduate offerings. This meant that they attempted to model some aspects of critical pedagogy in form and structure, providing a valuable lesson for me to think about my own teaching in the future: make it participatory, visionary, and committed to a pedagogical politics of justice.

The second way that the MiT program profoundly influenced my political and intellectual development as a critical educator was that it introduced me to *Pedagogy of the Oppressed*, which became my introduction to Freire and critical, liberatory pedagogy.[17] I remember reading the book, and I remember struggling with his prose style, abstractness, and overall approach. While I certainly understood some of *Pedagogy of the Oppressed* at the time, and I was immediately drawn to the politics of Freire's ideas, I also had a hard time reconciling his theoretical density with my developing practice as a teacher. Ultimately I didn't feel like I *really* understood Freire until later, when I studied his work in depth for my PhD at the University of Wisconsin–Madison. Regardless, his ideas have shaped my thinking, writing, and practice ever since.

The third way that the Evergreen MiT program shaped me politically and intellectually is that it allowed me to take advantage of two important student teaching opportunities. One was the chance to student-teach out of state with nationally known social justice educator, author, and long-time editor at Rethinking Schools, Linda Christensen. Linda and her husband, Bill Bigelow, were both teachers in Portland, Oregon, the hometown of my spouse Mira Shimabukuro. Mira had been one of Linda's and Bill's star students at Jefferson High School, and her connection to them allowed me to spend time student-teaching under Linda's masterful watch. There, I worked with Linda on teaching about the politics of language, and I felt lucky to be in that space as I developed my master's project—which turned out to be a curriculum for teaching critically about the racial, cultural, political, and historical issues surrounding Hawai'i. There, I also started to cement my relationship with Rethinking Schools, as I had both Linda and Bill to mentor me in curriculum development and in my writing about practice. My first article for *Rethinking Schools* magazine, on teaching critically about Hawai'i, grew directly out of that mentorship.[18]

My other student teaching opportunity was with a Seattle Public Schools program for dropouts/pushouts called Middle College High School at Seattle Central Community College.[19] Being a student teacher there felt like an extension of my work with Upward Bound students, and it was a direct application of the Freirian ways of understanding the relationship between education and liberation that I had been reading about. Middle College was guided by a very politicized curriculum, built upon the specific vision that these students, most of whom had been alienated from or tossed out of the regular school system for a variety of reasons, could become more critically conscious agents in their own lives. Within this vision, books like Zinn's *A People's History of the United States*—which purposefully and explicitly sides with the historical and political standpoint of the oppressed writ large—were our textbooks.[20] At Middle College I saw how the most marginalized students became excited at the knowledge being kept from them by more mainstream schools and texts, and to them it felt like they were being let in on critically important secrets about their own existences. In Freirian terms I was witnessing how curriculum could help students feel like the subjects of their own lives, rather than merely objects being acted upon by outside forces. It was here that I also started to think about what "critical consciousness" really meant—a concept I address in more depth in chapter 3.

Being a Radical Teacher

After I graduated from my teacher education program, I was fortunate enough to help establish a new Middle College program for dropouts/pushouts for Seattle Public Schools, this one located at South Seattle Community College.[21] I also continued to work for local Upward Bound programs, and generally saw myself creating curriculum in the Middle College tradition of building the critical consciousness of my students. Among the myriad of students I recall fondly, and among the memories of powerful graduations and personal triumphs, there are two teaching units that I find most remarkable from my years at Middle College. One was a mini-unit I taught on Marxism. I focused on two concepts for my mini-unit: historical materialism and surplus value. Historical materialism easily mapped onto our broader studies of US and world histories, where we continued to use *A People's History of the United States*, as well as Eduardo

Galeano's *Open Veins of Latin America* as one text for global history.[22] Historical materialism helped explain the major shifts in production, war and conflict, as well as changes in regime throughout the world. Similarly, Marx's concept of surplus value as drawn from the exploitation of resources (i.e., the planet) and people served the purposes of both explaining the rise in power of different classes and nations, as well as helping students understand contemporary economic relations that impacted their own low-wage existence.

The other teaching unit that was critical for me was the one my teaching partner Alonzo Ybarra and I did during the autumn quarter of 1999. That year was historic for Seattle and for the anti-globalization movement around the world because the World Trade Organization (WTO) was set to have its annual meeting in Seattle in November. In preparation for this, Alonzo and I focused our entire world history course on issues of globalization, neoliberalism, and the politics surrounding the global exploitation of people and their resources. It was a great unit that saw our students produce a class book of essays, poetry, and art that critically analyzed the WTO and neoliberalism.[23] Even better was the massive protest, later iconized as the "Battle in Seattle," that followed on November 30, 1999, as huge crowds took over the streets of downtown, and anti-globalization activists successfully shut down the WTO meetings.

Alonzo and I were at the protests, along with many other teachers, unions, and activist groups. And, on their own, many of our students voluntarily showed up to participate in the protests at varying levels as well. Seattle and the entire Puget Sound region, along with the rest of the world, vibrated for days after the protests, and the experience was transformational for all of us, teachers and students alike. In my mind's eye, I can still picture my students' faces in the class, days after the protests—vibrant and full of excitement about the history being made around them, and even the history they helped make themselves. Again, I was feeling and seeing what it meant to be a critical, and really, a Marxist, educator.

In 2001, Mira and I moved to Berkeley, California, to be in a more politically active area. I landed a job at Berkeley High School, where I taught ninth-grade ethnic studies, as well as Asian American history and Asian American literature. Berkeley High has its well-documented issues, but there I learned about what I might call "curricular solidarity" as I worked closely with a cadre of social justice teachers in the development and sharing of our ethnic studies curriculum. Here, teaching was an extension of my identity, and I was lucky to get to revisit these issues and teach about race and culture in very explicit ways.

A couple of key activities stuck with me and contributed to my development while teaching at Berkeley High School. The first was that the September 11, 2001, attacks on the World Trade Center happened just after our arrival in Berkeley. Once the United States launched its war machine on Iraq, I found myself in the midst of one of the largest demonstrations I've experienced—some five hundred thousand people marching in San Francisco. That was a powerful moment in and of itself, but I appreciated the student activism that emerged in its wake as well. On their own, Berkeley High students staged a massive die-in, sprawling throughout the courtyard, with an informational kiosk set up in the middle so onlookers could educate themselves as to why these students were "dying" on school grounds. Some of my students wanted to participate; some didn't; so we all went outside and I took attendance as I tip-toed through the bodies lying in symbolic protest of the latest US aggression into Iraq.

Another critically important moment for me at Berkeley High was focused on organizing. My time there was marked by massive California state budget cuts to education, with simultaneous increases in state spending on prisons. I and several of my colleagues felt the impact of these cuts viscerally because we had been laid off for two years running (California state rules require anyone who *might* be let go due to budget reasons be told by mid-March, thus leaving us to spend the last two months teaching without knowing if we would have our jobs or not). That said, we were also upset about the political implications of cutting education, essentially to fund prisons—a very concrete manifestation of the school-to-prison pipeline. In response a group of Berkeley High teachers met and began an organizing campaign called "Education Not Incarceration." We established connections with youth organizers, other education activists, parents, students, and prison activists (like Books Not Bars) as well. Using these networks, we established a core steering committee, and we met to plan our actions, media campaign, and build curriculum. In the end we had a very successful governmental education day at the state capitol in Sacramento, where students met with legislators; we held a large rally and protest at the state capitol as well. We generated a lot of media attention about the issue, and, perhaps more importantly, we essentially built an organization that survived beyond the event (Education Not Incarceration developed into a nonprofit organization that lasted a few years after). Education Not Incarceration also taught me a lot about organizing with students, parents, and community members as a radical and engaged teacher. It was a powerful lesson, illustrating the role that education can play in shifting people's consciousness critically.

I also have to briefly mention something here. During my last year at Berkeley High, the 2002–2003 school year, a master's of education student from the University of Wisconsin–Madison contacted me and wanted to study my classroom and my practice. She was working with Gloria Ladson-Billings as her degree advisor, and she wanted to come study how the teaching of ethnic studies impacted students generally, but with a particular eye to how the white students in my class responded.[24] It was this graduate student studying my classroom that introduced me to the name of Michael Apple at UW–Madison and his work in critical education. Between Apple's politics and the unionization of UW–Madison's teaching assistants, I was drawn to apply to graduate school there to earn my PhD as a Wisconsin Badger.

Becoming a Marxist, Activist Academic

The first question that arose for me when I got to Madison and started taking Apple's classes was, what the hell is a neo-Marxist anyway? And I was serious in asking that question. I was a Marxist, and I knew all kinds of Marxists and Marxist revolutionaries. My dad was a Marxist communist. I thought there were two categories: Marxist and non-Marxist. So I learned from Apple and others about neo-Marxism, which was essentially a two-fold reaction to "Marxism": on the one hand, a turn away from perceived economic determinism within Marxism, and on the other, a turn toward a more cultural understanding of class. I was very skeptical of much of the neo-Marxist turn in critical education, and rightly so. For instance, I found the general critique of Marxism as economic determinism to be thin, and often made by critics who it appeared had not actually read much Marx. In my reading of Marx there couldn't be a simple, deterministic relationship between the economic base and the sociopolitical superstructure, because Marxism places such a high value on understanding all relationships as complex processes.

I was critical of the neo-Marxist cultural turn as well. I saw much of this work (and today still see a fair amount of it) as a departure from materialism. At the time, I explored the neo-Marxist turn relative to Marxist dialectical materialism, finding neo-Marxism to be wanting on both of the counts of dialectics and materialism. In particular I revisited how Marx and Engels themselves discussed the relationship between economic production, culture, and the functioning of the state, and I also delved into the work of Althusser because of his popularity with neo-Marxists[25]; I found all of their work, particularly that of Marx and Engels, to be far more dynamic and nondeterministic than the critics were willing to recognize. I coauthored a chapter with Apple on this issue where we parsed through some of our differences and arrived at a general consensus surrounding the neo-Marxist project, as well as wrote my own paper on the topic, which I detail in chapter 3.[26]

It is important to note that, despite my critiques, I did not reject more-culturalist analyses outright, and I strongly embrace some for understanding how politics functions inside and outside of education. For instance, anyone who was one of Apple's PhD students has to become familiarized with a few key theorists as part of their experience, particularly Antonio Gramsci, Pierre Bourdieu, Basil Bernstein, Nancy Fraser, and Raymond Williams, all of whom helped shape my thinking about critical politics in education. Of these the work of Bernstein has been the most influential to me. I felt like his analysis, however dense, and at times confusingly written, helped provide a way for understanding how macro social, political, and economic relations translated into the micro level of classroom interactions vis-à-vis the politics of knowledge and the structure of pedagogic discourse. In this regard I have used Bernstein's work to explain specifically how high-stakes standardized tests function as an imposition of unequal power relations (external to schools) upon curriculum and classroom discourse.[27] Bernstein has also helped me sort through the ways a class fraction of technocrats, known as the professional and managerial new middle class, have conflicting interests within systems of high-stakes testing,[28] and how they rose to power within the bureacracies and data-processing systems associated with the Common Core State Standards and the Obama administration's Race to the Top initiative.[29]

The other thing I saw in neo-Marxism was critical scholars fundamentally running away from Marxism, based either on gross misunderstandings of it or on the fear of what their colleagues might think, because many scholars don't consider Marxism as a reasonable or legitimate framework within the academy. Indeed, it is important to remember that this flight from Marx was part of a broader rightward move both in academia and in society.[30] So as I read and was influenced by various scholars, I was beginning a personal and political project of essentially reclaiming what I saw as the Marxist roots of critical educational theory and practice, even if the field of critical education didn't seem to acknowledge the connection. For instance, I took up a deep study of Freire. I combed through his texts, old and new, and within them I saw someone who very much embraced dialectical materialism. To me the textual evidence was all there if one actually read his books, particularly if one knew dialectical materialism well enough to see it in Freire's writing. In the process, I engaged with several of his prominent critics and found many of their critiques to be based in misunderstandings and misconceptions of Freire's work. Materials drawn from several of my articles and book chapters on Freire form the basis of chapter 6.[31]

Lev Vygotsky's work in psychology has also proved to be of importance to me, particularly because I saw Marxist dialectical materialism in his work. My interest in Vygotsky was sparked in part because I saw his work cited regularly by mainstream and progressive scholars and practitioners for the concepts of "scaffolding" and the "zone of proximal development."[32] When I read Vygotsky myself, his work was so clearly Marxist to me that I felt as if these mainstream and progressive applications of his work either did not want to admit it out of a fear of Marxism, or didn't understand Marxism well enough to see it in his ideas. I specifically remember reading Vygotsky's discussion of the relationship between "spontaneous" or "everyday" concepts and "scientific" concepts, and recognizing that framing from Lenin's *What Is to Be Done?*, particularly his discussion of "spontaneous revolts" versus "conscious" and "strategic" actions. I outline many more connections between Lenin and Vygotsky in my paper "Vygotsky and Lenin on Learning," a revised and updated version of which also appears here as chapter 5.[33]

Even though I had been writing for them for some time, during this period of time I officially joined the editorial board of the social justice education magazine and publishing nonprofit, Rethinking Schools. I cannot overemphasize the role Rethinking Schools has had on who I am as a critical scholar/activist today. The Rethinking Schools editorial collective contains some of the most brilliant and most politically committed educational minds I know. From my earliest relationships with Linda Christensen and Bill Bigelow, to working with the founding editors like Bob Peterson or David Levine, to seasoned Rethinking Schools editors like Stan Karp, to the more recent editors like Jody Sokolower, Jesse Hagopian, Adam Sanchez, Dyan Watson, Grace Gonzalez, and Moe Yonamine, my analyses of educational politics and practices have been sharpened constantly through the years. In many ways I had a perfect combination of working in the academy with Apple (and others) on critical education theory in conjunction with my participation as an editor for the practitioner-based and activist-oriented Rethinking Schools.[34]

Of course, in the midst of all of this, I wrote a dissertation on high-stakes testing, which turned into my first book, *Unequal by Design: High-Stakes Testing and the Standardization of Inequality.* This work stitched together a lot of the thinking and writing I had been doing, and I saw that project as an explicit expression, from various critical angles, of Marxist analysis of testing. The book takes up the long conversation among critical scholars about the relationship between schooling and inequality, arguing for a dialectical view of (re) production in an attempt to recognize that schools produce culture and resistance even as they reproduce inequality. In it, I also offer a historical materialist analysis about the roots of standardized testing in the United States and its connection to the establishment of specifically race- and class-based inequalities. In *Unequal by Design* I look at the political economy of high-stakes testing, as well, outlining the corporate forces behind the tests and the gendered inequalities embodied within the political and bureaucratic education structures.

In a larger sense, much of my early work on Marx, Engels, Freire, Althusser, Vygotsky, and Lenin was an effort to reclaim the Marxist, dialectical materialist roots of critical education theory, or at least to defend the Marxist tradition against what I saw as simplistic and often erroneous attacks. Moving forward from that foundation, I continued to explore both Marxist and neo-Marxist traditions, still sorting out my own thinking and looking for useful constructs for understanding power and the relationship between education and consciousness. In this specific regard, I certainly carried forward the thinking of Marx, Engels, Vygotsky (and by extension Lenin), and Freire with regard to the concept of "consciousness" itself, which I see as grounded in a dynamic, dialectical relationship between people and their surroundings (including other people). More recently I've drawn upon the scholarship of Hartsock and Harding, who themselves drew upon Lukács's work around class consciousness, in an attempt to bring Marxist-feminist standpoint theory to my own dialectical materialist conceptions of both "critical consciousness" and "curriculum."[35] In doing so I continued to work on a conception of consciousness and epistemology that recognizes the relativity of perception from our subject positions while maintaining a firm grasp on the existence of material reality objectively beyond those very same subject positions (remembering that dialectics, among other aspects, sees relations between things such that we can choose "both" instead of being forced into choosing between disconnected, atomized options). Hartsock's and Harding's conceptions of "strong objectivity" are especially important because not only do they operate in opposition to positivistic notions of pure objectivity in research, but they also require us to embrace our subjectivity as a means of better understanding material reality.[36] I have found this framing to be of particular significance to critical educators because it emphasizes the ways that understanding who we are as educators and students is central to the project of understanding and changing the world.

My journey as a Marxist educator has also evolved into my identity as an academic activist and public intellectual who constantly tries to make formal scholarship accessible to a broader public of teachers and parents. I've always maintained a line of research on and critical analysis of education policy. This started with my dissertation on high-stakes testing and has since extended into critiques of charter schools as part of a broader analysis of the entire anti-union, anti-teacher, and anti-public school corporate education reform movement. In recent years, my research and writing has focused sharply on a critical racial analysis of education, explicitly taking up racism and white supremacy of high-stakes testing[37] and excavating the curriculum histories of communities of color in the United States.[38] In my local capacity as a professor in the Seattle area, I've lent my expertise publicly to activists and campaigns against a statewide charter school initiative that became law in 2012 (becoming a plaintiff in a successful constitutional lawsuit against the initiative, which is being tested in court again as I write) and have been supporting teachers and parents in their fight against high-stakes testing.[39] One of the most personally validating things that has happened in these recent local struggles is finding out that some of the teachers involved in organizing the Garfield High School teacher boycott of the MAP test were directly influenced by my first book, *Unequal by Design*.[40] This helped remind me that, while it is true that academic work is generally aimed at smaller audiences of professors and university researchers, committed and critical practitioners can and do benefit from serious conceptual analyses of education and power.

As I continue my journey as a critical, Marxist educational scholar and activist, I've noticed that there are two things that drive my critical politics. One is that I seek to uncover power relations in education and society—and not just along economic or political lines, but also along the lines of culture and identity more broadly. I'm still a committed dialectical materialist, *and* I also understand that as human beings we express our material relations through the multiplicity of our identities. The other thing that drives my critical lens is a constant search for ways of dialectically connecting the macro to the micro, of understanding just how individuals are expressions of broader social, cultural, and economic relations. As a Marxist dialectical materialist, I firmly believe that *we are our relations*. That is to say, our material and cultural existences are the products of a web of concrete relationships that extends far beyond our immediate grasp; as such, one of our most important roles in our research, pedagogy, and curriculum is to interrogate and understand these relations more deeply.

A Marxist Education

This book could have been organized in a few different ways and following a few different strands. The central philosophical and political core of this book is Marxist dialectical materialism. However, while Marxist dialectical materialist analysis is present in every chapter included here, as someone whose work focuses specifically on education—the politics of education policy, teaching for social justice, and curriculum—it has become clear to me that my work is always aimed at developing critical consciousness as a teacher and professor, a researcher, a public intellectual, and as an activist organizer. In this sense, developing the concept of "critical consciousness" is paramount because *that is what I do*. Finally, the other strands running through the book are wrapped up in the broader Marxist project of both critiquing capitalism and understanding the spaces we have to resist inequalities and build activist social movements.

Given the above, the chapters here unfold as follows: chapter 2, "The Heart of Marxism: Defining and Defending Marxist Dialectical Materialism," undergirds this book. It both explains dialectical materialism as the philosophy and methodology at the heart of Marxist analysis, and it addresses several critiques that posit Marxism as inherently Eurocentric and incapable of adequately attending to issues of race and colonization. Chapter 3, "Capitalist Inequality and Schools: Marxism, Neo-Marxism, and the Dialectics of Educational (Re)Production," looks at the long, ongoing debates about the role of schooling under capitalism and considers the relationship between schooling and capitalist production. Specifically this chapter takes up whether schools simply mirror capitalist relations and inequalities, or whether schools can be sites of resistance and interruption of capitalist inequalities. Chapter 3 also revisits some older arguments about schooling and capitalism, particularly that of Bowles and Gintis's "correspondence principle"—which suggests that schools will, on the whole, reproduce the kind of stratification of skills and credentials we see in the capitalist economy generally.[41] Chapter 4, "Dispossession and Defiance: A Race and Class Political Economy of Neoliberal Education Reform," is a more contemporary look at the ways current forms of schooling reproduce race and class inequalities relative to the rise of education policies built around neoliberal economic philosophy and practices, and discusses some ways that teachers, students, parents, and community activists have organized against these reforms. Chapter 5, "'It Is through Others That We Develop into Ourselves': Vygotsky, Lenin, and the Social Formation of Consciousness," offers a Marxist, dialectical materialist conception of critical consciousness and discusses the implications of this conception for individual learning and organizing. A Marxist framing of critical consciousness is important to this book because it helps us understand schooling as both a site of oppression *and* a site of potential resistance, including the roles that pedagogy and curriculum play in either process. Continuing this thread of the possibilities of resistance, chapter 6, "Teaching to Change the World: The Marxist, Dialectical Materialist Pedagogy of Paulo Freire," looks at the philosophical underpinnings of the revolutionary pedagogy of the late Brazilian educator, in order to better understand how we *teach* toward liberation and critical consciousness about the world. While chapter 6 looks at the pedagogy and instruction toward critical consciousness, chapter 7, "Curriculum to Change the World: Developing a Marxist-Feminist Standpoint in the Politics of Knowledge," plays as a companion in that it provides a Marxist, dialectical materialist framework for curriculum—the *what* we teach—in working toward critical consciousness. In the concluding chapter 8, "A Dialectical Life: Working to Change the World," I think through what this has all meant in terms of my own practices as an educator, scholar, and activist.

Chapter 2

The Heart of Marxism

Defining and Defending Marxist Dialectical Materialism

Warning: This is not a chapter about education. Nor is it a chapter about education and Marxism. There will, however, be a discussion of what I mean by Marxism and how I am using it throughout this book. This chapter is mainly devoted to two goals. First, I define what I mean by Marxism—namely, dialectical materialism. Please bear with me on this. Explaining dialectical materialism is always philosophical, and as such, can be abstract. I've tried to weave some examples and to make my discussion of dialectics reasonable and more readable, but I am keenly aware that dialectics is a different way of thinking about the world, and so it can be difficult to explain (and even wrap my own head around sometimes). Please be sure that I would not be taking the time to delve into dialectical materialism if I did not think it was centrally important to understanding Marxism, and, by extension, the Marxist analysis of capitalism, schooling, and education that happens across the other chapters of this book.

The second part of this chapter is a defense of Marxism and Marxist dialectical materialism. Marxism has long been critiqued on various grounds, sometimes fairly but mostly mistakenly. Here I mainly take up a defense and discussion of Marx and Marxism relative to race, racism, and settler colonialism in order to help buoy the Marxian tradition that understands the inseparability of class and race. Overall this chapter serves as the theoretical and conceptual backbone for the rest of this book.

Dialectical Materialism at the Heart of Marxism

It is widely agreed that Marx's methodological approach to analyzing capitalism was based on dialectical materialism, and for the intents and purposes of this book, dialectical materialism is what defines "Marxism." Essentially, dialectical materialism is a view of how the world works—a paradigm, an epistemology, a philosophy, a methodology—that is grounded in several core concepts. In a dialectical view everything (and I mean *everything*: people, materials, institutions, society) is in motion and is constantly changing. Even things that look still or stagnant, such as a hardwood table, are still made up of atoms that are moving. As such, in a dialectical view there are no "things" sitting idly, but rather every "thing" is a process that is developing. Further, in dialectics every "thing" is developing through the unfolding of its own internal contradictions in relation to contexts and conditions outside of that "thing," and these external conditions have a powerful effect: selecting exactly which internal process (contradiction) is resolved. This line of thinking also embraces the dialectical reality that everything is connected and is relational to other things. As Wilson Au, author of *Reclaiming Communist Philosophy* explains, regarding dialectics, "[A]ll things are *connected*, related to each other and determined by each other—not always directly, but ultimately—through chains of relations that are often of staggering complexity. Nothing exists entirely independent of other things."[1] Finally, in dialectics, all things/processes carry within them the kernel of their own destruction.

Thus, as Bertell Ollman discusses in *Dance of the Dialectic: Steps in Marx's Method*, a dialectical worldview requires a change in how we see everything:

> Dialectics restructures our thinking about reality by replacing the commonsense notion of "thing" (as something that has a history and has external connections with other things) with notions of "process" (which contains its history and possible futures) and "relation" (which contains as part of what it is its ties with other relations). Nothing that didn't already exist has been added here. Rather, it is a matter of where and how one draws boundaries and establishes units (the dialectical term is "abstracts") in which to think about the world. The assumption is that while the qualities we perceive with our five senses actually exist as parts of nature, the conceptual distinctions that tell us where one thing ends and the next one begins both in space and across time are social and mental constructs.[2]

For the sake of explanation, let's return to the example of the hardwood table—the one that looks like it is still, even though in reality it is in constant motion. Internally, at the molecular level, that same hardwood is going through a process of aging. It is deteriorating and degrading. This is its internal movement, and if left to just sit there in a vacuum, completely disconnected from the world, the hardwood table, of its own accord, would simply disintegrate into dust as part of an internal contradiction between the amount of energy needed to maintain the molecular bonds. The hardwood table is not a thing, but a process unfolding in front of us. It's just that in this case the table's process is so slow that we might not be able to observe its movement with just our eyes.

However, since nothing exists in isolation and everything is related, the process of aging that the table is going through is potentially conditioned by other external factors. For instance, perhaps the table sits in direct sunlight in a hot, moist climate. Perhaps it gets wet from the rain, or maybe it is just sitting outside in the elements. These external conditions (its relations) contribute to the aging of the hardwood table because the temperature, light, and moisture can all play a role in speeding up (or slowing down) degradation and deterioration. Depending on the context—its relationship with everything else—our table might last for two hundred years, or it might last for twenty. Or, our house might catch on fire and the table might meet a fiery end in a matter of minutes. (And in this case, the external conditions of a house fire causes the hardwood to release its oxygen in the form of heat and light [fire], thereby changing the process from aging to burning.)

Our hardwood table does not just have relations with its immediate physical environment either. It also has ecological-historical relations that play a role in its existence and development. Our hardwood came from a specific tree in a specific forest in a specific climate. The tree may have experienced drought or disease or a lightning strike, all of which may have impacted the grain and quality of the wood for our table (indeed, the tree itself represents its own developing process that may have come to an end when it was cut down for lumber). The hardwood table also carries with it sociohistorical relations that contributed to its existence. There was labor involved in the tree cutting and lumber shipping, as well as in the design and construction of the table. The workers may or may not have been unionized, may or may not have been kept safe in the process, and they may or may not have been paid a living wage. The harvest of the wood and the construction of the table might have come from a clear-cutting operation and a mass production line filled with machines and chemicals; or maybe it was the result of a singular woodworker who procured the tree from a friend's property where it had fallen and then set about creating a piece of art. The conditions of the wood's harvest depend on historical context and a chain of relations, all of which "live" in our hardwood table.

Further, understanding contradiction is central to dialectics. In dialectical thinking, there is a *thesis* (positive or conservative) side of a contradiction as well as an *antithesis* (negative or destructive) side of a contradiction. In the simplest terms, we see Marx's formulation of the contradiction between the working-class proletariat and the owning-class bourgeoisie under capitalism. In this case the bourgeoisie is the positive (conservative) side of the contradiction because it seeks to maintain or conserve the current relationship, because it benefits from the exploitation of workers in the production of capital. Conversely, the proletariat is the negative (destructive) side of this contradiction because it seeks to negate or destroy the relationship built on its exploitation. Indeed, Marx conceptualized history as moving and developing based on this kind of dialectical relationship, with different economies producing other kinds of unified opposites, and the tension among these opposites a key driver in social and economic change.

The *synthesis*, then, requires the resolution of the contradiction (where the old relationship has been destroyed—negation), as well as the creation of something new (where a new set of relations is produced—negation of the negation). Again, following the simplified example: As the negative side of the contradiction, workers would seek to destroy capitalism, thereby resolving the contradiction and "negating" it as a system of relations. However, once capitalism was destroyed, there would also be the creation of something new—a new set of relations, perhaps socialism, perhaps something else—and this would be the negation of the negation. Further, within a dialectical understanding of contradiction, whatever new relations were to come of the synthesis would contain aspects of the old relationship, but reorganized and subsumed in the new relation (in dialectics this subsuming of the old into the new is called "sublation"). In this way dialectics views the resolution of contradictions as a spiral movement. That is, there is a thesis, an antithesis, and a synthesis of the two into something new; but this process has movement and direction, because the synthesis represents a reconfiguration at another level of development.[3] In the Marxist ideal, the fundamental contradiction of capitalism would be resolved with a socialist revolution (negation), and the creation of a new set of socialist relations (negation of the negation) that would include some aspects of the old capitalist system like production and exchange (sublation), but done so in a more complex and advanced way that tended to the needs of human and the environment (spiral development).

Returning once again to the example of our hardwood desk: The hardwood tree was living and going through a process of cell regeneration and growth while still marching toward its own eventual death. If this tree was cut down by a lumberjack, then an external condition changed, and the process of tree growth was altered by harvesting—it was negated by the lumberjack. The harvested tree is now in the midst of another process—rotting, degradation, cell death as it is removed from the root and leaf systems that allowed it to produce energy, grow, and live. It is then transported, milled, and turned into lumber, which is dried in order to increase preservation. This final piece of lumber is qualitatively different than the wood that was in the living tree, and it represents an entirely different set of biochemical processes. In this way the finished lumber is a negation of the processes of the original tree. This pattern is reproduced again when the lumber is constructed into our hardwood desk, where the construction of the desk could be seen as negation of the lumber (a negation of the negation of the original tree) with the original lumber, the resources, and the labor having been subsumed (sublated) into our hardwood desk. The desk represents the reorganization of the tree into something new and qualitatively different than what it was previously, even if it contains aspects of the original tree within it. There is spiral development here, too, because in each round of negation the tree/wood takes on a qualitatively new reorganization of relations. (Note: this is not to say that the transformation from tree to lumber to wood is necessarily good, especially given the context of the overharvesting of trees and the exploitation of labor in the rapaciousness of capitalism.)

We can see one other illustration of dialectical thinking within the example of the hardwood desk: the relationship between quantity and quality and the transformation of one into another. As Wilson Au explains, "The *quality* of a thing, process, or phenomenon is the collection of features it possesses that distinguishes it from other things, processes or phenomena. Every quality, however, is based upon some quantitative definiteness. . . . In turn, quantity is based upon some qualitative definiteness."[4] While Wilson Au's work uses examples such as nucleosynthesis in stars and phase transitions in water to get at the complexities of how dialectical processes unfold in his book-length treatment of dialectical materialist philosophy,[5] we can think about this with more immediate examples. For instance, think about a tree versus a forest. An individual tree is an individual in that it is made up of its own cells and going through its own process as a tree. However, at some point, when enough trees grow together (quantity), they become something qualitatively different: a forest. A forest, even as it is made up of individual trees, has its own development *as a forest.* A forest is its own ecosystem and biome. A forest can support a greater variety of animals than a singular tree can. Through the creation of shade, water usage, and blocking wind, a forest can shape an environment in more powerful and different ways than a singular tree.

For instance, as reported in the *Atlantic* in 2017, in the US Eastern Seaboard, entire species of trees are moving westward.[6] Now, on the individual level, this happens tree by tree: a new tree grows, an old tree dies. However, looked at over time and at a more macro scale, as new trees grow on one side (the front of the movement), and as old trees die off on the other side (the back of the movement), we see an entire species of trees moving from one place to another. Each individual tree is going through its own process of growing and dying, but put enough of these trees growing and dying together, and a qualitative leap has been made: a species of trees is developing (in this case, moving across land) *as a species.* So the species of trees has its own qualitatively different process that includes, but is distinct from, the individual trees.

To use a more social example, we can look at schools in a similar way. Schools are made up of individual students and staff. All these individuals are undergoing their own individual processes: biological processes of aging or sickness or healing, as well as sociocultural processes of identity development and learning, among others. All these individuals also constitute a school. A school, as an institution, is qualitatively different from the simple quantity of individuals inside its walls. A school has its own history, culture, and development *as a school,* and this development is dialectically related to both the individuals inside of it, as well as the policy conditions at the district, state, and federal levels (by the way, the same argument can, then, be made with regard to individual schools relative to school districts). And all of this is fluid and dynamic as well.

For instance, gentrification might happen in a neighborhood over some number of years, such that the population of any given urban school might change from mostly working class, immigrant, and/or students of color to being mostly affluent and white. Across that time, as gentrification proceeds and individual students and families change, at some point the character of the school's population also changes. In the meantime the school in the gentrifying neighborhood might be making adjustments as the student body changes and as the new parents make different kinds of demands on school staff and administration. So the identity of the school might shift over time. Or the district might get a new superintendent and new senior-level district staff, all of whom have their own policy agenda for the schools. New policies (like lots of high-stakes testing) might come down from the district, changing the school culture, causing staff turnover, and perhaps causing some parents to try and change schools—thereby changing the school population. In either case the school, as an institution, as its own ecosystem, will shift and move and develop and change *as a school* in dialectical concert with changes of individual students, families, and staff members. This kind of fluidity, dynamism, and relationality are hallmarks of dialectical understandings of how our world works.

If you are familiar with *Capital* and Marxism, you can see the broad strokes of dialectics in Marx's analysis of capitalism beyond my above discussion of class antagonism.[7] Marx saw capitalism as a process of the production and accumulation of capital that was at once economic, historical, social, and physical, and driven by class contradictions that contained the seed of capitalism's demise. This thinking was the basis of historical materialism and his analysis of the rise of modern capitalism in Western Europe specifically. Marx also understood capital, products, commodities, and labor not as individual things, but as processes operating in relation to each other and everything else.

Up to this point I've devoted a significant amount of this chapter to explaining the "dialectical" part of "dialectical materialism." It is philosophical and it is complex, but it is also critical to understanding the heart of Marxist analysis. The "materialism" part of "dialectical materialism" is still philosophical, but more straightforward. The basic split is this: idealists believe that consciousness creates reality, while materialists believe that material reality, our material world, exists outside of human consciousness. Put differently (and more dramatically), most major religions posit that God created the world. This is philosophically idealist since it posits that some form of God consciousness created material reality. Materialists, on the other hand, posit that the world existed before human consciousness of it, and it would go on existing whether or not we were around to perceive it.[8] This is why Marxism, socialism, and communism are often associated with atheism. However, as Wilson Au explains, "This does not mean that materialism rejects the reality of the mind and human spirit. On the contrary, it recognizes mind and spirit as highly-developed forms of movement that occur in matter that has attained a certain degree of organizational complexity."[9]

In summary, a dialectical materialist analysis

- asserts that the material world exists outside of human consciousness of it;
- sees everything as in constant motion;
- understands contradiction as the basis for all movement, development, and change;
- sees everything as related and connected, where even opposites make up a relational whole;
- rejects "either/or" and instead sees "and/both," relationally;
- sees quantity and quality, and their transformation into each other, as part of the process of development;
- asserts that there are negative (destructive) and positive (conservative) sides to any contradiction;
- holds that the resolution of a contradiction contains within

it both the negation (destruction) of the original relationship and the negation of that negation, which is a new relationship (synthesis) at a different level of development;
- understands the new relationship created in the resolution of a contradiction as carrying aspects of the old relationship within it (sublation);
- sees the external conditions of a process as playing a strong, sometimes determining role in which internal contradiction is resolved;
- asserts that the development of a process happens in a spiral, not in a straight line.

To be absolutely clear, this is just a primer in dialectical materialist thinking and philosophy, and my goal here is to provide enough to both define what I mean by "Marxism" and frame out my own discussions and analyses of education within a Marxist, dialectical materialist framework.

Is Marxism Eurocentric and Therefore Racist?

There have long been critiques of Marxism based on assertions that Marx was, and Marxism is, fundamentally Eurocentric and therefore incapable of adequately addressing racism and colonization.[10] As Keeanga-Yamahtta Taylor highlights in *From #BlackLivesMatter to Black Liberation*, these critiques persist today as socialism and Marxism have been construed as the territory of whiteness by public intellectuals like Tim Wise and in the political commentary surrounding the 2016 presidential primary campaign of quasi-socialist candidate Bernie Sanders.[11] In order to address this critique and others, I think it is important to distinguish between *Marx* as a person who developed and learned over time, *Marxism* as a system of thought, analysis, and action (praxis) that actually transcends Marx individually, and *Marxists* as people who identify as believers and practitioners of Marxism.

Marx and His Analysis

Like all of us, Marx was human, and so it is important to understand that his views grew and developed over time. Marx was most certainly Eurocentric in his analysis and writings in that he focused mainly on Europe and that he relied on European perspectives as he gathered data about non-Western countries, histories, and cultures. As such, the historical development of class conflict that Marx and Engels outlined in their most widely read work, *The Communist Manifesto*, ultimately misses class conflict that existed outside of the European historical trajectory.[12] Citing the important African-centric work of Senegalese scholar Cheikh Anta Diop, Curry Malott notes that there were early and emerging forms of capitalism that existed in Egypt that did not become dominant, due to specific historical, economic, and cultural conditions.[13] Also consistent with Marx's earlier writings and analysis, *The Communist Manifesto* embodied Eurocentric racism through proclamations about the backwardness of China.[14]

It is important to recognize that Marx's focus on Europe is purposeful and understandable: capitalism had already taken hold in Europe as the dominant form of economic and social relations, Europe was at the heart of capitalism at the time, and capitalism had ravenously spread across much of the globe through European colonization and imperialism. In this regard, it makes sense to start a study and analysis of capitalism with Europe at the center, because Europe was the center of capitalism historically. However, as Marxist-feminist standpoint theorists like Nancy Hartsock and Sandra Harding remind us (and as I'll discuss at length in chapter 7 of this book), any knowledge project is limited by the positionality of the researcher relative to the object and process of study.[15] This was doubly true for Marx and Engels, considering most of the data they had access to was written in European languages and from the perspectives of European colonizers around the world. So their perspective was shaped not only by the fact that they were white European men writing in the mid-1800s, but also by the imperfect knowledge base they each employed in their study of capitalism regionally and globally.[16]

However, Eurocentrism carries with it the imperialistic weight of racism and settler colonialism, and, even though his views later evolved, Marx at times framed non-Western societies as backward and less progressive than their capitalist, Western counterparts. Marx's early writings were particularly Eurocentric and smacked of problematic notions of capitalistic progress. As Kevin Anderson documents in his meticulously researched book *Marx at the Margins*,[17] Marx initially saw capitalist production as a "progressive" force in the development of Europe and the world—inasmuch as it was necessary to create the conditions, infrastructure, and class structure to overthrow capitalism. He similarly (and mistakenly) thought other countries, particularly British colonies, would necessarily need to suffer the same growing pains of capitalist "progress" in order to eventually free themselves from capitalism and the oppression of British colonialism. For instance, he portrayed British colonialism as a "progressive" force in India, even as he also asserted that Indians needed to overthrow the British imperialists and were fully capable of ruling themselves as a sovereign nation.

Yet, by the late 1850s, Marx stopped framing capitalism as inherently progressive. He instead referred specifically to the "barbarism of bourgeois civilization," stopped asserting that colonialism benefited the British colonies, and began reporting on the widespread horrors of colonization.[18] As Glen Coulthard writes in *Red Skin, White Masks*,

> [I]n the last decade of his life, Marx no longer condemns non-Western and noncapitalist social formations to necessarily pass through the destructive phase of capitalist development as the condition of possibility for human freedom and flourishing. During this period, Marx had not only come to view more clearly how certain features of noncapitalist and capitalist modes of production "articulate" (albeit asymmetrically) in a given social formation, but also the ways in which aspects of the former can come to inform the construction of radical alternatives to the latter.[19]

Similarly, as Marx's thinking developed, he added a non-European, Asiatic mode of production to his analysis of the development of societies and economies, thus indicating that he in fact saw possibilities for the multilinear progression of societies, where the European model could not be universally applied to Asian (specifically Indian and Chinese) contexts. Indeed, it is very important to note here that, as Kevin Anderson explains in *Marx at the Margins*, Marx did not intend for the socioeconomic development of Europe outlined in *Capital* to be read as a universal development of all societies, as is often claimed by critics of Marx who pair the simplistic framing of *The Communist Manifesto* with that of *Capital*. Rather, in a footnote in the French edition of *Capital*, left out of other editions, Marx is very specific that his focus is purposely on the development of Western Europe alone.[20]

Although not extensive, Marx's growing analysis did also come to include slavery, with an eye toward the United States specifically. He clearly articulated that slavery played a critical role in the development of capitalism, and that the colonies were essential to the rise of modern industry.[21] Writing about the "genesis of the industrial capitalist," in *Capital*, volume 1, Marx fully recognized that "the discovery of gold and silver in America, the extirpation, enslavement and entombment in mines of the aboriginal population, the beginning of the conquest and looting of the East Indies, the turning of Africa into a warren for the commercial hunting of black skins, signalized the rosy dawn of the era of capitalist production."[22] Also in *Capital*, volume 1, Marx observed that "[i]n the United States of America, every independent movement of the workers was paralyzed as long as slavery disfigured a part of the Republic. Labor cannot emancipate itself in the white skin where in the Black it is branded."[23] As such, and going against many of the international socialists who were initially reluctant to support the capitalist North in the US Civil War, Marx himself was a strong supporter of radical abolitionists, a critic of Lincoln for moving too slowly, and linked the Civil War and abrogation of slavery to the global struggle for democracy.[24]

In thinking about Marx and his analysis, it is important to recognize that his focus on Western Europe in *Capital* was purposeful and methodological, and that both he and his analysis of capitalism grew and developed more nuance and complexity as the years progressed.

Non-Western Dialectical Thinking

In addition to asserting Marx's works as Eurocentric, critics also often label Marxism as a product of the European Enlightenment, casting Marx into the same milieu of white, European patriarchy at the center of Western conceptions of science.[25] In this Western tradition, the white male gaze has dominated, assuming its perspectives are universally true for everyone, building systems of formal logic that construct categories as either/or, viewing everything as stationary, separate, individual pieces that can be analyzed in pure isolation, and presuming simple, linear, and mechanical relationships between cause and effect. In terms of scientific philosophy, this Western conception is associated with positivism, empiricism, and mechanical materialism.[26] Western science then exercised its racism and sexism on the peoples of the world, disregarding non-Western approaches, taking deficit views of women's health and the health of people of color, and creating "scientific" justifications for race-, gender-, and class-based inequality and oppression.[27] Indeed, many of the feminist, postmodernist, postcolonial, and post-structuralist approaches to research are a direct response to the white male chauvinism that has been prominent in the social sciences.[28]

Now, as I noted earlier in this chapter, Marx was a white, European man, and, as we have seen, his analysis of things beyond the European context was limited at best, and suffered from Eurocentrism at worst. However, Marx also developed over time in ways that challenged this earlier Eurocentrism. We could argue that Marx was, in some key ways, an Enlightenment thinker, particularly relative to the Enlightenment ideas of the "natural rights of man" and progress, or even his specific lack of attention to women's labor in the production of capital.[29] However, Marx's dialectical materialism, with its focus on processes, movement, contradiction, interrelations, transformation, and duality (as opposed to either/or categories), actually stands in direct opposition to the positivism, empiricism, and mechanical materialism that has typically defined Western science.[30] This is an important distinction because liberal and left critics of

Marxism sometimes simply label it as part of the tradition of old, dead, chauvinistic, European, male, Western scientists that grew out of the Enlightenment, when in reality most of Marx's thought and methodology—his entire approach to analysis—fundamentally opposed that tradition. Indeed, a non-Eurocentric look at the history of dialectical materialism further challenges the supposition that Marxism is purely a Western, Eurocentric form of thought.

In most narratives of Marxist dialectical materialism, dialectics as a philosophy and worldview is traced through a Eurocentric lineage that stems from ancient Greece. For instance, Alan Woods, author of *Reason in Revolt*, views the origins of Western philosophy as being purely in ancient Greece.[31] In chapters on philosophy that were omitted from *Reason in Revolt* due to length considerations, Woods offers a typical outline for the Greek lineage of dialectics, starting with Heraclitus in the fifth century BCE through Socrates and Plato, and onward to Hegel and Marx.[32] However, there has been Western- and African-centric scholarship that challenges the Eurocentric narratives around the origins of Western "civilization," science, and philosophy in Greece.[33] These scholars argue that the Mediterranean Sea was a vibrant community of cultural and economic exchange and that ancient Egypt was the progenitor of much of what is considered to be Greek culture, science, and philosophy. In this vein, Cheikh Anta Diop, in his book *Civilization or Barbarism,* argues that the roots of dialectical materialism predate Heraclitus and are to be found in the philosophy of ancient Egypt. According to Diop there was a materialist philosophy contained within the Egyptian cosmogony (or conception of the origins of the universe), which asserted that matter existed before consciousness. Further, Diop presents evidence that Heraclitus's theory of opposites extends directly from the Egyptian cosmogonies, and that the Hermopolitan cosmogony specifically communicates a philosophy of dialectical movement due to the interactions of relational opposites. Diop also argues that the dialectical law of transformation (the evolution of matter through time) and the law of becoming (acting on matter through time to actualize being) were both expressed in the cosmogonies as well. After a lengthy account, Diop concludes, "One can measure, from this account which only scratches the surface of the subject, all that Greek philosophy owes to Egyptian thought of the Nile Valley's Blacks: Heraclitus's theory of opposites, Aristotle's dialectics . . . the diverse cosmogonies of the Pre-Socratic philosophers, etc."[34] To this end, contrary to claims of Marxist dialectics being inherently Eurocentric, dialectical philosophy and thinking are African in origin—even if Marx, Engels, and Hegel did not know it.

Additionally, even if we trace the lineage of dialectical materialism from Egypt through Greece to Hegel and Marx, we miss the fact that dialectical thinking has existed in other non-Western philosophical traditions as well. Most notably, China, which went on to adopt and recontextualize Marxist dialectical materialism after the communist revolution, had its own foundation of dialectical thinking to integrate with and map onto Marxism. Chenshan Tian, a Chinese scholar on the history of dialectics in Chinese philosophy and its relationship to Marxist philosophy, argues that Chinese dialectics is thousands of years old and is an expression of *tong-bian* philosophy.[35] Much like the dialectical materialist philosophy of Marx, as Tian explains,

> [i]t is appropriate to suggest an interpretation of the concept *tong-bian* that significantly involves four ideas: (1) Every thing (or event) in the world correlates with another; (2) The manifold and diverse relationships of things (or events) to any other things (or events) are of interconnectedness, and can be viewed as of a basic pattern as yin and yang, namely, the interaction and interdependence of complementary opposition; (3) It is this basic pattern that ceaselessly brings every thing (or event) in the world into constant change or movement; and (4) Everything is in a process of change and presents itself as a focus-and-field of relationship. Each item is understood as "this particular focus" which articulates the totality of things from its perspective; and, as of the totality, it focuses totality in its entirety. The totality is itself nothing more than the full ranges of particular foci, each defining itself and its own particular field.[36]

Tian goes on to discuss how dialectical unity is a relationship defined by "mutual becoming, or complementarity between any two interdependent things."[37] Thus, as Tian argues, when the Chinese turned toward Marxist dialectical materialism (via Qu Qiubai—one of the earliest to bring Western dialectics into China vis-à-vis translations from Japanese texts and lectures), they read it through the thousands-of-years-old Chinese cultural lens of tong-bian philosophy, resulting in a recontextualized and localized Chinese vernacular of Marxist philosophy.[38]

Dialectical thinking was also central to Nahua (Aztec) philosophy in the Americas of the fifteenth and sixteenth centuries. The Nahua believed that everything emanated from a single sacred force or spirit, *teotl*, and that everything was part of unified totality that itself was in motion and is constantly going through a process of self-generation and self-regeneration. Although they were not philosophically materialist (since for them everything flowed from a spirit force), the Nahua, consistent with dialectical thinking, did not see discrete or static "things"; instead they saw everything in movement. Further, the Nahua framed the processes of self-generation and self-regeneration as a product of the relationships between complimentary opposites (dialectial dualities) presented within teotl.[39] As James Maffie, author of *Aztec Philosophy: Understanding a World in Motion*, explains,

> *Teotl's* process presents itself in multiple aspects, preeminent among which is duality. This duality takes the form of the endless opposition of contrary yet mutually interdependent and mutually complementary polarities which divide, alternately dominate, and explain the diversity, movement, and momentary arrangement of the universe. These include: being and not-being, order and disorder, life and death, light and darkness, masculine and feminine, dry and wet, hot and cold, and active and passive.[40]

Further—and with striking similarity to the dialectical concepts of synthesis, sublation, and negation, discussed above—according to Maffie, while being/nonbeing exist as a dialectical duality in Nahua philosophy, the two were fundamentally stitched together as a whole that expressed continual *becoming*. Additionally, the dialectical movement in Nahua philosophy was also often graphically presented in spirals, where images of opposition, pairing, and intertwining were illustrated in weavings, paintings, ceramics, bowls, plates, board games, and architecture, among other forms.[41]

My point in making the above arguments is not to simply argue that dialectics came from nonwhite peoples, nor is it to suggest that the non-Western roots and forms of dialectical reasoning somehow "rescue" dialectics from "Marx the white man." Rather, in looking at the possible Egyptian roots of dialectical materialism, as well as other non-Western forms of dialectics, I am challenging the idea that Marxist, dialectical thinking is somehow inherently Western. This is a specific argument to be waged against specific critiques of Marxism as inherently flawed because of its perceived Eurocentric philosophy. Personally, as I argued earlier in this chapter, Marxist dialectical materialism offers such a powerful means for understanding the world and critiquing capitalism that it still provides useful tools for changing society. In this way dialectical materialism is somewhat transcendent of Marx himself, because it is a form of understanding how the world works. It just so happened that Karl Marx developed and used dialectical materialism to analyze capitalism in a particular geographic and historical context—one that centered the thinking of white men—such that it was named "Marxism." My argument in this chapter, then, has been that in order to understand Marxism, we need to ground Marxism itself in material history and context and understand its dialectical evolution across time and contexts. So yes, Marx was a political economist, and yes, Marxism is best known for its use, at length, to understand political economy and society under capitalism. However, Marxist dialectical materialism does far more than this: it is also a worldview, a philosophy, a methodology for analysis, and a system for being in the world—one that we can extend (and develop) well beyond political economy and Marx's original context.[42]

Even if we can recognize the growth of Marx and his analysis, and even if we can see the Egyptian origins of, and Chinese and Nahua (Aztec) corollaries to, Marxist dialectical materialism, we're still left with the arguments that Marxists and Marxist traditions like socialism and communism are mainly for white people, and white men in particular. While the above historical examples might challenge these arguments on historical-philosophical grounds, it is also important to challenge these arguments via the material histories of nonwhite Marxists.

#MarxistsSoWhite?

Because there are many, many thousands of people who identify as Marxist, interpretations of Marxism and what it means to be a Marxist range widely. As such, activists of color and women activists can easily attest to the number of times they've had a self-proclaimed Marxist "mansplain" sexism and patriarchy to them or "whitesplain" racism to them, with class politics seemingly taking precedent over concerns of race, gender, and sexuality. In this regard I and others would argue that sloppy applications, surface-level understandings, and thin commitments to Marxism have resulted in far too many white leftists relying on hegemonic tropes of power and identity in the name of Marxism—doing all Marxists a disservice in the process (and thereby reinforcing the constructed stereotypes of left Marxists as white men unable to understand or address other issues). As with any major system of belief and analysis, there are "better" and "worse" understandings and applications, and Marxism is no exception.

The diversity of understandings and applications of Marxism among self-identified Marxists notwithstanding, there is another basic point to make about arguments that Marxists are predominantly white men who can't adequately take up analyses of race and racism: this position effectively erases the long history of people of color within Marxist traditions in the United States and around the world. For over one hundred years, there have been strong non-Western Marxist, socialist, and communist traditions globally, many of which were grounded in anti-colonialism.[43] This also included indigenized Marxism and socialist governments in Latin America, other socialist and communist regimes in East and Southeast Asia, communist movements in India and the Philippines, and Marxist movements in Africa.[44]

In the United States there is a significant history of people of color identifying, and claiming identities, as Marxist, communist, or socialist. For instance, there is an established tradition of Black Marxist politics in this country that has been neglected (purposefully or not), where African Americans either sympathized with communist politics, were active in various Marxist/socialist/communist parties, or did cultural work, particularly from the 1920s to the 1940s.[45] Indeed, thousands of African Americans joined the Communist Party of the USA where, in 1921, after being pushed by Lenin to organize better among Black proletarians, they pronounced,

> The Negro workers in America are exploited and oppressed more ruthlessly than any other group. The history of the Southern Negro is the history of a reign of terror—of persecution, rape, and murder . . . Because of the anti-Negro policies of organized labor, the Negro has despaired of aid from this source, and he has either been driven into the camp of labor's enemies, or has been compelled to develop purely racial organizations which seek purely racial aims. The Workers Party will support Negroes in their struggle for Liberation, and will help them in their fight for economic, political and social equality . . . Its task will be to destroy altogether the barrier of race prejudice that has been used to keep apart the Black and white workers, and bind them into a solid union of revolutionary forces for the overthrow of our common enemy.[46]

Further, we tend to forget historically that towering African American figures such as C. L. R. James, Richard Wright, and W. E. B. Du Bois identified with Marxism and communism during important parts of their lives and work.[47] Black women such as Grace Campbell and Williana Burroughs were also key communist organizers in Harlem of the 1920s and 1930s, with Campbell cofounding the New York communist group the African Blood Brotherhood, and Burroughs being the first Black woman to address an international communist gathering, in Moscow in 1928.[48]

There were also Black men such as Harry Haywood, who traveled to the Soviet Union in the 1920s to study and became a strong Marxist-Leninist thinker, active in the Black liberation movement for decades in the United States, including the African Blood Brotherhood.[49] So even while it may have been imperfect and punctuated by internal struggle with white comrades (including some African Americans leaving the Communist Party USA out of frustration with sometimes racist leadership), there is most definitely a Black radical tradition that has embraced Marxism as an important component of Black liberation in the face of racialized capitalism. As Keeanga-Yamahtta Taylor so eloquently reminds us in *From #BlackLivesMatter to Black Liberation*, this tradition was carried on into the 1960s and 1970s through groups like the Black Panther Party for Self-Defense—perhaps the most famous and powerful Black socialist organization in US history—and anti-capitalist critiques have certainly been a piece of the #BlackLivesMatter movement.

Similar historical examples exist within different Asian American communities as well. For instance, in 1904 there were two Japanese American socialist groups formed in the San Francisco Bay Area, one in San Francisco and one in Oakland. These two groups joined in 1906 to form the Shakai Kakumeito (Social Revolutionary Party), with several members also active in socialist parties in Illinois and Iowa. The Japanese Labor League (essentially an independent union for Japanese American farmworkers) also published a newspaper, the *Rodo*, whose editorial team included key individuals from the Shakai Kakumeito.[50] There was also a San Francisco–based group, the Ghadar Party, which was formed by Sikh workers and Hindu students in 1913, as well as the New York–based Japanese Communist Group in 1920, whose leadership, specifically Sen Katayama, worked closely with the leaders in the African Blood Brotherhood to more deeply articulate an anti-colonialist socialism that dealt with the complex intertwining of race, society, and economics.[51] Spurred in part by the translation of Marxist texts from Japanese to Chinese, there were also pockets of socialist and Marxist organizing in the Chinese American community—including one of the earliest organizations, the Chinese Socialist Club, founded in 1914 in San Francisco.[52] In the 1930s Filipino/a Americans like Pablo Manlapit were very active labor organizers, and others like Carlos Bulosan and Chris Mensalvas were cultural workers among proletarian Filipino/a Americans. Even though the anti-communist pressures of the Red Scare and US government repression of Filipino/a radicalism kept many from openly declaring their communism, socialism, or Marxism, it was clear that these Filipino/a activists identified with working-class struggle and were fellow travelers with the communist movements of both the United States and the Philippines at the time.[53] These radical socialist, Marxist, and communist Asian American legacies were carried on into the 1960s, 1970s, and 1980s by Chinese American groups like I Wor Kuen and Wei Min She, Japanese American groups like the Japan Town Collective and East Wind, and Filipino/a American organizations like the Union of Democratic Filipinos (KDP).[54]

There is also a substantial tradition of Mexican American socialist/Marxist/communist organizing. In the 1920s and 1930s, Mexican American workers in California, throughout the US Southwest region, and into Texas joined the Communist Party and were quite active relative to labor organizing and the formation of various unions, with many taking leadership positions.[55] For instance, Emma Tenayuca, among a core of Mexican American women activists, became a leader in labor organizing in San Antonio. She became a state-level officer in the Communist Party there, and cowrote, with her husband Homer Brooks, an analysis of the "Mexican Question in the Southwest," for the publication the *Communist*.[56] This tradition was carried into the 1960s and 1970s through a myriad of community activist organizations and groups.[57] One such group was the Centro de Acción Social Autónomo (CASA), which grew out of the Hermandad Mexicana Nacional (Mexican Brotherhood)—

an explicitly Marxist-Leninist group in Southern California. CASA focused on labor organizing among Latinxs and providing support for immigrant services. Eventually, there were approximately ten different, relatively independent CASAs in different cities around the country, all working under the umbrella of the Brotherhood.[58]

My review here has been purposefully brief since the focus of this book is not to recapitulate the Marxist traditions in non-Western nations and among people of color in the United States. Rather, I simply want to remind us that there are Marxist traditions in many of our communities and that perhaps our understandings of these traditions has been whitewashed. Purposeful or not, such whitewashing of our radical histories can serve to keep people of color in the United States from feeling like they too can take up Marxist critiques of capitalism without succumbing to some kind of internalized oppression of whiteness. Similarly, then, if Marxism is inherently imbued with whiteness, then the only way we can explain the thousands upon thousands of nonwhite, US Marxists (or the millions of Marxists in non-Western countries around the world) is to say that they were all duped and fooled into submission to the "white man's Marxism." However, to believe that the Marxism of nonwhites is and has been a matter of submission to whiteness is functionally racist because it presumes that these peoples were not making their own powerful decisions to combat capitalism here and around the world, that somehow they were incapable of organizing in their communities of their own volition and by articulating their own anti-capitalist, anti-imperialist analyses. This is a presumption that we need to refuse outright.

Marxism, Indigeneity, and Settler Colonialism

Perhaps as a corollary for Marx's original lack of in-depth attention to the role of colonization in the formation of capitalism, there have also been tensions and appraisals regarding whether or not Marxism can adequately deal with issues of indigeneity and settler colonialism.[59] Historically, the bulk of these have been based on the assertion that

Marxism is purely Eurocentric, and therefore of little or no use to the struggles of Native Americans and other indigenous populations around the globe. While the issue of use value of Marxism to Native peoples in colonized America is not for me to decide, as I argued earlier in this chapter, Marxist philosophy is not as Western or Eurocentric as most have suggested. Other Native critiques have rightfully highlighted Marx and Engels's early assertions about the necessity of indigenous tribes to be broken in the development of society, as well as the Marxist trope of the human subjugation of nature, as antithetical to Native culture, understanding, and way of being in the world.[60] Between the above discussions about Marx's developing analysis of colonization and race and the compatibility of Marxism with environmental analysis, I have partially addressed these concerns here as well—particularly if we take dialectical materialism as transcending Marx's (and Engels's) personal, individual limitations. However, the indigenous critique of Marxism also raises another important consideration: a focus on capital and capitalism is in some ways precluded by the establishment and existence of a colonial state, with land and resources seen merely as fuel for "primitive accumulation" in the buildup to modern-day capitalist production. Further, this issue raises other complications for how we think about Marxist anti-capitalism. For instance, in simplistic terms, a socialist or communist revolution calls for the takeover of the state by the workers. However, what if the state itself was established through settler colonialism and the dispossession of Native lands? Without specific attention paid to indigenous sovereignty and colonization, socialism or communism could potentially imply the establishment of a settler-colonial socialist or communist state that is still based on the displacement of indigenous nations.[61]

To a certain degree, Lenin began to broach this issue in 1916 in his essay "The Socialist Revolution and the Right of Nations to Self-Determination."[62] At the time he was struggling with other socialists about the need for national unity versus the rights of self-determination, particularly at "the frontiers of a state that is based on national oppression."[63] To this end, Lenin was adamant that

> [t]he proletariat cannot but fight against the forcible retention of the oppressed nations within the boundaries of a given state, and this is exactly what the struggle for the right of self-determination means. The proletariat must demand the right of political secession for the colonies and for the nations that "its own" nation oppresses. Unless it does this, proletarian internationalism will remain a meaningless phrase; mutual confidence and class solidarity between the workers of the oppressing and oppressed nations will be impossible.[64]

While clearly not a fully articulated theory, Lenin's treatment here highlights how serious anti-capitalist movements must recognize the self-determination of nations within a nation, which in the contemporary context can and should be applied to indigenous nations in resistance to capitalist settler colonialism.[65]

Drawing on the work of anti-colonial Marxism suggested by Frantz Fanon, W. E. B. DuBois, and José Carlos Mariátegui (whose Marxism was grounded among indigenous Peruvians), Noah De Lissovoy has argued for a "decolonial Marxism" that decenters Europe and recenters the colonized "margins" in a way that "not only fills out an incomplete Marxism but actually reorients it in a basic way, undertaking a displacement of contradictions that exposes systemic violence and racism at the center of the logic of capitalism and its historical unfolding."[66] De Lissovoy's work here follows that of Glen Coulthard—an indigenous scholar from the Dene peoples in Canada—and his book *Red Skin, White Masks*. Coulthard centers colonial dispossession within a Marxist analysis, placing it at the heart of the development of capitalism. In doing so, Coulthard attempts to reconcile what is often perceived as a historical division between Marx's discussion of "primitive accumulation" and the production of capital. In the typical understanding of this division, primitive accumulation—the taking of land, water, and other resources in order to establish capitalism—is often constructed as a process that happened in the past and has since ended, with the ongoing production of capital that is now happening seen as a modern and separate process.

Instead, Coulthard suggests that "we should see [primitive accumulation] as an ongoing practice of dispossession that never ceases to structure capitalist and colonial social relations in the present. Settler colonialism is territorially acquisitive in perpetuity."[67] It is important to note that, in many ways, by making this argument Coulthard is actually recapitulating an analysis that Marx himself already made in *Capital*, volume 1, where, as Malott and Ford write, "Marx summarizes the process of expanding capital as cyclical, suggesting that primitive accumulation, rather than a one-time occurrence, is an ongoing necessity of the perpetually expanding property of capitalism."[68] Instead of there being a historical schism between primitive accumulation and capitalist development, as some critics of Marx and Marxism have suggested, Coulthard in fact agrees with Marx that their concurrence is ongoing.

Regardless, Coulthard's contribution is important because it brings a specifically indigenous politics to our understanding of the settler-colonial, capitalist present, where he further argues that

> [l]ike capital, colonialism, as a structure of domination predicated on dispossession, is not "a thing," but rather the sum effect of the diversity of interlocking oppressive social relations that constitute it. When stated this way, it should be clear that shifting our position to highlight the ongoing effects of colonial dispossession in no way displaces questions of distributive justice or class struggle; rather, it simply situates these questions more firmly alongside and in relation to the other sites and relations of power that inform our settler-colonial present.[69]

Coulthard's centering of colonial dispossession within Marxism also highlights the role of the capitalist state in enforcing settler colonialism at every turn, often under the guise of liberal programs supposedly enstated "for" Native peoples. Coulthard also offers an explicit recognition of indigenous labor in the production of capital during colonization and within the settler-colonial context, arguing that dispossession, not proletarianization, has been the dominant structuring force in the relationship between Native peoples and the state. Finally, drawing on this Marxism of the dispossessed, Coulthard also highlights how indigenous, place-based resistance recognizes the reciprocal relationship between people and the earth, and also challenges simplistic ecological critiques of Marxism and dialectical materialism.[70]

Coulthard's recentering of Marxism on dispossession and settler colonialism is creative and interesting on its own. However, it is even stronger when taken in conversation with David Harvey's analysis of neoliberalism and the process he refers to as "accumulation by dispossession"—which frames much of the current neoliberal capitalist project as a process of taking assets from the public and transferring them to the wealthy, capitalist class.[71] Coulthard's analysis also opens up some deeper implications for Marxist political economy: in understanding primitive accumulation as ongoing within the modern-day settler, capitalist state, we might also need to extend that shift more formally into a Marxist analysis of production, labor, and capital. For instance, this means accounting for enduring dispossession in the calculation of labor power. For Marx, "labor power" or the "capacity for labor" refers to the "aggregate of those bodily and mental capabilities existing in a human being"; it "only exists as a capacity of a living individual; its production presupposed his existence; and therefore the production of labour is dependent upon the worker's reproduction of himself, upon the worker's maintenance."[72] In this way Marx's analysis of labor power not only refers to the labor an individual worker can produce in a day, but also the aggregate resources (food, housing, health, etc.) it takes for an individual worker and for workers as a class to keep reproducing their labor power on a day-to-day basis. Coulthard's reframing then forces a different spin into our Marxist analysis of labor power: if we keep the ongoing maintenance of the capitalist settler state as part of our core analysis, then the reproduction of aggregate labor power (the reproduction of workers' capacities on a day-to-day basis) in part requires maintaining the ongoing dispossession of Native peoples within the capitalist present.

Another immediate implication of Coulthard's recontextualization of primitive accumulation in the settler-colonial capitalist present comes in how we might understand the production of capital and value. One of the forms of capital Marx analyzed is "constant capital." For Marx, constant capital referred to the "means of production"—the machines, the tools, the resources it takes to produce a commodity. Once a commodity is produced, some portion of the commodity's value arises from the contribution of constant capital. Marx referred to this portion of the value as "fixed capital" because it stays with the means of production while the rest of the capital circulates in the market with the commodity. Further, Marx explains that "[s]ome means of production do not enter materially into the product. Such are auxiliary materials, which are consumed by the instruments of labour themselves in the performance of their functions, like coal consumed by a steam-engine; or which merely assist in the operation, like gas for lighting, etc. It is only their value which forms a part of the value of the products."[73] Again, Coulthard pushes us here because if primitive accumulation is an ongoing process in our settler-colonial capitalist present, then Native dispossession exists within the means of production in the dispossessed land as well as the fuel and resources used in production. In this sense we could say that a portion of all value and all capital extends from the accumulation by dispossession of Native lands (facilitated by the settler-colonial capitalist state).

These issues are difficult and tangled, and I have consistently appreciated the work of Zeus Leonardo, Anthony Brown, Noah De Lissovoy (discussed below), and others who have recognized the materiality of racism and settler colonialism in their treatment of Marxism in educational research.[74] I think what the above colleagues and I have done is try to ameliorate the historical and theoretical tensions that have grown for a variety of reasons—reasons that include severe misunderstandings and misconstructions of Marxism and class analysis, as well as the missteps and mistakes of Marxists along the way. Suffice it to say, even if Marx himself was not up to the task of adequately addressing the specific relationship between indigeneity, settler colonialism, and capitalism, I do think that Marxist dialectical materialism is capable.

Race and Class and . . . in a Marxist Analysis?

I've argued here that even though Marx himself was Eurocentric at times (although he grew and developed over time), Marxism is not specifically Eurocentric, especially if we understand Marxism to be based on dialectical materialism and if we look at the actual history of nonwhite peoples identifying with Marxism, socialism, and communism in the United States and around the world. Indeed, I would also argue that serious Marxists understand quite well how different axes of power related to race, gender, and settler colonialism are tightly intertwined with capitalist production and exploitation. For instance, with regard to race specifically, Keeanga-Yahmatta Taylor incisively writes,

> Racism in the United States has never been just about abusing Black and Brown people just for the sake of doing so. It has always been a means by which the most powerful white men in the country have justified their rule, made their money, and kept the rest of us at bay. To that end, racism, capitalism, and class rule have always been tangled together in such a way that it is impossible to imagine one without the other. Can there be Black liberation in the United States as the country is currently constituted? No. Capitalism is contingent on the absence of freedom and liberation for Black people and anyone else who does not directly benefit from its economic disorder.[75]

Similar tensions regarding the relationship between racial and Marxist class analyses have long marked left and critical educational studies.[76] For instance, Zeus Leonardo specifically argues for the conceptual construction of *raceclass* as a unified term signaling that both the Marxist and critical race theory traditions have much to learn from each other and can be unified to increase the power of our analyses.[77] Anthony Brown and Noah De Lissovoy suggest a dialectical unification of race and class analyses. Using the example of racial segregation in schools, Brown and De Lissovoy go on to discuss how class and race intersect in education, where "capital builds race and class out of each other—throws them together and tears them apart, as suits it, and as assures the most effective subjugation and fragmentation of selves and societies."[78] Brown and De Lissovoy call for an analysis based on *economies of racism*, to bring "white supremacy and capitalist accumulation together in a single dialectic."[79]

In many ways, Brown and De Lissovoy express an educational version of Keeanga-Yamahtta Taylor's point regarding the relationship between race and capitalism, where she explains that "[t]o claim, then, as Marxists do, that racism is a product of capitalism is not to deny or diminish its centrality to or impact on American society. It is simply to explain its origins and persistence. Nor is this reducing racism to just a function of capitalism; it is locating the dynamic relationship between class exploitation and racial oppression in the functioning of American capitalism."[80] In the same spirit, I have reached outside of the field of education to the work of literary scholar Jodi Melamed and her framing of "neoliberal multiculturalism"[81] because it rests on the assumption that capitalism has always been racialized, and that capitalist anti-racisms get used to mask racist neoliberal projects.[82]

In these ways, a Marxist, dialectical materialist class analysis could never be reduced to just pure economic determinism, nor could it be reduced to some flat caricature of "class" being white and male. Our identities are intersectional, and capitalism has been adept at trying both to parse us into individual pieces and to use our identities against us. So a true class analysis, one based on our lived realities under capitalism, has to recognize this intersectionality. As political prisoner David Gilbert writes in his wonderful essay "Is Marxism Relevant?," there is a kind of intersectionality of identity that naturally flows from a Marxist analysis:

> To me, the best starting point for analyzing society is Marx's "the totality of [the] relations of production," (from the Preface to the *Critique of Political Economy*, 1859). He zeroed in on the relationship of wage labor and capital. Naturally, as insightful as Marx was, his perspective wasn't magically untethered from being a European male. What's even more relevant to his focus

> was the tremendously dynamic economic and social role industrialization was playing in mid-19th century Europe. But as I understand the sum total of the relations of production, they involve a lot more.[83]

Gilbert goes on to discuss the ways that, for instance, transphobia and homophobia play critical roles in enforcing patriarchy and violence against women as part of their subordination as an exploited class. Gilbert also highlights the central role of white supremacy in modern imperialism and the possibilities presented by Marxism for addressing environmental issues. In this way Gilbert suggests a kind of Marxist intersectionality that recognizes the many forms of violence and exploitation, based on different aspects of our identities, that the ruling class uses to maintain its power. Keeanga-Yamahtta Taylor also reminds us that

> [n]o serious socialist current in the last hundred years has ever demanded that Black or Latino/a workers put their struggles on the back burner while some other class struggle is waged first. This assumption rests on the mistaken idea that the working class is white and male, and therefore incapable of taking up issues of race, class, and gender. In fact, the American working class is female, immigrant, Black, white, Latino/a, and more. Immigrant issues, gender issues, and antiracism *are* working class issues.[84]

To this end, if you are reading this book and are merely seeing whiteness in my class and Marxist analyses, understand the following: (1) I am working from the basis that dialectical materialism as a worldview not only descends from Europe, but is also rooted in non-Western philosophies (Egyptian, Aztec, and Chinese, among others); (2) I see my work as part of a constellation and tradition of nonwhite Marxists and Marxism grounded in anti-colonial, anti-imperialist, and anti-capitalist struggles that have been taken up by communities of color in the United States and around the world; (3) I begin from a foundational understanding of class that embraces the more expansive, intersectional definition because that is the material reality of "class" as it exists in the world.

Building on the conceptual and philosophical base established here, in the next chapter I look at another foundational relationship: the role of schools and education under capitalism.

Chapter 3

Capitalist Inequality and Schools

Marxism, Neo-Marxism, and the Dialectics of Educational (Re)Production

> *What these [people] all lack is dialectics. They always see only here cause, there effect. That this is a hollow abstraction, that such metaphysical polar opposites exist in the real world only during crises, while the whole vast process goes on in the form of interaction—though of very unequal forces, the economic movement being by far the strongest, most primordial, most decisive—that here everything is relative and nothing absolute—this they never begin to see.*
>
> —Frederick Engels, "Engels to C. Schmidt in Berlin"[1]

What is the role of schools in our society? Are they pathways for upward mobility and for overcoming poverty and racism? Or do they operate mainly as vehicles for reproducing inequality? The liberal answers to these questions are that schools are, indeed, the great equalizer; that, while there are obvious obstacles like poverty and racism to overcome, if you just work hard and prove your worth, you will be successful in school; if you're poor, this success will translate into the chance to break the chains of poverty and racism as you climb up the socioeconomic ladder of life. This liberal logic of meritocracy holds that we are all individuals, and that structural and institutional inequalities don't really exist—because in our society, if you just work hard enough as an individual, you will be successful in school and elsewhere.[2]

Our system of education in the United States is overrun with policies and practices built on this liberal ideal. Using standardized tests to make high-stakes decisions around graduation, promotion between grades, teacher rating and pay, and student funding—as is the current practice nationally—is based on the assumption that these tests measure all individuals accurately and fairly based on the efforts of students, teachers, and administrators. The problem is that (as I discuss in greater detail in chapter 4) we have known for quite some time that factors outside of schools like food insecurity, housing insecurity, and access to health care, and livable wages account for up to 80 percent of any given test score.[3] Regardless of this fact, educational policymakers in the United States continue to blame individual children, teachers, schools, and parents for our educational woes, claiming that they are simply not trying hard enough. Failing poor kids are blamed not for being poor, but for believing in a "culture of poverty," or for being too wild and undisciplined, or for not having enough "grit," or for not caring enough to be successful in school.[4] In this liberal narrative of meritocracy, resources and structural inequalities shouldn't matter. Even if policymakers acknowledge these inequalities, they address them only at the level of the individual, considering structural changes like the provision of housing, food, and health care to be out of reach, unattainable, or unimaginable. And of course, challenging capitalism isn't even on the table.

However, Marxists ask different kinds of questions than liberals in analyzing educational inequalities. We ask, what is the relationship between schools and capitalism? And, can schools be sites of resistance and revolution, or do they simply reproduce capitalist inequalities? As a Marxist, I see education and learning as partly a product of student labor, as well as the labor of school staff and administration, and I don't deny the role that individual effort, care, and commitment plays in all of our labor. It is hard to get something done if you don't *try*. However, also as a Marxist, I am keenly aware of how our structural conditions—access to resources, cultural backgrounds, poverty, racism, citizenship status, housing, parental education, and so forth—create opportunities for us to do some things while simultaneously limiting our abilities to do others.

For instance, take the issue of parent or guardian help with homework. Instead of looking at purely individual effort, I tend to ask more structural questions: Does the parent or guardian have to work multiple jobs just to pay the rent, without much time to help with homework? Or does one parent or guardian make enough money that another has the time and energy to focus on their child's homework, and maybe even become involved with the parent-teacher association? Is the homework in the home language of the parent or guardian? Going to college is another example: What's the immigration status of the student, or, better yet, what is the current federal or university policy toward students' access to college if they don't have citizenship? Did the parents finish only high school, or do they have advanced degrees and have the institutional knowledge to navigate the tests, scholarships, and courses? The point is that structural conditions matter. The languages that are spoken at home, racialized community experiences with teachers and officials, prenatal and postnatal nutrition, likelihood of interacting with lead paint and other environmental toxins, or history as a refugee or immigrant—the list could go on forever—all make huge differences in how we understand, interact with, and perform in schools.

In this regard, there is a Marxian tradition of analyzing the relationship between schools and the inequalities of capitalism in the United States that goes back to the early 1970s. However, the problem is that this tradition has been marred by anti-Marxist tendencies from many who identify as leftist and even Marxist. In this chapter I defend the Marxist, dialectical materialist tradition of analyzing schools and capitalism. Because I think it is important for Marxist educators to have a strong grasp of history, I recount the struggle over Marxist analyses of education, particularly the turn to what was coined neo-Marxism. The terrain of this struggle is foundational in that it illustrates an erroneous attack on Marxism from within the Left itself as well as orients us toward what a Marxist analysis might look like. To make the Marxist corrective to these attacks, here I also turn to the actual words of Marx and Engels to explain their original dialectical materialist analysis of the relationship between the economy and parts of the state such as schools. I end this chapter with a discussion of the contradictions of capitalist schooling, including briefly addressing the role of schools in resistance and revolution.

Base, Superstructure, and Economic Determinism

It should be obvious to almost anyone that, on the whole, our system of education in the United States produces and reproduces inequalities largely on the basis of race and class. This reality is well documented in the research,[5] and has been for quite some time.[6] In order to explain this phenomenon, many Marxists (myself included) turn to Marx's own formulation of the relationship between the economy and society, summarized in "Preface to a Contribution to the Critique of Political Economy":

> In the social production of their life, men enter into definite relations that are indispensable and independent of their will, relations of production which correspond to a definite stage of development of their material productive forces. The sum total of these relations of production constitutes the economic structure of society, the real foundation, on which rises a legal and political superstructure and to which correspond definite forms of social consciousness. The mode of production of material life conditions the social, political and intellectual life process in general. It is not the consciousness of men that determines their being, but, one the contrary, their social being that determines their consciousness.[7]

These four sentences outline what is commonly referred to in Marxism as the base/superstructure model, where the "legal and political superstructure" rises out of the "relations of production" that make up the base "economic structure of society." Within this framing, schools are a part of the political superstructure, and they are implicated in reproducing "forms of social consciousness" that correspond with capitalist production.

However, it has been commonplace to critique Marx's formulation for being economistic—that is, for placing too much emphasis on the economy as the sole determinant of society, social relations, and sociopolitical institutions. Stuart Hall explains that economic determinism

> reduces everything in a social formation to the economic level, and conceptualizes all other types of social relations as directly and immediately "corresponding to the economic. . . . In this sense, "economism" *is* theoretical reductionism. It simplifies the structure of social formations, reducing their complexity of articulation, vertical and horizontal, to a single line of determination. It simplifies the very concept of "determination" (which in Marx is actually a very complex idea) to that of a mechanical function.[8]

In the field of education, such views resulted in Marxism being criticized for suggesting a direct, linear, mechanical, or simple correspondence between the capitalist economy and structures of schooling. Based on perceptions that Marx and Marxism are too economically determinist (perceptions that I will argue are patently wrong), critical educational scholars responded by placing more emphasis on the "superstructure" of society and culture through a focus on Gramsci's conception of "hegemony," as well as Althusser's arguments about the "relative autonomy" of the superstructure from the economic base.[9] This shift in focus within critical educational theory was significant because it signaled a tactical move away from Marxism that in the process essentially birthed neo-Marxism as a predominant trend, supposedly fixing the perceived economic determinism of the now-forsaken "orthodox" Marxism.[10]

Education, Social Reproduction, and the Correspondence Principle

Among neo-Marxist educational scholars, the most forsaken of them all were Bowles and Gintis and their 1976 book, *Schooling in Capitalist America: Educational Reform and the Contradictions of Economic Life*, which not only kick-started explicitly Marxist analyses of schooling in the United States, but also sparked the shift toward neo-Marxism in educational research. In their book, Bowles and Gintis advance the "correspondence principle" of educational relations, which asserts that "schooling has contributed to the reproduction of the social relations of production largely through the correspondence between school and class structure."[11] They go on to explain in more detail that

> [t]he educational system helps integrate youth into the economic system . . . through the structural correspondence between its social relations and those of production. The structure of social relations in education not only inures the student to the discipline of the work place, but develops the types of personal demeanor, modes of self-presentation, self-image, and social-class identifications which are crucial ingredients of job adequacy. Specifically, the social relationships of education—the relationships between administrators and teachers, teachers and students, students and students, and students and their work—replicate the hierarchical division of labor.[12]

Critical education theorists sharply criticized Bowles and Gintis's correspondence principle for ignoring the role of teachers, culture, and ideology in schools, for being too mechanical and overly economistic, and for neglecting students' and others' resistance to dominant social relations.[13] Thus, in response to the perceived economic determinism of Bowles and Gintis—and by extension, Marx and Marxism as well—neo-Marxist critics argued that schools do not exactly reproduce norms of behavior, attitude, and ideological dispositions required for capitalist production, and instead argued that individuals within schools possess *agency* and *consciousness* that allow them to mediate and *resist* the dominant social relations reproduced through institutions.[14]

I have to admit that as a graduate student I, too, fell prey to the canned critiques of *Schooling in Capitalist America*. In several publications I uncritically labeled Bowles and Gintis's "correspondence principle" as too mechanistic and overly economically determinist.[15] When I revisited Bowles and Gintis's book as I wrote *A Marxist Education*, I was surprised at what I found. For instance, and contrary to the canon of critiques, Bowles and Gintis were very clear from the outset that students, parents, and teachers do have power and that they do resist the inculcation of capitalist relations in schools. In the introduction, they write,

> [T]hough the school system has effectively served the interests of profit and political stability, it has hardly been a finely tuned instrument of manipulation in the hands of socially dominant groups. Schools and colleges do indeed help to justify inequality, but they also have become arenas in which a highly politicized egalitarian consciousness has developed among some parents, teachers, and students. The authoritarian classroom does produce docile workers, but it also produces misfits and rebels. The university trains the elite in the skills of domination, but it has also given birth to a powerful radical movement and critique of capitalist society. . . . Education in the United States is as contradictory and complex as the larger society; no simplistic or mechanical theory can help us understand it.[16]

Later, they also discuss how throughout US history "these reproduction mechanisms have failed, sometimes quite spectacularly," and how both the "internal dynamic of the education system" and "popular opposition" have countered the school's reproduction of capitalist relations.[17] Further, Bowles and Gintis spend significant time discussing freedom schools (radical community schools), equal education, and the potentials of revolutionary reforms—all of which they argue must be parts of larger mass movements for social change.[18]

To be sure, there are still critiques to be made of *Schooling in Capitalist America*. For instance, the utter lack of a developed analysis of the interplay of race and educational inequality within the context of capitalist schooling is glaring. This omission speaks volumes about their disregard for the role of racism and colonization in the development of capitalism, as well as for the role of schools in the ongoing maintenance of settler colonialism and racial hierarchies. Also, despite their many caveats, Bowles and Gintis's use of IQ test scores was (and still is) retrograde and backward, especially given the racist and classist history of standardized IQ tests themselves.[19] Further, it is true, as critics have argued, that Bowles and Gintis did not look at life within schools with the kind of nuance exhibited, for instance, in Jean Anyon's then-groundbreaking research on economic class in school curriculum.[20] However, on this point, in their defense (and for better or worse), I think Bowles and Gintis were focused purely on an analysis of the macro-structuring of schooling by capitalism, and they did not set out to describe how the correspondence principle operated at the individual classroom or school level. It simply was not a focus of their project.

The above critiques notwithstanding, contrary to the common neo-Marxist assertion that Bowles and Gintis offered a simple, mechanical correspondence between capitalism and schools, *Schooling in Capitalist America* actually recognized that schools were sites of contradiction, resistance, and potential change. However, despite this reality, neo-Marxists and others cast *Schooling in Capitalist America* as a prime example of the supposed flaws of Marxist analyses of education, and Bowles and Gintis's arguments became, a "straw-man against which more subtle and sophisticated accounts of the relationship between schooling and society can be favourably compared."[21] Faced with a formulation between the relations of production (economic base) and their reproduction in schools (the superstructure) that they *perceived* as a mechanical, functionalist, direct correspondence, critical educational theorists responded by developing a critique of capitalist relations in schools and society that allowed for resistance to those dominant relations—a consideration they suggested was missing from Marxist accounts. (Note that there were many reasons for this turn away from Marxist analysis by critical theorists and neo-Marxists, including anti-Marxism.)[22] Neo-Marxists thus looked to the works of Gramsci and Althusser for a solution to this perceived dilemma of Marxism.

Gramsci and the Concept of Hegemony

Antonio Gramsci was a founder of the Italian Communist Party who was imprisoned by Italian Fascists in 1926. While in prison he penned over three thousand pages of notebooks on Marxist theory and political strategy[23] that were subsequently edited and published in English translation as *Selections from the Prison Notebooks*. In particular Gramsci's elaboration of the concept of *hegemony* has become a central tenet in neo-Marxist educational theorizing. In the *Prison Notebooks* Gramsci posits that "social hegemony" is the "'spontaneous' consent given by the great masses of the population to the general direction imposed on social life by the dominant fundamental group; this consent is 'historically' caused by the prestige (and consequent confidence) which the dominant group enjoys because of its position and function in the world of production."[24] Gramsci further discusses how social hegemony takes on a kind of universal consciousness in the ways that "the development and expansion of the particular [dominant] group are conceived of and presented, as being the motor force of a universal expansion."[25]

Gramsci's concept of hegemony is intimately linked to his formulation of the relationship between the superstructure and the economic base. He specifies two ways in which the superstructure reproduces capitalist relations: the first is hegemonic—through ideology and universalized "spontaneous consent"—while the second is through "legal" enforcement of judiciaries and other institutions associated with the state.[26] With his focus on the processes of hegemony and domination and the state's role in the two, Gramsci places an emphasis on the autonomy of the superstructure from the economic base.[27] However, Gramsci does not elevate the superstructure to full independence. Rather, he conceives of the superstructure as dialectically related to the economic base:

> [Economic] structures and superstructures form an "historical bloc." That is to say the complex, contradictory and discordant *ensemble* of the superstructure is the reflection of the *ensemble* of the social relations of production. From this, one can conclude: that only a totalitarian system of ideologies gives a rational reflection of the contradiction of the structure . . . This reasoning is based on the necessary reciprocity between structure and superstructure, a reciprocity which is nothing other than the real dialectical process.[28]

Gramsci's description of the superstructure as a "complex, contradictory and discordant *ensemble*" (his emphasis) frames the superstructure as dynamic, fluid, and consisting of an assemblage of parts—all of which suggests a dialectical, complex, and nondeterministic conception of the base/superstructure relationship. By focusing on the superstructure, identifying two levels, expanding the concept of hegemony, and asserting the partial autonomy of the state from capitalist production, neo-Marxists used Gramsci to argue that schools were not being fully determined by the economic structure and to reinforce their potential for resisting bourgeois hegemony.[29]

Gramsci's conception of hegemony has also been used within critical educational theory to explain how consent of the subordinate is essentially "won" by those in power. Often, to maintain their legitimacy, dominant elites offer compromises or accords with subordinate groups, accords that can act as "an umbrella under which many groups can stand but which basically still is under the guiding principles of dominant groups."[30] Thus, Gramsci's conception of hegemony also allows for critical education theorists to recognize some amount of human agency in individuals and communities that purposefully relate to and navigate social, economic, cultural, political, and educational "structures."

It is important to recognize that various aspects of Gramsci's ideas have been claimed by a wide-ranging and often contradictory set of political perspectives, including educational conservatives like E. D. Hirsch, Marxists, Leninists, post-Marxists, neo-Marxists, feminists, post-structuralists, and postmodernists alike.[31] Bob Jessop explains this phenomenon as being possible because Gramsci's theoretical writing, a collection of notebooks, was of "incomplete and tentative character," thus making it "compatible with several other theoretical currents."[32] Additionally, Gramsci had to write cryptically in order to avoid prison censors, and he died before getting the chance to edit the notebooks himself—all of which allows for increased confusion as to the meanings of key terms like "ideology," "State," and "hegemony."[33] To further complicate matters, the editors and translators of *Selections from the Prison Notebooks* admit that Gramsci's own mixed usage of terms, along with translation issues, also contributed to such confusion.[34]

Althusser and Relative Autonomy

Another key theorist that neo-Marxist educational scholars looked to in their turn away from Marxism was French communist philosopher Louis Althusser; they were particularly interested in his specific framing of the "relative autonomy" between the state (superstructure) and the economic base. In his discussion of the relationship between the two in his book *Lenin and Philosophy and other Essays*, Althusser writes,

> It is easy to see that this representation of the structure of every society as an edifice containing a base (infrastructure) on which are erected the two "floors" of the superstructure, is a metaphor, to be quite precise, a spatial metaphor . . . this metaphor . . . suggests that the upper floors could not "stay up" (in the air) alone, if they did not rest precisely on their base. . . . Thus the object of the metaphor of the edifice is to represent above all the "determination in the last instance" by the economic base.[35]

Althusser goes on to explore the base/superstructure relationship, and given the superstructure's "determination in the last instance" by the base, he arrives at two conclusions: "(1) there is a 'relative autonomy' of the superstructure with respect to the base; (2) there is a 'reciprocal action' of the superstructure on the base."[36] Additionally, as part of his analysis Althusser distinguishes two different components of the superstructure: the "Repressive State Apparatus" (RSA) and the "Ideological State Apparatus" (ISA), used by those in power to maintain hegemonic control through physical force and ideology, respectively.

Althusser frames schools as part of the ISA because of their central role in maintaining ideological hegemony for the ruling class, stating, "I believe that the ideological State apparatus which has been installed in the *dominant* position in mature capitalist social formations . . . is the *educational ideological apparatus*."[37] He goes on to discuss how schools, as a tool of bourgeois hegemony, are presented as a universally neutral and natural mechanism: "The mechanisms which produce this vital result for the capitalist regime are naturally covered up and concealed by a universally reigning ideology of the School, universally reigning because it is one of the essential forms of the ruling bourgeois ideology: an ideology which represents the School as a neutral environment purged of ideology."[38] Althusser's conception of schools in relation to hegemony meshes with the Gramscian view in that schools transmit the "universally reigning ideology" while simultaneously maintaining the image of being a "neutral environment purged of ideology." Thus, they contribute to, in Gramscian terms, the spontaneous consent of the dominated.

Althusser's conception of "relative autonomy" is what has mainly been taken up by neo-Marxist education theorists. For instance, Michael Apple makes use of Althusser when he explains that "there was a dynamic interplay between the political and economic spheres which was found in education. While the former was not reducible to the latter—and, like culture, it had a significant degree of relative autonomy—the role the school plays *as a state apparatus* is strongly related to the core problems of accumulation and legitimation faced by the state and a mode of production."[39] Strands of Althusser's formulation can also be found running through the work of theorists in the field of sociology of education, including Pierre Bourdieu and Jean-Claude Passeron, as well as Basil Bernstein.[40] Althusser's concept of relative autonomy is also used within what is loosely referred to "resistance theory" in education and is especially prominent in the work of Henry Giroux, who offers that "in resistance accounts, schools are relatively autonomous institutions that not only provide spaces for oppositional behavior and teaching but also represent a source of contradictions that sometimes make them dysfunctional to the material and ideological interests of the dominant society."[41] Resistance theory, as evidence of the relative autonomy of schools, takes on issues of cultural production and reproduction as central fields of educational inquiry; it is perhaps epitomized by the ethnographic work of Paul Willis, who in his work about the "lads" in the United Kingdom found that working-class schoolboys "resisted the mental and bodily inculcations of the school and rejected students who showed conformist attitudes to the school authorities."[42] The concept of relative autonomy has thus proven useful for developing theories of resistance in schooling.[43]

Ironically, while he does challenge economic determinism broadly through the concept of relative autonomy, Althusser also is noted for denying human subjectivity and agency in relation to social, economic, and historical structures. This has been termed Althusser's "antihumanism," where "the self, the human subject, does not so much constitute but is constituted by the structural, systemic relations in which it finds itself. It is the belief not that [humans] make history but that history makes [humans] or that history makes itself."[44] Indeed, in *For Marx*, Althusser argues that Marx's early analysis of human agency should be thrown out in favor of an analysis that focuses solely on structures.[45] Critiques of Althusser's emphasis on structuralism also appear in critical educational theory, where his work is even grouped with Bowles and Gintis as being guilty of economic determinism.[46]

It is important to note that some Marxist educational theorists, such as Glenn Rikowski, have critiqued Althusser's conception of relative autonomy and theories of resistance as fundamentally anti-Marxist, arguing that they should be rejected entirely.[47] Further, I think that in modern times we have to raise questions about the distinction between Althusser's categories of the Repressive State Apparatus (RSA) and the Ideological State Apparatus (ISA), particularly when it comes to schooling in the United States, because for many children schools are both physically and ideologically repressive.[48] For instance, as I discussed in chapter 2, any analysis of the role of the state relative to the economy must recognize that the "state" is also a settler-colonial state directly involved in the ongoing primitive accumulation of capital from indigenous peoples and lands. While schools are undoubtedly (and generally, but not exclusively) doing the work of maintaining ideological hegemony under capitalism, their role as part of the settler-colonial state means that for Native/indigenous children and communities, schools are also playing a physically repressive function (and this does not even account for the history of schools being used directly in Native/indigenous oppression).[49] Similarly, schools have become much more prison-like for Black children in particular, and we know that schools and educational policies now play strong roles in the increased incarceration rates for Black youth and adults.[50] So for these communities, as well as others, there is no real distinction between the RSA and the ISA, because schooling for them has embodied both ideological and physical violence.

Challenging the Neo-Marxist Turn

The neo-Marxist turn in educational analysis has been *toward* Gramsci's concept of "hegemony" and Althusser's conception of "relative autonomy," and it has signaled a turn *away* from Marxism for being too structural, too overdetermined by the economy, and for not allowing space for individual or collective resistance vis-à-vis the relative autonomy of schools. There is a problem here, though: much of the neo-Marxist critique has erroneously confused functionalist economic determinism with Marxism. This has become common enough that critical scholars regularly dismiss "orthodox Marxism" for being too economistic, almost as if that claim was common sense.[51] However, as it should be clear from chapter 2 of this book, a Marxist, dialectical materialist analysis—with its focus on processes, contradiction, movement, and complex systems—cannot frame the relationship between the economic base and the superstructure (including schools) in a simple, linear, deterministic manner. Not only would that kind of economic determinism be counter to the Marxist, dialectical materialist project as a whole; it also would cut against what Marx and Engels actually wrote. Indeed, if we look at actual text, Marx and Engels themselves struggled against economistic and mechanical interpretations of Marxist theory, and as I argue here, their conception is complex enough to challenge the turn toward "neo" Marxism in the first place.

Beginning with *The German Ideology*, Marx and Engels offer a conception of the relationship between the economic base and the superstructure that is dynamic and non-functionalist[52]:

> The ideas of the ruling class are in every epoch the ruling ideas: i.e., the class which is the ruling *material* force of society, is at the same time its ruling *intellectual* force . . . The ruling ideas are nothing more than the ideal expression of the dominant material relationships, the dominant material relationships grasped as ideas . . . The individuals composing the ruling class . . . rule as a class and determine the extent and compass of the epoch, it is self-evident that they do this in its whole range, hence among other things rule also as thinkers, as producers of ideas, and regulate the production and distribution of the ideas of their age: thus their ideas are the ruling ideas of the epoch.[53]

They go on to add that

> [f]or each new class which puts itself in the place of one ruling before it, is compelled, merely in order to carry through its aim, to represent its interest as the common interest of all the members of society, that is, expressed in ideal form: it has to give its ideas the form of universality, and represent them as the only rational,

> universally valid ones . . . Every new class, therefore, achieves its hegemony only on a broader basis than that of the class ruling previously.[54]

The above discussion by Marx and Engels is open to a complex analysis of hegemony that does several things. First, it begins to interrogate the relationship between ideology and power in society in a way that recognizes how those in control have the power and capacity to produce and distribute their ideas, and that this power and capacity rests on their relative control over material production. Further, Marx and Engels's analysis includes the concept of ideological universality, where the interests of the ruling elite are presented as the commonsense interests of the whole society. Marx similarly addresses the concept of hegemony in *The Class Struggles in France, 1848–1850*, where he raises the role of inter- and intra-class conflict and compromise in the social, political, and economic turmoil in France at the time.[55] Thus, while Gramsci may have considered hegemony as a specific concept more deeply in his prison notebooks, Marx and Engels expressed what might be considered a proto-conception of hegemony that is fundamentally congruent with Gramsci's later work.[56]

Indeed, in his defense of Marx and Marxism, Engels in particular provided a nuanced, complex, and dialectical explanation of the relationship between the economic base and the superstructure. For instance, in a letter to Joseph Bloch, Engels critiques economistic interpretations of Marxism for gutting the "materialist conceptions of history," explaining,

> According to the materialist conception of history, the *ultimately* determining element in history is the production and reproduction of real life. More than this neither Marx nor I have ever asserted. Hence if somebody twists this into saying that the economic element is the *only* determining one, he transforms that proposition into a meaningless, abstract, senseless phrase. The economic situation is the basis, but the various elements of the superstructure—political forms of the class struggle and its results, to wit: constitutions . . . judicial forms . . . political, juristic, philosophical

> theories, religious views and their further development into systems of dogmas—also exercise their influence upon the course of the historical struggles and in many cases preponderate in determining their *form*. There is an interaction of all these elements in which, amid all the endless host of accidents, the economic movement finally asserts itself as necessary.[57]

In this passage Engels clarifies the Marxist, dialectical materialist conception of the base/superstructure relationship. After establishing that he and Marx never asserted that the economy was the sole determining factor, and recognizing that the superstructure does play a role in shaping history, Engels adds that the superstructure is "in many cases preponderate in determining [the] *form*" of class struggle. This point in particular speaks to issues of resistance, human agency, and mediation of bourgeois hegemony within the superstructure, including schools, because, as Engels suggests, the form that class struggle takes is fundamentally shaped by the cultural, political, and philosophical aspects of the superstructure. In essence, Engels posits a type of relative autonomy to the superstructural elements, thus opening the door for a Marxist analysis that asserts that these various elements, including human consciousness and human action, "exercise their influence upon the course of historical struggles" even as the "economic movement finally asserts itself as necessary."[58]

In another letter, Engels addresses the role of capitalist economic necessity in relation to the superstructure, while also discussing the power humans have as active agents within this relationship:

> Political, juridicial, philosophical, religious, literary, artistic, etc., development is based on economic development. But all these react upon one another and also upon the economic basis. It is not that the economic situation is *cause, solely active*, while everything else is only passive effect. There is, rather, interaction on the basis of economic necessity, which *ultimately* always asserts itself . . . So it is not, as people try here and there conveniently to imagine, that the economic situation produces an automatic effect. No. [Humans] make their history themselves, only they do so in a given

> environment, which conditions it, and on the basis of actual relations already existing, among which the economic relations . . . are still ultimately the decisive ones.[59]

Again we see Engels emphasizing that the economy is not the "solely active" cause for humans acting "passively" in the superstructure, asserting that humans "make their own history" and that there is "interaction" between the elements of the superstructure and the economic base. So even though capitalist production is a driver, it "ultimately always asserts itself" over the superstructure "in the last analysis," in Gramsci's words (or "in the last instance" in Althusser's phraseology).[60]

As we see from Engels's above letters, Marxist dialectical materialism conceives the relationship between the economic base and the superstructure in terms of dynamic relational interaction, not in terms of overly determined economic functionalism. However, this does not mean that Marx and Engels denied that the state could at times have "relative autonomy" from the economic base. For instance, Marx explained the "relative autonomy" of the state historically in *The Eighteenth Brumaire of Louis Bonaparte*, where he observed that "[o]nly under the second Bonaparte does the state seem to have made itself completely independent. . . . And yet the state power is not suspended in mid air. Bonaparte represents a class."[61]

In another letter Engels offers a more theoretical explanation of the relative autonomy of "particular spheres" from the "economic sphere": "The further the particular sphere which we are investigating is removed from the economic sphere and approaches that of pure abstract ideology, the more shall we find it exhibiting accidents in its development, the more will its curve zigzag. But if you plot the average axis of the curve, you will find that this axis will run more and more nearly parallel to the axis of economic history."[62] Not only does Engels advocate that other "spheres" can behave somewhat autonomously in relation to the "economic sphere," but he posits that we can only understand the economic base and superstructure *relationally* with each other. Engels further asserts that the more autonomous the state or aspects of the superstructure are from the economic base, the more they contradict the needs of the relations of production. This distance is expressed relatively through "accidents" in the development of a "particular sphere." None of these relations and accidents can exist within a non-dialectical, mechanical construction of the base/superstructure model.

However, it is apparent that, in stressing the power that the economic production wields relative to the superstructure, some of Marx and Engels's contemporaries interpreted their analysis as economically determinist, as many have today. For instance, Engels, in a letter to Franz Mehring, laments,

> Marx and I always failed to stress enough in our writings in regard to which we are all equally guilty. That is to say, we all laid, and *were bound to lay*, the main emphasis, in the first place, on the *derivation* of political, juridicial and other ideological notions, and of actions arising through the medium of these notions, from basic economic facts. But in so doing we neglected the formal side—the ways and means by which these notions, etc., come about—for the sake of content. This has given our adversaries a welcome opportunity for misunderstandings and distortions.[63]

In another letter, Engels also explains that he and Marx emphasized the economic base in relation to the superstructure because so many were actively denying the role of political economy: "Marx and I are ourselves partly to blame for the fact that the younger people sometimes lay more stress on the economic side than is due to it. We had to emphasise the main principle *vis-à-vis* our adversaries, who denied it, and we had not always the time, the place or the opportunity to give their due to the other elements involved in the interaction."[64]

There are other examples as well,[65] but suffice it to say that if we take dialectical materialism as the core philosophy of Marxism, as I discussed at length in chapter 2, then it is a logical impossibility to equate a Marxist account with a functionalist, economic determinist account of socioeconomic reproduction in education. Dialectical relationships are dynamic, interactional, fluid, and relational, and they do not allow for linear, mechanical, simplistic, one-to-one chains of causality.[66] We see some of the dynamic of dialectics in Engels's explanation of the relationship between the economy and society, discussed above, which he characterizes as comprising "zigzags," "the wills of individuals," "exhibiting accidents," and "interactions" between various aspects of the superstructure and the base of capitalist economic production. It is also apparent that Engels in fact disagreed with his contemporaries who interpreted Marx's analysis to mean that there was a direct, automatic cause-and-effect relationship between the economy and society. To posit a functionalist, deterministic, and simplistic one-to-one causality between schools and capitalist production is decidedly anti-dialectical—or "undialectical" using Engels's word—and therefore arguably should not count as a Marxist analysis.

Schooling and Capitalist (Re)Production

The question remains: What is the relationship between schools and the reproduction of capitalist social relations? While some advocate that the base/superstructure metaphor within Marxist, critical educational analysis be completely rejected,[67] it is not clear to me that the problem is with the metaphor itself. Rather, the central problem seems to have been maintaining a dialectical materialist analysis when we think about how schools function under capitalism. As Sean Sayers points out, and as I stressed in chapter 2, one of the key tenets of Marxist dialectical materialism is that in order for us to understand things as they concretely exist as part of material reality, "it is vital to see them in the context of their interconnections with other things within a wider whole."[68] Arguably, this has been the intent of all Marxist and neo-Marxist formulations of the relationship between schools and capitalism—the empirical evidence of schools reproducing capitalist economic and racial inequality is too overwhelming to deny such a relationship. The devil, however, is in the details: in *how* we conceive of the interconnections between things, including the complexity of the overall web of relations. Again, Sayers offers a Marxist dialectical explanation of how we should understand social processes, when he writes that they

> have their own internal dynamic, their own inner contradictions. The different aspects of society—forces and relations of production, base and superstructure—are aspects of a single whole, internally and organically interrelated, in dialectical interaction and conflict. It is these interactions, these conflicts, these contradictions—which are internal to society—that lead to historical change. In the process, none of these aspects is inert or passive: the forces and relations of production and also the superstructure are all transformed and developed.[69]

The importance of understanding social and economic processes as having their own internal dynamics cannot be overstated, for it recognizes that there are dialectical logics of development at play within these relationships, that influential external processes abound, and that social and economic systems have their own life *and* are made up of the lives of individual humans (themselves the subject of their own unfolding internal processes).

In a Marxist conception of the relationship between schools and capitalist production, then, we need to recognize multiple layers and processes, including some that operate in contradiction to the simple reproduction of capitalism. We know that overall schools reproduce the socioeconomic inequalities associated with capitalism (inequalities that themselves are raced, gendered, and cultured),[70] and that this inequality is reproduced from the level of education policy on down into the ways knowledge is constructed and communicated in the classroom.[71] The evidence of this overall material inequality is so overwhelming and has been consistent for so long that to suggest schools do not reproduce capitalist inequalities would be foolish. However, it is important to understand that schools do more than reproduce capitalist inequalities; they also do ideological work to justify the existence of those same inequalities. Schools in the United

States have played a key role in legitimating existing socioeconomic and racial inequalities, because our system of education is predicated on the idea that hard work and individual merit are the keys to overcoming any and all structural inequalities presented by society at large.[72] That is to say, in our mythical American meritocracy, all it takes to succeed is grit and determination, whereas failure can be attributed to individual cultural or racial shortcomings, laziness, or lack of effort.[73] As Michael Apple explains, there is an inherent contradiction in this relationship created between the need for structural reproduction and the promise of individual freedom:

> On the one hand, the school must assist in accumulation by producing both agents for a hierarchical labor market and the cultural capital of technical/administrative knowledge. On the other hand, our educational institutions must legitimate ideologies of equality and class mobility, and make themselves be seen as positively by as many classes and class segments as possible. In a time of fiscal crisis, the structural contradiction is exacerbated. The need for *economic* and ideological efficiency and stable production tends to be in conflict with other *political* needs. What we see is the school attempting to resolve what may be the inherently contradictory roles it must play.[74]

Schools, on behalf of the state superstructure, have to simultaneously accomplish the fundamentally contradictory goals of reproducing the social and material relations of capitalist production while hegemonically working to win the "spontaneous consent" of the students and the broader public through appeals to individual equality within the educational, economic, and social meritocracy. In essence, schools materially reproduce structural capitalist inequalities for groups of students based on race and class while advancing an ideology of individual equality and achievement. Further, some individual students, teachers, and schools may ultimately "beat the odds" (overcome structural constraints), thereby providing evidence to prove the liberal myth of meritocracy, but institutionally the odds still prevail as a general rule. This contradiction presents a dialectical relationship between production of capitalist social relations and the maintenance of bourgeois hegemony vis-à-vis education.

However, the ideological role that capitalist schools play also holds its own internal contradiction: it is hard to continually tell students that they are all equal and not have a good portion of them actually expect equality. This contradiction points to some of the space to challenge capitalist inequalities that do exist within schools, particularly the role that education has played in developing student consciousness and how students from K–12 schools to universities have been critical as activists fighting for justice in our modern history.[75] Not only are schools incapable of simply controlling students, but schools themselves can be, and have been, spaces of resistance and for building critical consciousness—even if that process has been more the exception than the norm.

In arguing that schooling in fact does contradictory work by both reproducing capitalist relations and simultaneously producing limited space for resistance to those same relations (vis-à-vis legitimating ideologies of individual equality and access), I also want to complicate my analysis a little bit by highlighting how this contradiction is racialized. For instance, as I discussed at length in chapter 2, the capitalist state in part functions through the ongoing process of primitive accumulation, one that is based on the ongoing settler colonialism of Native lands and peoples.[76] Schools, as part of the state, are thus generally complicit in the maintenance of settler colonialism and have generally operated against the cultural and material needs of indigenous students and communities historically and in contemporary times.[77] Of course, this is a generalization because there are Native and non-Native teachers who have used their classroom spaces and curriculum to engage Native students in ways that work to decolonize their identities and build resistance to the white supremacy embedded in schooling.[78] However, in the same ways that the state can never fully operate against the economic base, schools, as part of the state, cannot wholly overcome their functions of reproduction and legitimization, and so in the current context are incapable of operating wholly in the interest of Native student liberation.

The same argument could be made for the schooling of Black students as well, where even though there are instances of individual Black student success and limited spaces for the development of liberatory consciousness among Black students,[79] the functioning of schooling under (racialized) capitalism means that Black children are failed disproportionately, pushed out, and generally mistreated and oppressed by our school system.[80] So even though we need to fully recognize that the ways schools serve capitalism are always enveloped in maintaining class differences for all races (making sure the poor stay poor), we also need to fully recognize that there is significantly less space for resistance among Black students because schooling for them is even more restrictive and tied even more tightly to the inequalities of the economic base. As I detail in the next chapter, this increased restriction is evidenced by the hyper-disciplining of Black students in schools, as well as the ways that more-restrictive teaching and curriculum happen in classrooms of working-class Black children. Further, this tighter tethering of students of color to capitalist inequalities means that the legitimating function of schooling through appeals to individual equality and merit hold significantly less meaning for them than for white and/or affluent students, who tend to see the system working for them. In this way, even though we may be correct in our broad understanding of how schools simultaneously reproduce inequality and produce sites of resistance, we would be even *more* correct to also recognize that even this reproduction and production itself is relational to how race is structured under capitalism.

Can Education Change Society?

While I have thus argued extensively that the neo-Marxist turn in critical education was largely misguided and based on thin understandings of Marxism and perhaps based on anti-Marxism itself, it is important to recognize that some of the neo-Marxist impetus was driven by a need to acknowledge that human beings are not totally determined, and that we have the power to act and shape both history and our conditions. Of course, this exact point was expressed by Marx and Engels repeatedly. Indeed many (myself included) would argue that this human "agency" in making history was the basis for Marx and Engels's work and it lives at the heart of a Marxist, dialectical analysis.[81] As Marx himself asserted in the oft-quoted *Eighteenth Brumaire of Louis Bonaparte*, "[Humans] make their own history, but they do not make it as they please; they do not make it under self-selected circumstances, but under circumstances existing already, given and transmitted from the past."[82] Or, in Engels's words, "In the history of society . . . the actors are all endowed with consciousness, are [humans] acting with deliberation or passion, working toward definite goals; nothing happens without a conscious purpose, without an intended aim."[83] Despite the claims and worries of neo-Marxists and others, within a Marxist conception, humans do have agency; they can be and are subjects of history. Indeed, as I discuss in later chapters of this book, this was the goal of both Lenin's and Vygotsky's conceptions of consciousness, as well as Freire's conception of liberatory pedagogy: that humans, as subjects, as agents, as interrelated individuals, and as individual classes, develop consciousness of the imposition of structures on their lives and, based on that consciousness, take action to change it.[84]

However, given that the terms "agency" and "subjectivity" are used regularly by neo-Marxist, postmodernist, Marxist, and, more broadly, "critical" theorists to highlight our abilities to resist and act at individual (micro) and structural (macro) levels, it is important to recognize that, as Anderson points out, the terms "agent" and "subject" are both internally contradictory.[85] "Agent" can signify an active initiator (as it has been used in critical theory) as well as an instrument acting on behalf of another body (e.g., the "agent" of a foreign power). Similarly, the word "subject" can signify forms of sovereignty (e.g., being a "subject" of history as opposed to being an object) as well as subordination (as in "subjection," or being the king's subject). Perhaps what the internal contradictions of these terms highlight, as well as our ambiguous use of them, is that when we take action—when we negotiate structures through our own subjective positions—we are never operating as the fictive autonomous individual, nor are we operating in politically neutral terrain: we are instead always taking action amid ongoing historical processes and relations, and, ultimately, on behalf of some set of interests.

Such internal contradictions point to the appropriateness of both terms, for they provide analytic space, in a Marxist conception, for both individual consciousness and schools to be "relatively autonomous" from the relations of production associated with the economic base. Thus, while schools primarily reproduce socioeconomic and racial inequalities, their contradictory role in legitimating ideologies of equality also allows room for resistance to this reproduction.[86] It is absolutely crucial for us to recognize this room for resistance because students *do* resist the inculcations of schooling on all levels,[87] and teachers, as laborers within the political economy of education, also resist the reproduction of inequitable capitalist socialist relations in their classrooms and schools.[88] However, at the heart of this issue about the relationship between schooling and capitalism is a broader question: Just how powerful are schools? This question was raised by Apple in his 2012 book, *Can Education Change Society?*, itself a conceptual reiteration of George S. Counts's 1932, *Dare the Schools Build a New Social Order?*[89] Given the discussion here, the dialectical materialist answer is yes and no, simultaneously: schools are powerful, and they are not. As part of the state, schools have some relative autonomy, but in the end, the *general* functioning of schools cannot contradict the capitalist economic base. But that is the *general* function, and because of the relative autonomy of schools and the power of people to resist inequalities and hegemonic ideologies all the time and everywhere, individual schools and classrooms have been and can be seeding grounds for building critical consciousness and building revolutionary resistance among teachers and students alike.

Chapter 4

Dispossession and Defiance

A Race and Class Political Economy of Neoliberal Education Reform

There is a specter haunting public education in the United States—the specter of neoliberalism. Like other "public" services in our country, our system of public education is being transformed in fundamental ways. It is being financialized and turned into a profit-making sector while whatever semblance of democratic, public control and accountability—however imperfect—is steadily eroded in the name of individual "choice" and models of free market competition. This unfurling of neoliberalization in public schools, most often in the name of individual freedom and racial equality, consumes the poor and communities of color, preparing the bulk of our graduates for jobs in the service sector, the unstable hustle of the "gig" economy, and, for Black and Brown kids in particular, transition from hyper-disciplinary school systems to the prison system. As I discussed in chapter 3, this is the reproductive side of capitalist schooling—the educational creation and maintenance of the dispossessed[1]—and it is a project that is simultaneously raced and classed.

Here I explore the entanglements of neoliberal education policy and white supremacy, as well as the forms of popular resistance to those entanglements that have arisen in recent years. In many ways this chapter is an extension of the previous one, on the Marxist analyses of the relationship between schools and capitalism. While many of the basic structures of public schooling in the United States—like tracking, using bells and periods, having grade levels, using standardized tests, and even modeling schools almost as factories—haven't changed all that much since the Marxist analyses of the 1970s, the application of the logics of capitalism in schooling has become even more entrenched and intensified. The creation of quasi-markets in education, the sharp increase in the quantification and measurement of students and teachers, and the conception of public education as a source of great profit for private industry have all become hallmarks of the more recent shifts in capitalist schooling. This chapter is thus an application of a Marxist analysis to modern-day education reforms and practices; it is an analysis that outlines the structural race and class inequalities perpetuated by today's education reforms as styled by the capitalist free market and highlights the kinds of grassroots and community resistances that have grown in the struggle for educational justice.

Neoliberalism and the Transformation of Public Education

In his article "Neoliberalism as Creative Destruction," Marxist geographer David Harvey explains neoliberalism as "a theory of political economic practices proposing that human well-being can be best advanced by the maximization of entrepreneurial freedoms within an institutional framework characterized by private property rights, individual liberty, unencumbered markets, and free trade."[2] Similarly, the critical educational scholar Pauline Lipman defines neoliberalism as "an ensemble of economic and social policies, forms of governance, and discourses of ideologies that promote self-interest, unrestricted flows of capital, deep reductions in the cost of labor, and sharp retrenchment of the public sphere," where "[n]eoliberals champion privatization of social good and withdrawal of government from provision for social welfare on the premise that competitive markets are more effective and efficient."[3]

Fundamentally, neoliberalism is the idea that market competition operates to the benefit of everyone, and that any barrier to free market competition needs to be done away with in order to let the market run free. For neoliberals, regulations associated with environmental protections, minimum wages, unions, worker protections, or taxes are all seen as barriers to the free market, and as such, they should be highly curtailed or abolished completely. In this sense, a fundamental principle of neoliberalism is deregulation. Another principle of neoliberalism that extends directly from deregulation is that the public sector is best served by free market competition as well. This means that, according to the neoliberal ideal, anything we might associate with being a "public" service—parks, roads, military operations, public transportation, health care, welfare, state universities, and public schools, among others—would be better and more efficient if they were turned into private, competitive markets. In the neoliberal imaginary anything public is bad, and anything private is good.

The neoliberal vision of public education is one of a competitive market where students, teachers, schools, and administrators are ranked against each other using high-stakes standardized test scores as the primary metric for comparison.[4] In this vision, teachers' unions are a barrier to the competitive hiring and firing of "good" or "bad" teachers—as determined by student test scores—teacher labor becomes more controlled through test-aligned curriculum, and the teaching profession itself is deregulated through fast-track teacher training programs (i.e., Teach for America), resulting in both the deprofessionalization of teaching and an attack on university-based teacher education programs. Further, within the neoliberal revisioning of public education, and as something akin to small businesses, public schooling is turned into a competition for students through the advent of deregulated charter schools—run by for-profit or nonprofit charter management organizations and governed by appointed boards—again to be compared, judged, and potentially closed, all based on test scores.[5]

We can also see the neoliberal transformation of public education through the changes in discourse about, and even the underlying purposes of, education. For instance, the very language of educational bureaucracies has changed. Borrowing from the corporate sector, high-level district administrators are now referred to as chief executive officers (CEOs), chief financial officers (CFOs), and chief operations officers (COOs); and instead of being concerned with learning, schools are enmeshed in paradigms built around growth targets and benchmarks in test scores. Students and parents are subsequently reframed as consumers and customers, and teachers, schools, and principals are similarly reframed as service providers.[6] This neoliberal shift in language also signals a more profound shift in the very purposes of education: under neoliberalism, education is increasingly focused on the production of "human capital," "adding value," and meeting the needs of the economy, instead of, for instance, serving the social good or meeting collective needs of communities.[7]

Under neoliberalism, responsibilities for governing are also increasingly shifted from democratically elected state governments toward private bodies that are unelected and unaccountable to the voting public. As Lipman explains, this is a radical shift from *government* to *governance*:

> The "triumph of market ideology" is coupled with an erosion of the idea that informed citizens should make decisions based on the general welfare. The shift from *government* by elected state bodies and a degree of democratic accountability to *governance* by experts and managers and decision making by judicial authority and executive order is central to neoliberal policy making . . . Public-private partnerships, appointed managers, and publicly unaccountable bodies comprised of appointed state and corporate leaders make decisions about urban development, transportation, schools, and other public infrastructure using business rationales. In these arrangements, the state acts as an agent of capital.[8]

In education we see this move toward neoliberal governance in very particular ways. For instance, in several urban school districts there has been a push to discard publicly elected school boards and replace them with autocratic, top-down mayoral control.[9] We can also see the rise of neoliberal governance through the role that billionaires like Bill Gates Jr., and their respective foundations, play in setting local and national education policy agendas. Through individual personal donations and via their philanthropies, these elites have leveraged their vast wealth to push their own educational policy agendas through funding a complex network of nonprofit organizations, political advocacy groups, individual candidates running for offices, research centers, endowed university professorships, education reporting, and former employees placed in high-level federal education positions (particularly under the Obama administration).[10] They are aided by a neoliberal tax policy that has lowered taxes on the top income earners, transferring wealth from the state—which could have been pumped into cash-strapped public schools—back into the hands of the wealthy. As such, among others, Bill Gates Jr. and the Bill and Melinda Gates Foundation were essential in bringing the Common Core State Standards to the United States along with all the itinerant tests, Common Core–aligned textbooks and curriculum, Common Core–aligned standardized tests (the PARCC and the SBAC), and the technological platform required to deliver these tests entirely on computers.[11] Gates and other billionaire philanthropists have also pushed for charter schools at the local and national levels, among other policy initiatives.[12]

One of the central problems for this form of neoliberal governance of education is that these billionaires are setting policy agendas for public schools. These billionaires were never elected, and they are powerful purely because of amassed wealth. What is worse is that they cannot be held accountable for any damage they cause or any of the failures of their policies.[13] For instance, in 2013, in a talk he gave at Harvard University, Bill Gates Jr. commented, "It would be great if our education stuff worked, but that we won't know for probably a decade."[14] In the meantime, what happens if his policies are failures, as was the case with the Gates-funded small schools movement of the 1990s?[15] Who will be held accountable for the potential hurt done to students, schools, and communities in the wake of these neoliberal education policies being driven by wealthy elites? And this points to yet another issue with this kind of neoliberal governance by the wealthy: they are experimenting on other people's children, not their own. The children of Bill and Melinda Gates attended selective, extremely well-resourced private schools—the kinds of schools that don't bother with high-stakes testing, Common Core standards, or restrictive curriculum reserved for the rest of us, especially the poor.[16]

Bill Gates Jr. is just a convenient example here, and I use him not only because I think he is destroying public education and trampling on whatever limited democracy we have left, but also because I think he embodies a set of class interests and commonsense ideology that is an expression of neoliberal education reform in action. These folks, and others like the Walton and Broad families, simply see the world in terms of markets, profits, and financialization. Again, for the sake of consistency, here is something Bill Gates Jr. said in a 2009 speech to the National Conference of State Legislatures as part of the ramp-up to the implementation of the Common Core State Standards: "When the tests are aligned to the common standards, the curriculum will line up as well—and that will unleash powerful market forces in the service of better teaching. For the first time, there will be a large base of customers eager to buy products that can help every kid learn and every teacher get better."[17] It is a vision of the world, education included, as one giant market, ready for production, purchases, and profiteering.

In this light, the neoliberal transformation of public education is not just about recreating policy and practice as a financial market; it is also about generating profits from public education resources. As Fabricant and Fine explain in *The Changing Politics of Education*,

> In public education, we have witnessed the ascent of charter schools, virtual learning, market curricula development, and an expansive number of firms engaged in the measurement and assessment of teachers, with a host of entrepreneurs making large

> and small profits. More specifically, profit making extends from publishers capitalizing on the new standards-based testing curricula, to high-tech companies experimenting and testing their curricula interventions, to real estate operators leasing property to exorbitant fees, to alternative certification programs, and finally for-profit schools. Each of these fragments, pieces of profit making, are part of a new "gold rush" to capitalize . . . public assets being redistributed from neighborhood K-12 public schooling to the marketplace.[18]

Further, as education professor Patricia Burch has found in her research, substantial amounts of the profit making from public schooling comes through "hidden markets" generated through federal policy—namely in areas like transportation, tutoring, and other services that are contracted out to private firms.[19] Both high-stakes standardized testing and charter schools are central to the entire endeavor of the neoliberal transformation of public education.

Testing, Charters, and Neoliberal Education Reform

High-stakes standardized tests are just one form among many possible forms of assessment of learning. They are "high stakes" because official and unofficial consequences are attached to test results, including graduation, receiving funding, moving from one grade level to the next, earning college credit, getting a certificate or diploma, and maintaining one's public reputation. Tests are "standardized" in that the intent is to give the same test, in the same format, under similar or the same conditions, to a variety of students in different school and classroom contexts. The test questions themselves are also "standardized" because they are (supposedly) constructed to measure whether or not test takers are meeting standards (specific subject matter standards, the Common Core State Standards, or other sets of goals or objectives), and they are built on the ideal that they measure "normal" levels of performance among student populations.[20]

Most of us know standardized testing through our own experiences in schools: depending on your age, where you lived, and your level of education, any one of us might have taken the CAT (California K–12 test), STAAR (Texas K–12 test), ACT (college entrance), AP (college credit in high school), ITBS (older K–12 test), SAT (college entrance), SBAC (Common Core–aligned K–12 test), PARCC (another Common Core–aligned K–12 test), PRAXIS (teacher education subject matter test), EdTPA (teacher education performance evaluation), LSAT (law school entrance), the state bar exam (lawyer licensure), GED (general education high school graduation exam), or MAP (K–12 test), among many, many others. All of them are timed tests, usually delivered under the watchful eye of an official proctor or teacher, and mainly consist of a lot of multiple choice questions, a lot of reading, and some short-answer questions; your answers and results are determined by either a computer or some unknown, far-away person (or a combination of both). Most importantly, all of them take your effort, time, and testing conditions and boil them down to a single number or a small set of single numbers. And this gets at the official point of all standardized testing: to create simplified metrics to efficiently compare students, teachers, schools, states, and countries to each other, in order to say, *this* kid knows more than *that* kid, *that* teacher must be better than *this* other teacher, and *this* school/state/country is better at educating than *this other* school/state/country.

Comparison is central to the neoliberal transformation of public education: high-stakes standardized tests provide the metrics for neoliberals to determine the value of student performance as a product, thereby also creating the conditions for viewing the system of education as a competitive market. Then, individual consumers (parents) can use the test scores—almost like stock values—to choose which producer (schools) will make the best product (their "educated" children). Those schools that produce low test scores (a low-quality, low-value product/student) will lose customers and ultimately close, and those schools that produce high test scores (a high-quality product/student) will thrive. Subsequently, so the logic goes in this neoliberal edutopia, the quality of all schooling will improve as the market mechanism works itself out and "bad" schools close while only the "good" schools remain open for business. As an example, here is what George W. Bush said in a 1999 presidential campaign speech delivered to the conservative think tank, the Manhattan Institute, regarding his own business-like vision for public education free market competition:

> Federal funds will no longer flow to failure. Schools that do not teach and will not change must have some final point of accountability. A moment of truth, when their Title 1 funds are divided up and given to parents, for tutoring or a charter school or some other hopeful option. In the best case, schools that are failing will rise to the challenge and regain the confidence of parents. In the worst case, we will offer scholarships to America's neediest children.[21]

Bush said this almost twenty years ago, just as the neoliberal, corporate education reform juggernaut was really being put into motion. In a way, he was prescient in that most of these policies came to fruition in 2002 when No Child Left Behind was signed into law (which lent federal support to both high-stakes testing and charter schools), and the idea of offering "scholarships to America's neediest children" is being advanced at the federal level through the Trump administration's Secretary of Education Betsy DeVos's plan to implement a voucher system in the United States—allowing children to use public monies to enroll in any school, including religious private schools.[22]

In this way, charter schools are also strongly linked to high-stakes testing within the project of neoliberal educational reform: the tests establish the metric for the comparison and charter schools establish market-like competition between schools. In theory, charter schools are just that—schools that are granted a charter by some authority to provide education to students using public school dollars. The idea is that the charter schools would be exempt from most of the regulatory requirements and agencies connected with public schools (i.e., unions, elected school boards, school districts) in order to be more flexible in terms of curriculum, teaching, structure, and style.[23] Then, with this added flexibility and deregulation, charter schools could become hothouses of educational innovation, giving parents and communities more choices for the education of their children apart from the regular public school system. Or in the language of neoliberalism, charter schools could compete with regular public schools for market share (parent "investment" vis-à-vis student enrollment), under the assumption that the good charters would increase the quality of education and raise student achievement, thereby attracting more students from other charter or public schools (which might eventually close due to loss of market share). Importantly, in this neoliberal vision of the school marketplace, the public tax dollars will follow the children into their school of "choice."[24]

Combined, high-stakes testing and charter schools illustrate two theories of action that underlie neoliberal education reform:

1. The threat of disciplinary action, public scrutiny, and loss of resources attached to standardized tests will cause students, teachers, and schools to try harder, do better, improve teaching and learning, increase test scores, and raise the overall quality of education. Consequently, as a result of such improvement, and as a result of the improved transparency arising from test score data, such testing will also work to close gaps in test scores between the rich and poor, as well as between different racial groups.
2. The deregulation of a specific set of schools—charter schools—will grant more flexibility to those schools, allowing them to be more innovative in program and structure, thereby also allowing them to meet the needs of a variety of students and increasing achievement. Thus, charter schools, operating in competition for students and using high-stakes test scores as the main metric, will raise the overall quality of education because only good charter schools will survive, while the less effective schools (charter or public) will wither and close as they lose students.

There are, of course, all sorts of problems with this entire model—foremost among them the idea that opening and closing schools as part of market competition, with total disregard to what school closings do to communities, is somehow healthy and good. Further, this model does not hold up under any kind of empirical scrutiny.

The Troubles with Charters

Charter schools, for one, are not living up to any of their promises. Setting aside the numerous scandals involving embezzlement, cheating, and other illegal practices that have manifested due to deregulation and lack of public oversight,[25] charter schools fall short on promises to innovate, increase achievement, and serve all students. Regarding innovation, even staunch supporters of charters—many working in institutes, programs, and research centers paid for by charter and "choice" advocates like the Gates and Broad Foundations—are finding in their research that charter schools are not more innovative than regular public schools in form, structure, curriculum, personnel, space, bell schedules, grade levels, or use of technology.[26]

The research findings of charter school performance are similar. A 2012 review of eighty-three charter school achievement studies, spanning twelve years, found that charter schools perform similarly to public schools.[27] The largest of these studies of charter performance were done by the Center for Research on Education Outcomes (CREDO). Interestingly, despite CREDO's openly pro–charter school stance, in their 2009 study they found that 17 percent of charters outperformed public schools in mathematics test scores, but also that 46 percent were indistinguishable, while the remaining 37 percent performed significantly worse than public schools.[28] Similarly, in their updated 2013 study, while charter school performance in math improved somewhat—with 29 percent now outperforming public schools, 40 percent were still indistinguishable, and 31 percent performed worse than public schools.[29] A 2016 study of Chicago's charter schools found that by nearly every measure they performed worse than Chicago's public schools, with the report's authors explaining,

> This study uses comprehensive data for the 2012–13 and 2013–14 school years to show that, after controlling for the mix of students

> and challenges faced by individual schools, Chicago's charter schools underperform their traditional counterparts in most measurable ways. Reading and math pass rates, reading and math growth rates, graduation rates, and average ACT scores (in one of the two years) are lower in charters all else equal, than in traditional neighborhood schools. The results for the two years also imply that the gap between charters and traditionals widened in the second year for most of the measures. The findings are strengthened by the fact that self-selection by parents and students into the charter system biases the results in favor of charter schools.[30]

Apparently charter schools are not the magic bullet for student achievement that proponents claim them to be.

Charter schools also fail when it comes to serving all students. As Stephanie Simon found in her 2013 report for Reuters, charters have several ways of controlling who walks through their doors:

1. Applications that are made available just a few hours a year
2. Lengthy application forms, often printed only in English, that require student and parent essays, report cards, test scores, disciplinary records, teacher recommendations, and medical records
3. Demands that students present Social Security cards and birth certificates for their applications to be considered, even though such documents cannot be required under federal law
4. Mandatory family interviews
5. Assessment exams
6. Academic prerequisites
7. Requirements that applicants document any disabilities or special needs[31]

This process is commonly called "creaming," where charter schools attempt to selectively enroll students—one way to try to improve test scores. Whether purposefully through selective enrollment or not, it is clear from multiple studies that charter schools enroll students with disabilities and English-language learners at much lower rates than public schools.[32] These students are both more expensive to educate (because they require more resources) and tend to perform more poorly on standardized tests.

A brief look at Dr. Steve Perry's Capital Preparatory Magnet School, a much-lauded charter school in Hartford, Connecticut, serves as a prime example. Dr. Perry, the school's principal, has become a darling of neoliberal corporate education reformers because Capital Prep, as it is commonly referred to, annually boasts 100 percent college acceptance rate for its graduates. However, we need to look more closely at Dr. Perry's school to understand its apparent success. For instance, when compared to surrounding schools in Hartford, Capital Prep serves far fewer English-language learners, far fewer students with disabilities, and far fewer students in extreme poverty—sometimes on the order of 30 to 50 percent less in each category.[33] As the blogger Jersey Jazzman explains, "Simply put: Capital Prep does not serve the children of Hartford who are the most difficult and expensive to educate."[34] Further, Capital Prep loses lots of students between ninth grade and graduation, where, for instance, the class of 2010 had a 36 percent attrition rate, and the class of 2011 had a 35 percent attrition rate. And finally, despite having a selective school population, Dr. Perry's Capital Prep actually performs worse on the SAT and only does marginally better on state math and reading tests compared to surrounding Hartford schools.[35]

The Troubles with Testing

The use of standardized tests to make high-stakes decisions about students, teachers, and schools is equally problematic as, if not more than, the use of charter schools. Policymakers and much of the public generally assume that the scores generated through high-stakes standardized tests are fairly objective and hence are accurate measures of teaching and student learning. The entire apparatus of neoliberal education reform is built upon this assumption because without it, there would be no way to compare students, teachers, and schools, and hence no way to create a competitive market or use those test scores to threaten discipline or loss of resources. If we don't presume the accuracy of the test scores, the entire system cannot function. It is the fuel for their machine.[36]

The thing is, researchers have regularly and continually found high-stakes standardized tests to be wholly inaccurate measures of teaching and learning. For example, there has been a movement to try to use high-stakes tests to evaluate teachers, called "value-added measurement" (VAM). The idea is that if the teacher is effective, then student test scores will increase, and that therefore we can accurately measure how much value the teacher added to the student's learning (test score).[37] Of course, if these tests offered accurate measures of learning, and if learning happened in a simple linear, additive progression, then we might be able to find such causality to be true. However, in one 2010 report by the US Department of Education's National Center for Education Statistics, researchers found a statistical error rate of 35 percent when using one year's worth of test data to measure a teacher's effectiveness, and an error rate of 25 percent when using data from three years.[38] This means that the data produced by tests is so inaccurate that, even with three years of scores, there is still a one-in-four chance that using those scores to evaluate a teacher will be entirely wrong.

Another study found that students' test scores fluctuated wildly from year to year, with the same teacher rated in the top 20 percent one year and in the bottom 40 percent the following year.[39] Unless this teacher committed self-sabotage in the second year, the only real variable that changed was the students, not the teaching. Another issue that belies the accuracy of high-stakes standardized testing to measure teaching and learning is the change in test scores based on one-time, random, day-of-testing occurrences. One study found that factors like whether or not a child ate breakfast on test day, whether or not a window was open and a distracting dog was barking outside during the test, whether or not a child got into an argument with parents or classmates on the way to school, which students were in attendance while taking the test, who happened to be administering the test, and so forth, actually account for 50 to 80 percent of any improvement or decline of a student's standardized test score. If these tests were accurate measures of teaching and learning, then the scores should not be so sensitive to random occurrences, nor subject to such wild fluctuations.

While there are a whole host of other reasons high-stakes standardized tests are not accurate measures of teaching and learning (and therefore should not be used for evaluation),[40] it is also important to question the objectivity of the test scores themselves. The lack of objectivity of test scores becomes most clear when it comes to the grading of standardized writing tests. In one account, Dan DiMaggio worked as a writing test grader for the US testing company Pearson for several years and wrote about what it was like to be a part-time worker on a temporary contract for them:

> In test-scoring centers, dozens of scorers sit in rows, staring at computer screens where students' papers appear (after the papers have undergone some mysterious scanning process). I imagine that most students think their papers are being graded as if they are the most important thing in the world. Yet every day, each scorer is expected to read hundreds of papers. So for all the months of preparation and the dozens of hours of class time spent writing practice essays, a student's writing probably will be processed and scored in about a minute. . . .
>
> Scoring is particularly rushed when scorers are paid by piece-rate, as is the case when you are scoring from home, where a growing part of the industry's work is done. At 30 to 70 cents per paper, depending on the test, the incentive, especially for a home worker, is to score as quickly as possible in order to earn any money.[41]

Perhaps even worse, DiMaggio goes on to explain how he and other scorers were told to change their scores to create results consistent with the previous year's tests:

> Usually, within a day or two, when the scores we are giving are inevitably too low (as we attempt to follow the standards laid out in training), we are told to start giving higher scores, or, in the enig-

> matic language of scoring directors, to "learn to see more papers as a 4." For some mysterious reason, unbeknownst to test scorers, the scores we are giving are supposed to closely match those given in previous years. So if 40 percent of papers received 3s the previous year (on a scale of 1 to 6), then a similar percentage should receive 3s this year.[42]

These kinds of practices led Todd Farley, a former employee in the US testing industry of fifteen years, to reflect,

> [T]he test-scoring industry cheats. . . . It cheats on qualification tests to make sure there is enough personnel to meet deadlines/get tests scored; it cheats on reliability scores to give off the appearance of standardization even when that doesn't exist; it cheats on validity scores and calibration scores and anything else that might be needed. . . . Statistical tomfoolery and corporate chicanery were the hallmark of my test-scoring career, and while I'm not proud of that, it is a fact. Remember, I was never in the testing business for any reason other than to earn a pay check, just like many of the testing companies are in it solely to make a buck.[43]

So if high-stakes standardized tests are not as objective as we think and are not very good at measuring teaching and learning, what are they good at measuring? Among other things, poverty.

Noted educational researcher David Berliner explains that our high-stakes test scores mostly correspond with the kinds of experiences and resources available to children outside of schools:

> Virtually every scholar of teaching and schooling knows that when the variance in student scores on achievement tests is examined along with the many potential factors that may have contributed to those test scores, school effects account for about 20% of the variation in achievement test scores. . . .
>
> On the other hand, out-of-school variables account for about 60% of the variance that can be accounted for in student achievement. In aggregate, such factors as family income; the neighborhood's sense of collective efficacy, violence rate, and average income; medical and dental care available and used; level of food

> insecurity; number of moves a family makes over the course of a child's school years . . . provision of high-quality early education in the neighborhood; language spoken at home; and so forth, all substantially affect school achievement.[44]

This is perhaps one of the greatest tricks of the current neoliberal education reform project: their primary tools for reform—charter schools, high-stakes testing to hold teachers and schools accountable, and deregulated teacher education programs, among others—are premised on holding individual teachers and schools wholly accountable for achievement, when we have known from decades of research that non-school factors associated with socioeconomic inequality are overwhelmingly important to school outcomes (including flawed test scores).

We should not be surprised by this, however, because it is entirely consistent with the logic of neoliberalism. In the case of the neoliberal reform of education, instead of addressing the systemic inequalities that produce hunger, housing insecurity, lack of health care, and so forth—all of which could improve a child's educational performance in ways more substantial than any single school-focused intervention—the neoliberal's approach is hoist all responsibility on the individual who is supposed to hustle, innovate, or gig themselves out of poverty. This is critically important given how rampant poverty is in the United States, and it has been steadily getting worse. As the US Federal Reserve reported in 2017, the top 1 percent of families controlled 38.6 percent of the country's wealth, amounting to almost twice that of the bottom 90 percent of families, meaning we are currently experiencing some of the highest levels of income inequality in our country's history.[45] In terms of what this means for children in our schools, the National Center for Children in Poverty reports that 43 percent (or 30.6 million children) under the age of eighteen live in low-income families, and 21 percent (or 14.8 million children) live in poor families officially below the federal poverty line—a trend that has been fairly consistent since 2010.[46]

There are three important points about high-stakes testing that I want to follow up with here. The first is that the above argument—that schools and teachers only account for about 20 percent of any standardized test score—is also often employed by the same neoliberal education reformers to argue that schools and teachers aren't that important, and thus that it doesn't really matter who is teaching students or how many resources a school (or school system) has. Ironically, and contrarily, these reformers also often argue, at the same exact time, in order to justify using test scores for teacher evaluation, that teachers are the most important factor in student success.[47] Regardless, we need to be clear that, when it comes to high-stakes standardized test scores, non-school factors are the most determining factors. However, there are a host of important things that standardized tests do not measure—like cultural awareness, empathy, intersocial relations, artistic and creative abilities, curiosity and sense of wonder, honesty, and resourcefulness, among others[48]—and schools and teachers are critical to educational experiences and how students learn these things. Teachers and schools are important, just not in the ways demanded by the tests (a fact that also belies the tests as an accurate measurement of teaching and learning).

The second point I'd like to make regarding testing is that, despite growing poverty, scores have generally risen over the last fifteen years on the National Assessment of Educational Progress (NAEP), a standardized test given to a random sample of students in the United States. This would seem to contradict the nearly ironclad relationship between test scores and socioeconomic status. However, even though those scores have risen overall, it is important to note that the gaps in scores between white and Black students, for instance, have grown. So, yes, the scores of Black students have risen, but the scores of white students have risen even more[49]—indicating that the test-and-punish approach to educational equality has failed. However, I would argue that we can explain this contradiction between rising poverty and rising test scores very simply: students have become better standardized test takers.

Research has long shown that one way to raise standardized test scores is to practice taking standardized tests, and that schools have engaged in that kind of test preparation in response to the pressures of high-stakes testing.[50] The passing of the No Child Left Behind Act in 2002 made high-stakes testing a requirement for all US states for the first time in our country's history. Since then, there has been an avalanche of standardized tests for students to take. For instance, according to a study of sixty-six school districts by the Council of the Great City Schools, as of the 2014–2015 school year students took 112.3 tests on average between kindergarten and the twelfth grade. The same study found that there were 401 unique tests given across the sixty-six districts, and that most students took an average of 8 standardized tests per year.[51] Another study of fourteen mostly urban districts during the 2013–2014 school year found that students were tested once a month on average, with some tested as frequently as twice a month; students in grades three through eight were tested ten times a year on average, and some students in those same grades took as many as twenty standardized tests a year. In the report, educational researcher Melissa Lazarin commented, "There is a culture of testing and test preparation in schools that does not put students first."[52]

The third point that is important to understand about high-stakes testing is technical, and it has to do with how standardized tests are designed. Fundamentally, all standardized tests are designed to produce what is often referred to as a bell curve of test scores—a line that literally is in the shape of a bell, or perhaps something like a one-hump camel. That is to say, the tests are made such that when a group of students takes the standardized test, some will score high, some will score low, and the bulk will score in the middle. This is what test makers (also called psychometricians) commonly call a "normal" distribution, and when they design the tests, they intend for it to produce this kind of curve. As the educational blogger Jersey Jazzman so clearly explains,

> [W]e only test students on what we reasonably expect them to be able to do. We don't test fourth graders on trigonometry because we know most of them can't solve those kind of problems

> and wouldn't be able to even if we drilled them on it repeatedly. Similarly, we don't test high school juniors on adding one-digit numbers because we know that would be too easy. . . . Are there fourth graders that know the difference between a sine and a cosine? Are there juniors who can't add 5 and 4? Of course there are, but we know they are far away from the norm; we don't set our standards based on these outliers. Because we like to see ourselves as normally distributed, we create standards and tests that give us normal distributions. . . . This can't be stressed enough in the testing debates: we design tests not based on objective criteria, but on socially constructed frameworks that assume some of us are above average, some of us are below, and most of us are in the middle.[53]

There are two common kinds of standardized tests. One is called "norm referenced." Norm-referenced tests are designed to measure students against each other, and these produced bell curves in their initial design. The other type of common standardized test is called a "criterion-referenced" test, and it is designed to test students against a set of criterion. Many of the major K–12 tests given today, especially those that are "standards based" and connected to state standards or the Common Core standards, are criterion-referenced tests. Theoretically, these tests are designed so that it is possible for everyone to demonstrate that they've met the standards—which means it is theoretically possible for everyone taking these tests to meet proficiency and pass. These tests do not immediately produce a bell curve as do the norm-referenced tests. However, criterion-referenced tests still fall prey to the bell curve of performance: when statisticians interpret, analyze, and report the data from criterion-referenced, standards-based tests, they manipulate the raw data to produce a bell curve anyways (something they call "scaled scores"), again based on the assumption that there is a "normal" distribution of scores across the student population.[54] So no matter which kind of standardized test is given, in the end it will produce a bell curve of student test score results.

This technical discussion is important because it draws our attention to a fundamental principle that governs our current standardized tests: they are designed to fail some portion of our student population, because failure is literally built into the very paradigm of these tests. This is vital to understand about standardized testing because it means that we cannot test our way to equality, and in fact we can only test our way to inequality. Additionally, the construction of tests to require failure means that talk about "closing achievement gaps" in test scores between rich and poor students, or between Black/Brown students and white students, is generally misleading. Closing the test score achievement gap between rich and poor students, and between Black/Brown students and white students in particular, has become a mantra for education reform spanning both the Bush and Obama presidential administrations and connecting conservative Republicans and liberal Democrats alike.[55] It is used to suggest that if we can close these achievement gaps, we will have reached a state of educational equity. However, the reality is that, because of the presumed bell curve structured into the outcomes of our standardized tests, "closing the achievement gap" does not mean that everyone succeeds on the tests. Rather, because of the test-designed failure, "closing the achievement gap" means that we reach a point of equal passing and equal failure on the tests—of having proportionate numbers of rich and poor students pass and fail the tests, proportionate numbers of Black/Brown and white students pass and fail the tests, and so on. Within the paradigm of the tests, the goal of closing the achievement gap is simply a goal of achieving equally mixed results for everyone.

Testing, Charters, and the Colonial Plunder of Communities of Color

If high-stakes standardized tests do not really measure learning or work as a tool to improve educational outcomes, and if charter schools do not really innovate or increase educational achievement, then what do they do? Well, for one, both high-stakes testing and charter schools negatively impact communities of color and contribute directly to the school-to-prison pipeline.

Given that non-school factors associated with socioeconomic status and poverty most strongly correlate with high-stakes standardized test scores, we are led to an important conclusion: because the tests are designed to produce certain amounts of failure, and because the tests essentially function as a measure of poverty, then we have to recognize that high-stakes standardized testing concentrates failure among poor and working-class children, their schools, and their communities. Further, since Blacks, Latinx, indigenous/Native Americans, Pacific Islanders, and Southeast Asians are disproportionately impoverished,[56] test-designed failure is also most densely concentrated among those students, their schools, and their communities. Combined, this means that the effects of testing and other neoliberal education reforms like charter schools and school closing become focused on communities of color, with particularly deleterious effects. For instance, kids of color from low-income families are tested more than their more affluent, white counterparts in higher-scoring schools. Low-income kids of color also experience the greatest loss of time spent on non-tested or less-tested subjects like art, music, science, and social studies, and they don't have access to multicultural, anti-racist curriculum, because those subject areas are not on the tests. Further, because the tests inhibit process-based, student-centered instruction in favor of rote memorization, Black and Brown students in particular lose opportunities for culturally relevant instruction.[57]

Additionally, because of the increased intensity and more restrictive curriculum and educational environments created by the tests, for children of color high-stakes testing serves to acculturate them to a norm of being disciplined by state authorities.[58] The disciplining of Black and Brown children by high-stakes standardized testing also manifests in very concrete and material ways: a study by the Economic Policy Institute found in one state that attending a school with a high-stakes exit exam was correlated with a 12.5 percent increase in the rate of incarceration.[59] This is particularly concerning given that the implementation of exit exams increased the drop-out rates up to 300 percent in some cases, with the drop-outs being disproportionately

Black and Latinx[60]—suggesting that high-stakes standardized tests are a conduit for the school-to-prison pipeline.

Charter schools are also becoming notorious for the hyper-discipline of working class Black and Brown children because they suspend and expel students at higher rates than public schools. A 2016 report by UCLA's Center for Civil Rights Remedies found that, nationally, charter schools' student suspension rates were just over 1 percent higher than those of public schools. This difference seems small because the findings were based on the aggregate whole of charters, and it was found that a fair number of charters reported zero suspensions—which is not statistically possible and likely means they were not keeping track of, or purposefully not reporting, suspensions. However, more specific data in the report was more damning of charter school discipline. In Connecticut, for instance, elementary charter schools suspended and expelled students at a rate of 14 percent, while the public elementary schools reported a rate of 3 percent. As another example, in Massachusetts charter schools are disproportionately represented among the state's highest-suspending schools, with some suspending as many as 35 percent of their students at least once per year.[61] Reporting for the *Atlantic*, George Joseph points out that in 2014 in New York City, despite counting for just 7 percent of the city's student enrollment, New York's charter schools were responsible for almost 42 percent of the district's suspensions.[62]

These charter school disciplinary issues have led Carla Shedd, professor at CUNY Graduate Center, to observe that "[c]harter schools are providing a seamless transition for [low-income, Black] students in terms of how they are already treated, watched, and surveilled outside."[63] What's especially troubling about these charter school suspension and expulsion rates is that numerous studies show suspensions and expulsions correlate strongly with lower educational achievement, increased dropout rates, and increased likelihood of getting caught up in the juvenile justice system.[64] Dropping out of schools is a particularly racialized issue, where, for instance, three in ten white male drop-outs have served time in the federal penal system compared to the almost 60 percent of Black male drop-outs who will be imprisoned at some point in their lives.[65] While public schools also have troubles in this area, we have to remember that charter school advocates keep promising that their model is *better*, whereas the evidence points to the opposite: charters are in fact contributing to the school-to-prison pipeline in very racialized ways.

In addition to contributing to the school-to-prison pipeline, charter schools are also producing another sharply racialized outcome: intense racial segregation.[66] This racial segregation works in two directions, too. While we tend to think of segregation mainly as the concentration of students of color in a particular school or classroom (which is happening), the other side of racial segregation in charter schools is that white families are using charters to self-segregate from nonwhite children and communities. There is a long history of white families making choices to send their children to schools that are either all white, mostly white, or at least "white enough," and this includes charter schools.[67] A 2005 national study of white flight to charter schools found that "even when whites are the majority in a school district and among their schools, whites who attend schools with nonwhites continue to look for options that are even more white" in their search for charter schools, and that these white families were not basing their choices on the academic performance of schools.[68] In North Carolina, for instance, researchers found that white parents preferred that their children attend schools that had less than 20 percent Black students, and thus chose to pull their children out of schools with "too many" Black students in favor of enrolling them in predominantly white charter schools—resulting in a decline of the white population of North Carolina's public schools and a notable increase in white enrollment in their charter schools.[69] In 2014, the president of the school board in Hoboken, New Jersey expressed concern that the charter schools there were becoming havens for white flight from public schools, which he said was both bankrupting the public schools system and creating a separate school system entirely.[70]

While high-stakes testing and charters both have racialized outcomes, they also do something else: add to the profits of wealthy elites. In 2011, a Rupert Murdoch–affiliated investment firm valued the entire K–12 public education market in the United States at $500 billion,[71] and a more recent estimate came in even higher, at $788 billion.[72] As an example, the Common Core State Standards have been a huge financial windfall for testing companies, consultants, textbook corporations, and the educational technology sector. The Fordham Institute estimated that the Common Core cost $12.1 billion from 2012 to 2015.[73] The conservative Pioneer Institute and American Principles Project estimate a mid-range cost of $15.8 billion over seven years for the Common Core State Standards, with $1.2 billion spent on assessments, $5.3 billion on professional development, and $6.9 billion for tech infrastructure and support.[74] According to the *New York Times*, in part due to Common Core, venture capital investment in public education has increased 80 percent since 2005, to a total of $632 million in 2012—a figure that has, no doubt, increased in the years since.[75] Not surprisingly, given that the Gates Foundation invested $200 million in promoting and lobbying for the Common Core,[76] Bill Gates Jr. and Microsoft have cashed in on this lucrative market too: in February 2014, Microsoft announced it was partnering with the Pearson textbook company to install Pearson's Common Core materials onto Microsoft's Surface tablet.[77] Considering these billions of dollars, one thing in particular is important to keep in mind: these are public tax dollars moving into the pockets of private corporations vis-à-vis systems of public education.

Charter schools, like high-stakes tests, are also proving to be profitable for investors. As Kristin Rawls reports for *Alternet*, hedge fund managers and real estate developers are making money off the charter school sector by taking advantage of a federal program, the New Markets Tax Credit, which rewards investment in low-income communities with a 39 percent tax credit on loans made to those communities.[78] The promise made to investors and developers is that, between the hefty tax credit and the interest rates on the loans they invest in, they can double their investment in as little as seven years, causing Rawls to opine,

> Maybe this helps explain why, in 2011, former tennis champion Andre Agassi helped set up a $500 million startup fund for his Canyon-Agassi Charter School Facilities Fund, the first for-profit organization of its kind. . . . The credit may also explain why Facebook CEO Mark Zuckerberg donated $500 million in stocks to a variety of organizations that distribute charter school funding in 2012, or why he opened his own foundation, called Startup: Education, to build new charter schools.[79]

With federal backing, charter schools—whether for-profit or nonprofit—thus become seen as a good investment. As David Brain, head of the Entertainment Properties Trust, told CNBC in 2012 regarding charter school investment, "Well I think it's a very stable business, very recession-resistant. It's a very high-demand product . . . [I]t's our highest growth and most appealing sector right now of the portfolio . . . And a great opportunity set with 500 schools starting every year. It's a two and a half billion dollar opportunity set in rough measure annually."[80]

In addition to pure investment, these real estate firms can then turn around and charge charter schools rent on their properties, which in some cases amounts to 20 to 30 percent of a charter school's annual budget and can be quite lucrative given the high cost of rent in cities like New York or Chicago.[81] In some states, like Arizona, charter school law is written such that the physical properties revert back to the charter operator if the charter school closes down—essentially transferring property that was maintained by public monies, and perhaps where public monies paid for rent or mortgage, directly to the charter operators.[82] In other cases, like the state of Ohio, the state's contract with the charter school operator specified that, even though bought with public taxpayer dollars, all school property purchased by the charter school (e.g., computers, textbooks, or desks) became property of the charter school operator.[83] Further, in this case, if the state of Ohio wanted to recoup this property—which was already purchased once with public funds—they would have to buy it back from the operating charter, essentially using public monies to pay for it twice. Recent research on charter school expansion has consistently shown that charter school growth has a short-term and long-term negative fiscal impact on public school systems,[84] reminding us that, again, like with high-stakes testing, between federal programs, state laws, and charter contracts, these are public monies being transferred into the coffers of private industry vis-à-vis the system of public education.

As we can see with the above examples of Common Core testing and charter schools, in the words of Fine and Fabricant, "Entire sectors of the social reproduction side of the welfare state, most critically in health care and education, are being rapidly capitalized as entrepreneurs search for new profitable markets."[85] This process of the neoliberal movement of capital from public projects and institutions into private enterprises is what Marxist geographer David Harvey calls "accumulation by dispossession," where the public is simultaneously dispossessed of its assets as wealthy elites accumulate those very same assets in a massive transfer of wealth from the poor and working class to the capitalist class.[86]

In these ways, neoliberal, corporate education reform is fundamentally a racist, colonial enterprise. Even as individual kids, classes, and maybe even a school or two may beat the odds, the economic inequalities that correlate with test scores guarantee failure for working-class kids of color in general. Rather than address the structural inequalities facing these children and their communities, dismal test results become the basis for concentrating the market-based education reforms like charter schools, school closings, hyper-disciplinary programs, Teach for America, and the like, in those communities. In turn, these reforms result in the direct transfer of public wealth from working-class communities of color into the pockets of entrepreneurs, investors, real estate developers, and tech moguls, who profit directly from this relationship.

The colonial reality of these reforms is also present in the fact that the wealthy elites advancing these reforms are not doing so for their own children—as I noted in the beginning of this chapter, they have no interest in sending their children to charter schools or under-resourced public schools that feel the weight of high-stakes testing and the Common Core. Bill Gates Jr.'s eldest child, for instance, attended an elite, private school in Seattle called Lakeside, which boasts small class sizes, a well-endowed facility, a rich liberal arts curriculum, and pays no attention to the Common Core or most high-stakes tests.[87] Rather, these predominantly white, wealthy elites are interested in making education policy for other people's children: the rest of us in the 99 percent generally, and for working-class kids of color specifically.[88]

Finally, the colonial nature of neoliberal, corporate education reform is present in the ways that these wealthy elites and their foundations fund, promote, and reward individual people of color (i.e., Michelle Rhee, Kevin Johnson, Steve Perry, Howard Fuller, Geoffrey Canada, Cory Booker, etc.—the list is long) and mainstream organizations speaking on behalf of communities of color (e.g., the League of United Latin American Citizens, National Urban League, and UnidosUS [formerly National Council of La Raza], among others) as a means of suggesting that testing, charters, and so forth, are really in the best interest of racial justice—ignoring any indicators to the contrary.[89]

Communities of Color Resist Corporate Colonization

Just looking at the evidence of this chapter, the influence of capitalism on schools in the United States—discussed here as neoliberalism—is in many ways overwhelming. Much like Bowles and Gintis observed over forty years ago,[90] the current neoliberal model of schooling advanced by corporate reformers reproduces inequalities that very strongly correlate with capitalism. Further, it is clear these neoliberal education inequalities are simultaneously *raced* and *classed*—they are disproportionately implemented among poor communities and communities of color, meaning they are sucking financial resources out of these communities as well. However, as I discussed in chapter 3, we also need to understand this relationship between the capitalist economy and education dialectically: while the neoliberal educational reforms are hegemonic and they feel universal in their power and reach, human consciousness and action are not so easily controlled. To that end, communities of color have actively resisted and rebelled against these policies and their deleterious effects.

For instance, there has been a sizable resistance to high-stakes standardized testing. As just one important example, in January of 2013 the teachers at Garfield High School in Seattle, Washington, held a press conference where they informed the world that they would not administer the Measure of Academic Progress (MAP), a district-mandated high-stakes standardized test. It was a brave act that brought threats from school authorities as well as an outpouring of support locally and around the world. The Garfield Parent-Teacher-Student Association (PTSA) officially endorsed the boycott, and Garfield student government leaders and leaders of the Black Student Union vocally supported this action. Soon, other schools in the district joined the boycott. Activists in the teachers' union, the Seattle Education Association, lent their support, and the Seattle National Association for the Advancement of Colored People (NAACP) also endorsed it.[91] National support for the Garfield test boycott also grew. Teachers in Hawai'i, Florida, California, Oregon, and Illinois expressed their solidarity. The national teachers' unions sent letters of support to the Garfield teachers,[92] and over one hundred scholars from universities around the country signed a petition expressing their solidarity as well.[93]

The Garfield PTSA circulated a flyer informing parents of their rights to opt out of the MAP test, which resulted in dozens of parents informing the school that they were not allowing their children to take the test. Students also circulated their own flyer telling peers that they did not have to take the MAP. On the day of the test, many Garfield students refused to leave their seats, essentially performing an impromptu sit-in by refusing to go to the library to be tested. Other students went to the library but sabotaged the computer-based MAP test by rushing through their answers so fast that the computers automatically registered their exams as invalid.[94] The combined resistance of teachers, the student body government, the Black Student Union, parents, scholars from around the country, civil rights leaders, and colleagues from around the city defeated the ninth-grade MAP test at Garfield and the district—which was made optional by Seattle Schools for the following academic year.

It is important to note that the MAP test resistance started at Garfield High School. Garfield is historically at the heart of Seattle's African American community, and it has been a center for community resistance and action for decades, reaching back to Seattle's chapter of the Black Panther Party for Self-Defense.[95] It is also important to note that, although the Garfield/Seattle MAP test boycott was a single event, it served as a watershed moment for the national movement against high-stakes standardized testing. In the years since, we have seen large protests by students in places like Santa Fe, New Mexico, and Long Island, New York, and massive opt-out numbers in New York State (two hundred thousand in 2015) and Washington State (over sixty thousand in 2015), among others.[96] Further, despite claims that the opt-out movements are mainly for white suburbanites,[97] students, parents, and communities of color are leading voices in urban test resistance, as we have seen in Seattle, Chicago, Portland, Philadelphia, and elsewhere.[98] The collection *More Than a Score: The New Uprising against High-Stakes Testing*[99] documents several of these, including an interview with New York City parent and public school teacher Jia Lee, who tells the story of how she organized with her community at the Salt of the Earth School to lead an opt-out movement and make a public protest to the NYC schools chancellor—a protest that spread to other schools like the Brooklyn New School.[100] Additionally, Sarah Chambers tells the story of how she and colleagues at Saucedo Academy in southwest Chicago lead a successful boycott of their state exam, the ISA.[101] And Dao Tran, a parent at Castle Bridge School in New

York City, discussses how she helped organize a successful high-stakes test opt-out and boycott movement at her school.[102]

Additionally, people of color–led groups like the Journey for Justice Alliance (J4J) have organized powerfully not only against high-stakes testing, but also most other aspects of neoliberal, corporate education reform. J4J is a "national network of intergenerational, grassroots community organizations led primarily by Black and Brown people in 24 U.S. cities" that leads workshops, organizes protests and actions, and speaks at conferences around the country.[103] J4J's educational platform calls out educational equity as a central issue for racial inequality in public schools today, and they denounce charter schools, privatization, school closings, racist disciplinary practices, and the destabilization of urban schools as core aspects of the neoliberal, corporate education policy agenda. They go on to explain, "J4J believes that we do not have failing schools. We have in fact been failed by a system that has ignored savage inequities in public education, using civil rights rhetoric while violating the human rights of Black and Brown families through privatization schemes like state takeovers, school closings, for profit charter and alternative schools."[104] Consequently, J4J's seven-point education platform calls for "a moratorium on school privatization," "federal funding for 10,000 sustainable community schools," an immediate end to zero-tolerance discipline policies, a "national equity assessment," a stop to the attacks on Black teachers, an end to "state takeovers, appointed school boards, and mayoral control," and an end to the "over-reliance on standardized tests in public schools."[105]

Similarly, the #BlackLivesMatter (BLM) education platform also identifies the privatization of public schools as a major problem, including the undue (and undemocratic) influence of billionaire philanthropists like the Bill and Melinda Gates Foundation, racist zero-tolerance discipline policies, the cutting of staff positions that directly serve Black students, the under-resourcing of classrooms and schools of Black children, and the exclusion of teachers, students, and parents from decision-making processes. The BLM platform then goes on to suggest an end to school closings, charter schools, "corporate-backed market reformer programs such as Teach For America and the Broad Superintendents Academy," having police in schools, and mayoral control, among others—while also calling for substantial increases in school funding, positive discipline practices, and local, democratic control of schools and school boards.[106]

It is also important to note that even more-mainstream organizations representing communities of color have resisted aspects of neoliberal corporate education reform. For instance, despite its support for high-stakes testing, the NAACP caused a stir in 2016 when its national board ratified a resolution calling for a moratorium on charter school expansion.[107] After explicitly affirming the NAACP "School Privatization Threat to Public Education" resolution from 2014, the NAACP's 2016 moratorium calls for an end to charter school expansion until

> 1. charter schools are subject to the same transparency and accountability standards as public schools;
> 2. public funds are not diverted to charter schools at the expense of the public school system;
> 3. charter schools cease expelling students that public schools have a duty to educate and;
> 4. charter schools cease to perpetuate de facto segregation of the highest performing children from those whose aspirations may be high but whose talents are not yet as obvious.[108]

The NAACP's call for a moratorium was particularly upsetting to corporate education reformers because, like high-stakes testing, charter schools were marketed on the promise that they would improve educational equity and achievement for Black students, among other marginalized populations. The call for a moratorium on charters served as a rebuke of that false promise.

Some teachers' union organizing has also embodied ways that communities of color have resisted neoliberal, corporate education reforms. Most notably, behind the leadership of Karen Lewis, the Chicago Teachers Union responded to the intense privatization of

Chicago's schools by organizing with parents there under the banner of fighting for a quality education. This campaign included critiques of privatization efforts vis-à-vis charter schools, school closings, and high-stakes testing, among others. Similarly in Milwaukee, Wisconsin, under the leadership of Bob Peterson, the Milwaukee Teachers' Education Association built relationships with immigrant rights groups and the local NAACP to fight for public school funding and to resist school closings. In Saint Paul, Minnesota, the teachers' union there invited the community to participate in the shaping of the union's contract demands. This work all foreshadowed the 2013 convening of the Alliance to Reclaim Our Schools, which brought together the major teachers' unions with groups like J4J, the Alliance for Educational Justice, the Gamaliel Network, and the Center for Popular Democracy, among others.[109] This model has spread to other cities as well, where, for instance, in 2015 contract negotiations, the Seattle Education Association included demands for racial equity teams across the district.[110]

Of course, as I discussed earlier in this book, attacks on communities of color have only increased with the election of President Donald Trump, and this has created sharpened tensions for Black, Muslim, and Asian and Latinx immigrant students and communities in particular as they navigate the growing violence of white supremacy that is appearing both in person and in policy.[111] Also, Trump's pick of Betsy DeVos as his secretary of education and their insistence on school choice and vouchers only serve to remind us of the racism of those policies. However, it is important to recognize the resistance of communities of color to the neoliberal, corporate education reform agenda, especially because, as Fine and Fabricant point out,

> [M]ore and more parents of color have come to realize that school closings do not yield school improvement; that over-testing steals instructional time; and that charter schools do not generally outperform local schools even though they under-enroll students in need of special-education services, extremely poor youth and English-language learners. Shuttering neighborhood schools and

> dispersing their students, meanwhile, severs the links between communities and local schools, and redistributes real estate, contracts and public funds away from poor communities and into private pockets.[112]

Concretely, the failure of these reforms and the popular pushback from students, parents, and communities forced the administration of President Obama to recognize that there was too much testing, and the US Congress to recognize the right of parents to opt out of testing in their 2016 reauthorization of the Elementary and Secondary Education Act (dubbed the Every Student Succeeds Act, or ESSA).[113] Further, as *Education Week* reported in the summer of 2017, a poll completed by the conservative, free market–supporting think tank Education Next (housed at the Hoover Institute), found that national support for charter schools plummeted from 51 percent in 2016 to 39 percent in 2017. The poll also showed that support for charters was down among both Democrats and Republicans, as well as among Blacks and Latinxs. In their reporting, *Education Week* suggested that the NAACP charter school moratorium, the anti-charter platform of #BlackLivesMatter, and the unpopularity of Trump's presidency—with its focus on charters and "choice"—might explain the recent shift.[114]

While we do not know the exact cause of the shift in the public's attitude toward charter schools, the resistance to charters and other neoliberal, corporate education reforms—by teachers, students, parents, and community activists—illustrates that schools and education are not entirely dominated by the hegemony of capitalist relations. Rather, even as those relations are dominant, if we are to understand the relationship between schooling and capitalism dialectically, then we have to also recognize that schools and education can potentially play an important role in building critical consciousness that is itself resistant to capitalism. Indeed, this is one of the reasons that right-wing conservatives are constantly attacking public education.[115] In the next three chapters I examine this educational space for building critical, resistant consciousness along three different lines: learning, teaching, and curriculum.

Chapter 5

"It Is through Others That We Develop into Ourselves"

Vygotsky, Lenin, and the Social Formation of Consciousness

> *Consciousness is, therefore, from the very beginning a social product, and remains so as long as [humans] exist at all. Consciousness is at first, of course, merely consciousness concerning the immediate sensuous environment and consciousness of the limited connection with other persons and things outside the individual who is growing self-conscious.*
>
> —Karl Marx and Frederick Engels, *The German Ideology*[1]

I was a teacher when the World Trade Organization (WTO) meetings took place in Seattle, Washington, in 1999. The Seattle school I worked at was for high school "drop-outs" (really, better described as "push-outs") who wanted to return to a public school and get their diplomas. Our students were working class through and through; some had kids, some had drug issues, many had police records or were on the edge of gangs or homelessness, and others simply could not fit into the regular public school system. My teaching partner and I embraced our students by building our curriculum to specifically help them understand their own social, historical, racial, and economic conditions. We wanted them to develop a meta-understanding of how our systems produced and reproduced the very inequalities they were living, in hopes of building their capacities to seek to change both their own lives and the structures that created their conditions. In that particular autumn of 1999, we took the teachable moment provided by the WTO meetings and the planned protests to teach about global capitalism, environmental issues, and labor issues both here and around the world.[2] At the individual level we could see student understanding about global capitalism and its impact on them and their communities deepen. Then, when the actual date of the WTO meetings and protests arrived (November 30, or N30 as it is burned into our collective memories here in Seattle), many of our students made the choice to participate in the protests. As they joined the mass protests, which shut down the city of Seattle and eventually led to a police riot (where, unprovoked, the police violently attacked peaceful neighborhoods with tear gas and batons), our students saw that they were not alone in the world, that they were a part of something far bigger. In doing so they made a leap from individual consciousness to mass consciousness about these issues.

My teaching experiences constantly remind me of the process of the development of critical consciousness that happens both in classrooms and in community organizing, which is why the work of Soviet psychologist Lev Vygotsky became so important to me when I was introduced to it later in graduate school. In Vygotsky's work I saw a beautiful analysis of how learning happens, one that was considered mainstream and quite popular among educational researchers. Indeed, Vygotsky has been hailed as the "Mozart of Psychology" and as "one of the great theory makers of the first half of the [twentieth] century,"[3] and his theories and findings have been used in powerful ways in contemporary settings.[4] As I read Vygotsky in my graduate courses, I saw that he was offering us a Marxist, dialectical materialist theory of learning, and it was one that to me clearly ran in parallel with Lenin's work on the role of the party in the development of class consciousness and revolution. What was interesting was that, even though a handful of scholars within educational psychology have at least recognized some connection between Vygotsky and Marxism over the years,[5] most of the folks I saw making use of Vygotsky in educational research and practice did not mention Marx or Marxism, let alone Lenin.[6] Vygotsky's Marxism was almost like a ghost: a lurking presence that was there, but you could only see it if you looked at it in the right way.

Part of the absence of Marx or Marxism within educational research and practice based on Vygotsky is historical. When Vygotsky's *Thought and Language* was first translated into English and edited,[7] all references to Lenin, and almost all his references to Marx and Engels, were purposefully taken out.[8] It was not until twenty-five years later that the revised and edited edition by Alex Kozulin reinserted Vygotsky's references to Marx, Engels, and Lenin, and included more of the original text.[9] Essentially there was an entire generation of educational researchers and scholars who, by omission, could not see Vygotsky's own connections with Marx, Engels, and Lenin. This of course was a vestige of Cold War anti-communism, where it was largely assumed that nothing good could also be socialist, and that the socialism in work like Vygotsky's needed to be purged. However, another part of this absence of Marx and Marxism is also connected to the anti-Marxism of academia.

Vygotsky himself referenced Lenin in his work,[10] and a few scholars have noted that Vygotsky used Lenin's theory of reflection and activity,[11] but Vygotsky simply is not fully recognized as working as part of the Marxist-Leninist theoretical tradition. This is despite Vygotsky's own words; for instance, in a notebook he wrote,

> I want to find out how science has to be built, to approach the study of the mind having learned the whole of Marx's method . . . In order to create such an enabling theory–method in the generally accepted scientific manner, it is necessary to discover the essence of the given area of phenomena, the laws according to which they change, their qualitative and quantitative characteristics, their causes. It is necessary to formulate the categories and

> concepts that are specifically relevant to them—in other words, create one's own *Capital*.[12]

The lack of recognition of Vygotsky's Marxism and Leninism is something I seek to remedy here, because in my reading not only did Vygotsky's concepts extend from Marxist dialectical materialism (and Leninism), but he also actively made parallels between individual learning and the development of class consciousness discussed by Lenin in *What Is to Be Done?*. If we're interested in social change and ending capitalist inequalities, then it is important to understand how learning happens, how consciousness develops, and, subsequently, how we can develop class consciousness toward mass movement. A comparison of Vygotsky and Lenin helps us both understand these processes and rightfully reclaim Vygotsky as part of the Marxist-Leninist, dialectical materialist tradition, and a good place to start is to look at how Lenin understood the development of proletarian class consciousness and how Vygotsky's conceptions of everyday versus scientific concepts bring Lenin's framing to the level of individual learning.

Lenin's Conception of Proletarian Spontaneity and Consciousness

In organizing for the 1917 socialist revolution in Russia, Lenin was deeply concerned with understanding how the working class came to class "consciousness" against capitalist exploitation. Arguably, this is the basic impetus for *What Is to Be Done?*, which Lenin wrote in ideological struggle with other political organizations about which strategy would best lead to a socialist revolution. For instance, in *What Is to Be Done?* Lenin praises the newspaper *Rabocheye Dyelo* because they were doing the important work of highlighting "different appraisals of the relative importance of the spontaneous and consciously 'methodical' element" as central to grasping the political differences among Russian Social Democrats at the time.[13] He explains, "That is why the question of the relation between consciousness and spontaneity is of such enormous general interest."[14]

Lenin thus takes the question of the relationship between what he termed "spontaneous" revolts and "conscious," organized strategic actions by workers as central to understanding class consciousness and the socialist revolution in Russia.

Lenin never delineates a clear or specific definition of "consciousness" in *What Is to Be Done?*, but one emerges from the text in his analysis of the labor movement of the time. For instance, Lenin discusses the Saint Petersburg strikes of 1896 as an example of a spontaneous movement, but one that spread throughout Russia and demonstrated a "wholesale character" of a deepening understanding of Marxism. Lenin contrasts this action with the strikes in the 1860s and '70s, and the "spontaneous" destruction of machinery that happened then. These earlier strikes qualified as "riots" to him versus what he saw as the "conscious" Saint Petersburg strikes marking the progress of the "working-class movement of that period."[15] In Lenin's terms, then, "riots" are spontaneous worker uprisings that happen in a nonsystematic manner and without long-term goals or strategic plans.

Lenin further analyzes the differences between "spontaneity" and "consciousness" in the two types of strikes. For him the "riots" of the 1860s and '70s were an early expression of an "awakening of consciousness" that were "outbursts of desperation and vengeance."[16] Conversely he sees the strikes of the 1890s as showing "far greater flashes of consciousness" since "definite demands were advanced, the strike was carefully timed, known cases and examples in other places were discussed." Lenin further asserts that "while the riots were simply revolts of the oppressed, the systematic strikes represented the class struggle in embryo," claiming that, "this shows that the 'spontaneous element,' in essence, represents nothing more nor less than consciousness in an embryonic form."[17] Lenin then summarizes his observations of the workers' movement, and names the distance he saw between their spontaneous awakening and their overall consciousness of the entire social system: "Taken by themselves, these strikes were simply trade union struggles, but not yet Social-Democratic struggles. They testified to the awakening antagonisms between workers and employers, but the workers were not, and could not be, conscious of the irreconcilable antagonism of their interests to the whole of the modern political and social system, *i.e.*, theirs was not yet Social Democratic consciousness."[18] Similarly, in discussing the development of student movements and how they often get crushed "spontaneously," Lenin points out that these actions often end in large arrests, "precisely because these open hostilities were not the result of a systematic and carefully thought-out and gradually prepared plan for a prolonged and stubborn struggle."[19]

Lenin's goal is to move workers toward a "genuine" class consciousness built on a materialist analysis of the world around them as part of a movement of workers explicitly conscious of how the social, political, and economic systems were operating in direct contradiction to their interests and well-being. In this regard Lenin explains that "[t]he consciousness of the masses of the workers cannot be genuine class consciousness . . . unless they learn to apply in practice the materialist analysis and the materialist estimate of all aspects of the life and activity of all classes, strata and groups of the population."[20] Importantly, Lenin later discusses the "conscious" thought of the growing working-class movement in terms of people developing abstract generalizations of concrete social conditions, proclaiming, "[I]t is possible to 'begin' only by inducing people to think about all these things, by inducing them to summarize and generalize all of the diverse signs of ferment and active struggle."[21]

Based on these examples from *What Is to Be Done?*, we can begin to glean Lenin's definition of more class "conscious" workers, whose uprisings he saw as more "systematic" and "methodical"; with "known cases . . . discussed" and "definite demands . . . advanced"; working with a "gradually prepared plan" that is "carefully thought-out" and strikes that were "carefully timed"; with workers able to "apply . . . materialist analysis," "summarize and generalize," and to see their "antagonism to . . . the whole social system."[22] In this sense Lenin defined consciousness as being self-aware, planned, thought-out, and using systematic analysis to develop strategy and take action as part of a larger working-class movement against a system that is not operating in their class interest. In Lenin's original context—pre-Socialist Russia—his rhetoric was directed at the goal of workers developing consciousness as a class, so that their revolts, rebellions, and strikes would be strategic acts as a part of a mass working-class movement with the revolutionary aim of overthrowing the Tsarist government and establishing a socialist state.[23] Lenin's fundamental argument about consciousness was that it was crucial for workers if they wanted to achieve liberation from their exploitation in Russia through a socialist revolution. Further, Lenin was arguing specifically against the "economists" who at that time were focusing solely on workers' rights as opposed to the liberation of workers through the overthrow of the whole exploitative economic system. This argument is consistent with the Leninist tradition that holds that workers must challenge racism and become champions of all oppressed people, as I discussed in chapter 2.

Lenin's general conception of "consciousness" might be summarized as the willful application of a *systematic* and *materialist* analysis of socioeconomic conditions and relations, making use of *summation* and *generalization* as forms of abstraction for understanding what is happening in the world, and as preparation for *purposeful action* to change that world. This is consistent with Marx and Engels's understanding of a materialist development of consciousness, which they explain thus: "We set out from real, active [humans], and on the basis of their real life-process we demonstrate the development of the ideological reflexes and echoes of this life-process. The phantoms formed in the human brain are also, necessarily, sublimates of their material life-process, which is empirically verifiable and bound to material premises. . . . Life is not determined by consciousness, but consciousness by life."[24] Indeed, this very idea that consciousness comes from human activity, "on the basis of their real life-process," is a foundational concept within the cognitive psychology subfield of "activity theory," of which Vygotsky is considered a founder.[25] Additionally, with a little further analysis we can see that Vygotsky's conception of conscious awareness and scientific concepts paralleled Lenin's definition of consciousness in workers' strikes and rebellions.

Vygotsky's Conscious Awareness and Scientific Concepts

Conscious awareness is an act of consciousness whose object is the activity of consciousness itself.

—Lev Vygotsky, "Thinking and Speech"[26]

The importance of Vygotsky's conception of "conscious awareness" cannot be overstated, because it serves as the cornerstone of his theorizing, including his conceptualization of "scientific concepts" and the ever-popular and widely used "zone of proximal development." For Vygotsky, conscious awareness was a form of generalization—that is, taking a concept and connecting it to a broader system of concepts. Or in his words, "[T]he generalization of the concept leads to its localization within a definite system of relationships of generality. . . . Thus at one and the same time, generalization implies the conscious awareness and the systematization of concepts."[27] Much like Lenin, Vygotsky connects conscious awareness to the processes of generalization and the systematization of thinking. While Lenin specifically addresses how workers' developing consciousness of the "whole social system" functions so that they can transform it, Vygotsky writes more generally about how understanding the system of concepts allows one to gain "mastery" over its use.[28]

We can use the racial concept of whiteness as a simple example here. In the United States, white people grow up with a common-sense understanding that they are designated as "white" in a racial sense. They may speak on it, live their life based on the idea, use it to their advantage on purpose or by accident, and choose to just be "white" in the world. However, this sort of day-to-day understanding of whiteness differs from a more systematic, consciously aware understanding of whiteness. Such conscious awareness of whiteness might instead entail understanding the history and development of whiteness in relation to racial categories and as part of a system of racism; it might also look at whiteness relative to structural advantage compared to nonwhites, or look at how whiteness in the United States was entangled with Christianity, patriarchy, and the dispossession of land. In this regard, conscious awareness of whiteness requires generalizing it away from only the individual experience and understanding its connection to an entire system of concepts.

Vygotsky's link between conscious awareness and generalization within a system of concepts then allows him to connect conscious awareness and what he calls "scientific concepts": "It is apparently in this domain of the scientific concept that conscious awareness of concepts of the generalization and mastery of concepts emerges for the first time. . . . Thus, conscious awareness enters through the gate opened by the scientific concept." He further explains, "[B]ecause it is scientific in nature, the scientific concept assumes some position within a system of concepts. This system defines the relationship of scientific concepts to other concepts."[29] Thus, based on Lenin's conception of consciousness, Vygotsky develops the idea of "scientific" concepts and their counterpart "everyday" or "spontaneous" concepts.[30] Staying with our above example, we might say that, just growing up, many white people develop everyday, spontaneous concepts about race, including their own whiteness. However, by generalizing and developing these more systematic understandings of whiteness, white folks are in fact developing a more scientific concept of whiteness, and are moving toward conscious awareness of whiteness specifically and race generally.

Everyday and Scientific Concepts

In much the same way that Lenin never directly defined "consciousness" and instead delineates it through examples, Vygotsky also never exactly defines scientific concepts. However, he does provide a meaning through textual references and in relation to their opposite: everyday or spontaneous concepts.[31] As Vygotsky explains, "everyday concepts" are those that come from our daily life experiences: "We must explore the common characteristics of the processes involved in the formation of scientific concepts and those involved in the formation of the concepts that . . . emerge from the child's own everyday life experience, we will refer to the latter as everyday concepts."[32]

Elsewhere, Vygotsky describes everyday concepts as "characterized by a lack of conscious awareness."[33] To be clear, Vygotsky's point is not to say that we walk around asleep and unconscious in our daily lives. Rather, Vygotsky is suggesting that "conscious awareness" develops as "an act of consciousness whose object is the activity of consciousness itself."[34] So to be consciously aware in Vygotsky's framing is to be *thinking about* your thinking, be systematically *conscious of* your consciousness. Lenin characterized workers' class consciousness in much the same way; for workers may have been upset about everyday work conditions—hence the unplanned "riots"—but they did not necessarily exhibit a meta-understanding of their own consciousness in systematic relation to Russian economic, political, and social structures. Lenin saw them reacting based on their everyday concepts or conditions, rather than applying a more systematized, strategic, "scientific" analysis to their actions.

Further, Vygotsky placed an importance on a systematized, conscious understanding of our relationships with the material world because this kind of conscious awareness allows us to make what he termed "supra-empirical connections" between concepts within—and as part of—a system, thus allowing us to see things in new ways (as new processes and relations).[35] This framing also mirrors that of Lenin, who was, in part, concerned with workers developing an understanding of such supra-empirical connections between their day-to-day struggles over working conditions and their relationship as workers within the economic and social system of Tsarist Russia as a whole. We see this in Lenin's emphasis that workers need not only focus on their day-to-day "trade union struggles," such as better pay and improved working conditions,[36] but that the workers also need to reenvision their relationship to the social and economic system (thus his discussion of the necessity of dreaming of a new future), as well as to understand that their contradiction is not only with their employers over everyday work conditions, but also with the whole system. This requires the development of supra-empirical connections by the workers themselves regarding their condition as a class and their relationship to a social-economic system that exploits their labor. In Lenin's analysis, it is this form of "consciousness" that is necessary for workers to take collective revolutionary action.

Vygotsky supports this developmental need to see relationships in new ways when he claims, "In receiving instruction in a system of knowledge, the child learns of things that are not before his eyes, things that far exceed the limits of his actual and or even potential immediate experience."[37] The learning of concepts within a system—scientific concepts—enables us to understand things differently than we might have merely within the immediacy of our everyday lives. Doing so allows us to learn something new we might not have noticed previously, or it allows us to learn something new about an object that is beyond our immediate physical perception and experience. This is the power of "receiving instruction in a system of knowledge": it opens new horizons in our conceptual development, and old horizons may be recast to offer new understandings. Further, for Vygotsky, learning new things and seeing things differently is critical because it allows us to conceptualize *new relationships* and *different actions*: "To perceive something in a different way means to acquire new potentials for acting with respect to it. . . . By generalizing the process of activity itself, I acquire the potential for new relationships with it."[38] One of the key ways that Vygotsky suggested concepts develop is in the movement from spontaneous to scientific concepts.

From Spontaneous to Scientific Concepts

It is important to begin with a recognition that Vygotsky did not see spontaneous and scientific concepts as separate: they do not have distinct individual identities or develop on their own distinct paths. Indeed, for Vygotsky, spontaneous and scientific are dialectically related: "Whether we refer to the development of spontaneous concepts or scientific ones, we are dealing with the development of a unified process of concept formation."[39] Further, spontaneous and scientific concepts are interrelated because, according to Vygotsky, "the learning of a system of scientific concepts presupposes the widely developed conceptual fabric that has emerged on the basis of the spontaneous activity of the child."[40] In Vygotsky's analysis, our "spontaneous concepts" begin in the concreteness of our day-to-day experiences, and it is from there that we begin to generalize and understand individual concepts as part of a larger system of concepts: we move from spontaneous, commonsense understandings of the world toward developing conscious awareness through more systematic, scientific understandings. Importantly, as Vygotsky explains, "The link between these two lines of development reflects their true nature. This is the link of the zone of the proximal development and actual development. . . . Scientific concepts restructure and raise spontaneous concepts to a higher level, forming their zone of proximal development."[41] The last sentence of the above quotation is critical because it highlights how scientific concepts raise spontaneous concepts from the level of actual development toward conscious awareness, and this leads directly one of Vygotsky's most popularly used conceptions of learning: the "zone of proximal development"—which I will detail shortly.

Again, Vygotsky's conception of the development of scientific concepts from spontaneous concepts as part of a unified process of concept formation follows that of Lenin's discussion of the character of worker revolts. As I highlighted previously, Lenin characterized the spontaneous worker revolts and strikes as "consciousness in embryonic form" and as an "awakening" to the contradictory interests of the owners and workers.[42] Lenin's framing points to the way that spontaneous consciousness among the workers regarding economic issues was important, necessary, and contained the potential—with leadership—to develop into "Social-Democratic" (i.e., socialist) consciousness with the goal of establishing a socialist state.[43] Lenin explains, "Everyone agrees that it is necessary to develop the political consciousness of the working class. The question is, how is that to be done, what is required to do it? The economic struggle merely 'brings home' to the workers questions concerning the attitude of the government towards the working class."[44]

By raising the above issues, Lenin addresses how the spontaneous conceptions that arise from their "everyday" experiences are central in the development of a more scientific consciousness of the workers' movement. Further, for Lenin it was necessary for workers in Russia to reach a certain level of spontaneous awareness before they developed a more "conscious" understanding of their position as workers within the context of a broader class-based resistance, as well as within the socioeconomic system. Lenin saw that the workers' spontaneity had specific strengths and potentials that the Social Democrats of the time needed to seize upon in their organizing. In the language of Vygotsky, we could say that the spontaneous consciousness of the workers was within a zone of proximal development for developing a stronger class consciousness and moving a socialist revolution into being.

Instruction and Moving through the Zone of Proximal Development

For Vygotsky, the relationship between instruction and development was at the core of the dialectical movement between spontaneous and scientific concepts: in the process of instruction, spontaneous concepts are the cognitive framework, the seeding ground, for the emergence of nonspontaneous (scientific) concepts. Instruction, then, is the impetus for the development of this new type of concept.[45] Similarly to the way he articulates the relationship between spontaneous and scientific concepts, Vygotsky sees the relationship between instruction and development as, "two processes with complex interrelationships," asserting that "the zone of proximal development—which determines the domain of transitions that are accessible to the child—is a defining feature of the relationship between instruction and development."[46] The "zone of proximal development" (hereafter ZPD) is one of Vygotsky's most widely accepted and widely used concepts, and he most succinctly defines it as "the distance between the actual development level as determined by independent problem solving and the level of potential development as determined through problem solving under adult guidance or in collaboration with more capable peers."[47]

Most good teachers and community educators would recognize the ZPD as common sense because we know that effective teaching starts where students are already "at" in terms of conscious understanding (Vygotsky's "actual level of development," or ALD), and positions the teacher as a "more capable peer" to help move the learner through the ZPD. Thus, the ZPD is "an essential feature of learning" that "awakens a variety of internal developmental processes that are able to operate only when the child is interacting with people in his environment and in cooperation with his peers."[48]

Two things are worth noting here. First, Vygostky's conception is very much an extension of Marxist dialectical materialism. This is clear, for instance, when Vygotsky explains that the ZPD and the ALD form an interrelated pair and that as the process of learning happens, the ZPD dialectically transforms into the ALD.[49] In this process the zone of proximal development at one level of learning becomes the actual level of development at a second level of learning. That is to say that, through the process of learning, something that was once within our grasp (ZPD) becomes integrated into our current understanding (ALD). This, in turn, establishes another level of ZPD. For Vygotsky, learning thus happens as a dialectical spiral, with the first level ALD being negated by the ZPD, which in turn is itself negated with the establishment of a new ALD—a dialectical negation of the negation. Second, it is also worth noting that the ZPD does not extend infinitely. As Vygotsky explains, learners are "restricted to limits which are determined by the state of [their] development and [their] intellectual potential. . . . There always exists a definite, strictly lawful distance that determines the differential between [their] performance in independent and collaborative work."[50] In this sense Vygotsky informs the curriculum and instruction of teachers and "more capable peers" in that we need to always be working within the ZPD, ahead of the ALD, but if we overestimate and move beyond the ZPD, then our teaching will not necessarily contribute to successful learning; stated another way, if we overshoot where our students are "at" in terms of their level of understanding, then we run the risk of creating confusion instead of learning.

Working-Class ALD and ZPD

Vygotsky's conception of the relationship between the zone of proximal development and actual level of development also parallels Lenin's analysis of the development of the consciousness of workers. Lenin sees spontaneous understanding within the workers' strikes and other acts of rebellion in pre-socialist Russia, based on their focus on immediate working conditions and lack of a broader analysis of the social and economic system as a whole. Lenin thus asserts that if the level of consciousness of the workers remains focused purely on working conditions associated with "economic struggle," then Social Democratic progress will not be made.[51] In Lenin's analysis, the immediate "economic struggle" was at the ALD of workers, and remaining at that ALD would not allow them to make the full and necessary push to end their systematic class exploitation through socialist revolution. Further, for Lenin, the actual level of spontaneous worker consciousness—which was antagonistic with their employers—meant that the development of "political consciousness" (as Lenin put it) or "conscious awareness" (as Vygotsky put it) was within the ZPD of the working class at the time. Lenin thus asserts that the workers' spontaneous consciousness and ALD could grasp a socialist, revolutionary class consciousness, especially with the right strategic, systematic leadership (by a teacher or more capable peer) toward the necessary qualitative leap in both class consciousness and socioeconomic structure.

Indeed, Lenin summarizes the process of working-class consciousness moving through the ZPD with the aid of a teacher or "more capable peer" thus:

> Hence, we had both the spontaneous awakening of the masses of the workers, the awakening to conscious life and conscious struggle, and a revolutionary youth, armed with the Social-Democratic theory, eager to come into contact with the workers. In this connection it is particularly important to state the oft-forgotten (and comparatively little-known) fact that early Social-Democrats of that period zealously carried on economic agitation . . . but they did not regard this as their sole task. On the contrary, right from the very beginning they advanced the widest historical tasks of Russian Social-Democracy in general, and the task of overthrowing the autocracy in particular.[52]

This rich quotation illustrates all the major components of Lenin's and Vygotsky's respective theories of social class and individual development. Lenin's reference to the "spontaneous awakening" of the workers to "conscious life and conscious struggle" speaks to their ALD, which functionally is the level of spontaneous understanding that serves as the foundation for more conscious or scientific understanding. Lenin also identifies the role of leadership through his reference to the "revolutionary youth, armed with the Social-Democratic theory," who, while starting with the workers' ALD through "economic agitation," sought to move workers through a revolutionary ZPD to "the widest historical tasks of Russian Social-Democracy in general, and the task of overthrowing the autocracy in particular."[53] Here we also see the relationship between consciousness and the ability to form system-wide or supra-empirical connections: such "supra-empirical" connections were central to the "revolutionary youth" organizers who sought to develop the workers' understanding of the entire system of relationships in which they were enmeshed—the goal being for the workers to be able to do independently tomorrow (i.e., develop consciousness and lead a revolution) what they did "in collaboration" with revolutionary leadership today. In essence, whether he was conscious of it or not, Lenin had a sense of revolutionary learning, and Vygotsky seems to have built upon this in his own learning theories. Also critical here is how both Vygotsky and Lenin center the important relationship between teaching, political leadership, and the development of consciousness through learning.

Political Leadership, Teachers, and "More Capable Peers"

In Lenin's analysis the workers would only develop a systematic understanding of their class position and class strategies for socialist revolution with the aid of political leadership that, in part, comes from outside of the working class itself. This most controversial of Lenin's ideas has been understood and discussed in a variety of ways, some of which contradict each other. Lenin argued that there must be an organization, party, or group of people whose main task is to make revolution—including doing consciousness-raising work among the working class itself—otherwise the development of revolutionary consciousness would not happen (and historically did not happen). Alan Shandro recasts this argument of Lenin's in terms of two distinct claims:

> first, that the working-class movement cannot establish a position of strategic independence vis-à-vis its adversaries without attaining a recognition of the irreconcilability of its interests with the whole politico-social system organized around the dominance of bourgeois interests; second, that such recognition cannot be effectively brought to bear upon the class struggle in the absence of an organized leadership informed by Marxist theory.[54]

The contentious piece of Lenin's framing revolves around who is in political leadership. In one read it appears that Lenin is calling for an elite group of intellectuals to come from on high and tell the working class how to make a revolution. However, I would argue that Lenin was not the elitist he was portrayed to be,[55] and that, in Vygotsky's terms, teachers and/or "more capable peers" that come from the working class would be directly involved in helping develop conscious class awareness.

If we compare Lenin's and Vygotsky's texts, Vygotsky's conception of leadership and the ZPD runs in parallel with Lenin's conception of the role of political leadership in the development of revolutionary worker consçiousness. For instance, Lenin is clear in his discussion of how consciousness only develops with the support of leadership from outside of the working class. He writes that Socialist consciousness

> could only be brought to [the workers] from without. The history of all countries shows that the working class, exclusively by its own effort, is able to develop only trade union consciousness, i.e., the conviction that it is necessary to combine in unions, fight the employers and strive to compel the government to pass necessary labour legislation, etc. The theory of Socialism, however, grew out of the philosophic, historical and economic theories that were elaborated by the educated representatives of the propertied classes, the intellectuals. . . . In the very same way, in Russia, the theoretical doctrine of Social-Democracy arose quite independently of the spontaneous growth of the working class movement.[56]

This quotation from Lenin highlights the contentious point that consciousness among workers can be developed "only from without." This has been interpreted to mean that a vanguard group of disconnected, outside intellectuals should intervene and tell the workers how to save themselves. However, it is important to look closely at what Lenin actually says regarding this "outside" group. For instance, Lenin specifically says that the necessary political leadership should come from a group of "people who are professionally engaged in revolutionary activity."[57] He also says that "the organizations of revolutionaries must consist first, foremost and mainly of people who make revolutionary activity their profession."[58] So for Lenin, what distinguishes political leadership from the working class is that it is the political leadership's "job" to develop a systematic, materialist understanding of current conditions and make strategic decisions and take strategic actions toward revolution—and this includes helping workers develop their consciousness as an exploited class, albeit a powerful one. People making revolution their "profession" is the defining characteristic of Lenin's conception of political leadership.

Relative to the class makeup of the political leadership, Lenin is also clear that he is not referring to non–working class or intellectual elites. Rather, he asserts that "the spontaneously awakening masses will advance *from their own ranks* increasing numbers of 'professional revolutionaries.'"[59] Lenin goes on to assert that "the masses will never learn to conduct political struggle until we help to *train leaders for this struggle, both from among the enlightened workers and from among the intellectuals.*"[60] Lenin does not assume that intellectuals are automatically part of the political leadership, while asserting that they need training just as the leadership from among the workers need training. Further, Lenin sought to have political leadership that challenged all distinctions of class and profession, stating, "In view of this common feature of the members of such an organization, all distinctions as between workers and intellectuals, and certainly distinctions of trade and profession, must be utterly obliterated" and that "we must have a committee of professional revolutionaries and it does not matter whether a student or a worker is capable of becoming a professional revolutionary."[61] Contrary to various claims about the elitism of Lenin's conception, in reality he saw political leadership as consisting of workers, intellectuals, and students, and the defining aspect of this leadership as their "job" of carrying out revolutionary struggle.[62]

Vygotsky's idea of a teacher or "more capable peer" helping the learner move through the ZPD—from everyday concepts toward scientific concepts—parallels that of Lenin's conception of the working class developing more revolutionary consciousness with the assistance of political leadership made up of both intellectuals and fellow workers. The importance of the teacher or "more capable peer" is central to Vygotsky's conception of learning because, for him, a more knowledgeable person is necessary to help the learner move from the ALD and into the ZPD, in the development of scientific concepts: "In a problem involving everyday concepts he must do with volition something that he does with ease spontaneously. In a problem involving scientific concepts, he must be able to do in collaboration with the teacher something that he has never done spontaneously."[63] In a commonsense way, we know intuitively that none of us knows everything, and that someone else may know more about any one given subject than we do ourselves.[64] More important to the present discussion regarding leadership is that the role of the teacher or "more capable peer" is partially defined by their ability to assess where a learner's knowledge is presently (the ALD) and adapt instruction according to the ZPD. In this regard, both the act of teaching and the act of revolutionary leadership require working with others from their ALD and through their ZPD in the process of dialectically moving from spontaneous concepts toward scientific ones.

Of course, none of this speaks to pedagogy and how teachers, "more capable peers," or revolutionary leadership actually teach in this process. Regarding pedagogy, Vygotsky did not elaborate nearly as much as he did about learning,[65] but he was clear that rote memorization was not good enough for the process of learning in stating that "scientific concepts are not simply acquired or memorized by the child and assimilated by his memory but arise and are formed through an extraordinary effort of his own thought."[66] More contemporary Vygotskian scholars, including Vera John-Steiner and Holbrook Mahn, have also argued that Vygotsky did not promote a simple "transmission" model of learning.[67] Further, if we recognize that Vygotsky's conception of the process of learning consists of a dialectical, dynamic process where the ALD and ZPD of the learner are constantly unfolding and developing into each other, then we need to understand teaching as process oriented as well, including the kinds of ebbs and flows, zigzags, and leaps and pauses that characterize the dialectical process generally.[68] Additionally, to envision the ZPD of a student in such a way similarly means embracing the acts of learning and teaching as intertwined, dynamic, dialectical processes, too. Such a view of learning does not lend itself well to a simple transmission or rote model of education. Rather, viewing learning as a dialectical process means being student centered in our understanding of where a learner's actual level of development may be, by basing our teaching and curriculum on their ALD with an eye toward moving them in and through their specific ZPD, and by helping them in this process. Further, it is important to keep in mind that teachers and "more capable peers" are themselves developing as individual learners who have their own ALD and ZPD, both in their subject areas and in their understanding of teaching practice and their students. As Freire correctly argues, and as I talk about in the next chapter, such a conception of teaching and learning does not allow for didactic forms of instruction; because neither teacher nor student are perfectly formed, all those involved in educative relationships are in the process of learning and relearning themselves and each other.[69]

As we might expect, Lenin did not focus on pedagogy as much as Vygotsky. However, in at least one key passage of *What Is to Be Done?*, Lenin does speak against didactic instruction within the context of addressing the role of workers in creating socialist ideology:

> This does not mean, of course, that the workers have no part in creating such an ideology. But they take part not as workers, but as socialist theoreticians . . . in others words, they take part only when, and to the extent that they are able, more or less, to acquire the knowledge of their age and advance that knowledge. And in order that workingmen may be able to do this more often, every effort must be taken to raise the level of the consciousness of the workers generally; the workers must not confine themselves to the artificially restricted limits of "literature for workers" but should learn to master general literature to an increasing degree. It would even be more true to say "are not confined," instead of "must not confine themselves," because the workers themselves wish to read and do read all that is written for the intelligentsia and it is only a few (bad) intellectuals who believe that it is sufficient "for the workers" to be told a few things about factory conditions, and to have repeated to them over and over again what has long been known.[70]

It is worth noting that, as part of the political leadership, Lenin saw workers taking part as "socialist theoreticians" who indeed were interested in reading and thinking about how to best move the revolution forward in Russia. However, in terms of his commentary on teaching and pedagogy, it is important to highlight that Lenin critiqued "bad" intellectuals who, in their approach to political leadership, dogmatically explained the workers' struggles to the workers themselves (workers who already knew more about factory conditions than the intellectuals of whom Lenin speaks). Lenin further insisted that "every effort must be taken to raise consciousness" for workers so that they could study on their own—a framing that fits well with Vygotsky's conception of ALD and ZPD. Lenin was also a materialist in his sense of working-class education, which he felt should be based in revolutionary struggle: "The real education of the masses can never be separated from their own independent, and especially their revolutionary, struggle. Struggle alone educates the exploited class, reveals to it the measure of its strength, broadens its horizons, raises its capacity, clears its mind, and forges its will."[71] In this way perhaps Lenin saw revolutionary struggle as a form of pedagogy as well. However, Lenin's educational programs post-revolution were pragmatic with regard to increasing the industrial and economic capacities of the Soviet Union, and thus did not carry the same vision and aspiration as he had for the building of working-class consciousness before the revolution.[72] Regardless, the connections that Vygotsky made with Lenin's analysis of class consciousness and organizing in making the socialist revolution point to a brilliant breakthrough in Vygotsky's theorizing and research: the connection between the individual mind and society.

Vygotsky and the Social Mind

> *To paraphrase a well-known position of Marx's, we could say that humans' psychological nature represents the aggregate of internalized social relations that have become functions for the individual and forms of his/her structure.*
>
> —Lev Vygotsky, "The Genesis of Higher Mental Functions"[73]

In many ways Vygotsky's theorizing about the process of learning and concept development is an individually scaled-down version of

Lenin's social/macro analysis of class development. This individualization of social relations is illustrated through one of Vygotsky's most fundamental and groundbreaking claims: that the structure of social relations external to the individual person becomes internalized and effectively structures what he calls the "higher mental functions" of the individual.[74]

Vygotsky describes "higher mental functions" in several ways. First, referring to Karl Bühler's model of "three stages in the development of behavior," Vygotsky talks about the highest and final stage among them as being "of intellect or intellectual responses that fulfill the function of adaptation to new conditions."[75] Here Vygotsky uses "higher mental functions" to refer to conscious, thought-out responses to the environment (a philosophically materialist understanding) and as one step "above" reflexive reactions—essentially running parallel with his framing of spontaneous and scientific concepts. Vygotsky also discusses how humans interact socially through sign systems (i.e., language), arguing that the social interaction through the use of these signs represent "higher" or more complex forms of mental development. Essentially this is Vygotsky extending Engels's materialist conception of human use of physical tools in their interactions with the environment;[76] however, in Vygotsky's case he was seeing sign systems as the "tool" for human evolution and development.[77] Following this chain of logic, Vygotsky concludes, "Any higher mental function necessarily goes through an external stage in its development because it is initially a social function."[78] That is to say, because we are reliant on language to make sense of the world, and because language is fundamentally a product of human social interaction, our consciousness is also fundamentally social. Vygotsky then asserts that "voluntary attention, logical memory, the formation of concepts, and the development of volition" appear on the "social plane" before being internalized, themselves constituting "higher mental functions."[79] So for Vygotsky, "higher mental functions" originate socially and are concerned with volition (willful decision making) and concept formation.

In several different settings and studies, Vygotsky pursued the idea that the structure of external social relations is internalized in the individual's "higher mental functions." For instance, in his theorizing about the cultural development of children, he states that "[t]he child, after mastering the structure of some external method, constructs the internal processes according to the same type."[80] He also sees this process unfolding through the ways that sign systems serve as mediating tools in the cultural development of children, writing, "If it is correct that the sign initially is a means of social interaction and only later become a means of behavior for the individual, it is quite clear that the cultural development is based on the use of signs and their inclusion in a general system of behavior that initially was external and social. In general, we could say that the relations among higher mental functions were at some earlier time actual relations among people."[81] Vygotsky extends this analysis further in a "law of cultural development," where, "[a]ny function in the child's cultural development appears twice. . . . First it appears between people as an interpsychological category, and then within the child as an intrapsychological category."[82] Never one to lose his point, Vygotsky summarizes this process yet again: "[T]he very mechanism underlying higher mental functions is a copy from social interaction; all higher mental functions are internalized social relationships. These higher mental functions are the basis of the individual's social structure. Their composition, genetic structure, and means of action—in a word, their whole nature—is social."[83] For Vygotsky there is little to no distinction between the individual and the social: the individual is the social and the social is the individual, and structures of social relations shape the cognitive structures of the individual. It is important to note that other scholarship and research beyond that of Vygotsky has established this dialectical link between individuals and society through studies of culture and the sociology of knowledge.[84] Lenin's analysis shows the dialectical opposite as well: it illustrates how, under the right conditions and connected to a revolutionary class consciousness, the structure of individual and class consciousness and cognition can also reshape the structure of society.

Developing through Each Other

I have waged a few different arguments in this chapter. Most immediately, I have connected the cognitive psychology of Lev Vygotsky with the revolutionary socialist analysis of V. I. Lenin, drawing out the ways Vygotsky's conception of the process of learning and the construction of consciousness parallels Lenin's conception of the role of political leadership in the development of working-class consciousness. As Vygotsky said, "[I]t is through others that we develop into ourselves."[85] In making these connections, I have also reclaimed Vygotsky's work as an important, yet rarely recognized, part of the Marxist, dialectical materialist tradition. Together Lenin and Vygotsky provide a dialectically unified explanation of how the development of consciousness unfolds in both the individual and society. Lenin's political project was the development of class consciousness as part of a vision of macro-level socioeconomic transformation, and Vygotsky's analysis helps us think concretely and pedagogically about Lenin's organizing at the individual, micro level of the transformation of consciousness through learning. Thus, Vygotsky's work buttresses Lenin's in that it helps us understand how changes in social consciousness operate among individuals. Further, Vygotsky's conceptions of learning and the development of concepts help political leadership gain a deeper grasp of the cognitive aspects involved in the growth of scientific, revolutionary consciousness. Indeed, in a dialectical way, Vygotsky ends up giving back to the Marxist, dialectical materialist theoretical tradition from which he drew: by explaining the social nature of individual consciousness, he provides a more nuanced understanding of how individuals develop as agents of socioeconomic change. Perhaps this is Vygotsky's own answer to Lenin's question, *What Is to Be Done?*

If consciousness is indeed a product of our material and social relations, then we have to cede the notion that there is no neutral, nonpartisan, or nonideological form of consciousness. What we think, how we think it, and how we communicate our thinking to others is all political because it is produced by experiences with the world. Schools, then, become sites of struggle over both the materiality of our experiences and how they shape our consciousness about the world. The next two chapters engage this issue by looking at the kinds of teaching and curriculum that can develop critical, revolutionary forms of consciousness.

Chapter 6

Teaching to Change the World

The Marxist, Dialectical Materialist Pedagogy of Paulo Freire

While schooling and education do generally reproduce race, class, and other inequalities of capitalism, schooling and education are not wholly controlled by the economic base: there is some relative autonomy, and schools, as part of the state, may not always be tightly tied to the needs of the economy, just as they may also produce consciousness that runs counter to capitalism. What this means is that education and learning have some space to develop forms of consciousness that are contradictory to, and can challenge, capitalist social and economic relations.[1] Indeed, if this were not the case, then right-wing conservatives in the United States would not be so continually worried about the politics of school curriculum or the policing of student bodies through anti-LGBTQ, zero-tolerance discipline, and abstinence-only policies. Conservatives are so unhappy with the cultural politics of public education in the United States that they constantly work to try and control it.[2] So there is hope in education as a site of resistance to oppression and as a site for changing the consciousness of individuals as part of broader mass movements. This is why I became a teacher, and why I understand teaching fundamentally as a form of activism and community organizing—because for me there was always this link between teaching, learning, developing critical consciousness, and the potential this created for developing a more collective class consciousness as well.

In the last chapter, using the work of Soviet revolutionary Vladimir Lenin and Soviet cognitive psychologist Lev Vygotsky, I talked about the relationship between the development of critical consciousness at both the individual and social levels, highlighting how everyday understandings of the world can evolve into more-systematic understandings actively aimed at transforming that very same world. Drawing this parallel orients us toward thinking about the power of education and social change, and it reminds us that, despite the seemingly overwhelming influence of capitalism over schools, they can be places to build and support resistance movements. For instance, as I discussed in chapter 4, there has been significant organizing by educators, parents, and students who oppose the neoliberal reforms of high-stakes testing and charter schools, and much of this organizing has been centered in the schools themselves. However, one of the things missing from the discussion so far is *how* to develop critical consciousness, the kinds of teaching or pedagogy that can help us move toward a more critical understanding of the processes we see and experience in the world. The revolutionary Brazilian educator Paulo Freire offers us one such example of a pedagogy that helps us develop a more critical consciousness in the interest of working for social, economic, and cultural justice.

Freire originally developed his version of critical, liberatory pedagogy within the specific sociopolitical contexts of Brazil and Chile.[3] Freire became involved in popular literacy campaigns among the poor in Brazil in the late 1950s and early 1960s, where he ultimately ended up coordinating the Brazilian National Literacy Program. Under Freire's direction, the National Literacy Program sought to increase literacy rates among the population, which in turn would help politicize the masses of Brazil—the vast majority of whom were impoverished—by enabling them to become voters. The literacy program became seen as a threat to the Brazilian power structure, and the military government ended the program in 1964. Freire was arrested by the Brazilian government twice, and for his own safety he eventually felt compelled to leave Brazil.[4] It was while living in exile in Chile, drawing on the anti-capitalist vision of Karl Marx, the postcolonial theories of Franz Fanon, Amílcar Cabral, and Albert Memmi, and building from his experience in literacy programs with the poor in Brazil, that Freire wrote the now-famous *Pedagogy of the Oppressed*, as well as the less known *Education for Critical Consciousness*.[5] Freire's work on building consciousness through critical pedagogy—as an act of revolutionary resistance and transformation aimed at upending the race, class, and gender inequalities systematically created through colonialism and imperialist capitalism—arrived in a post-1968 world that felt like it was on the edge of revolution.[6]

In many ways, the publication and distribution of *Pedagogy of the Oppressed* was a defining moment in the development of critical education. To be clear, there certainly were antecedents to Freire's critical pedagogy—before "critical pedagogy" had been named as such. For example, the Harlem Socialist Sunday schools and the critical pedagogies enacted in socialist, communist, and other countries offer examples of liberatory education that predated Freire.[7] Also, even though he has often been mythologized as a "founding father" of critical pedagogy in the United States, Freire's work was not really popularized here until the mid-1980s, when the shift toward critical politics in education research and practice was already well under way.[8] All of that said, it is hard to overemphasize Freire's importance to progressive, social justice, radical, and critical educators.[9] The cover of the Thirtieth Anniversary Edition of *Pedagogy of the Oppressed*, published in 2000, boasted that the book had sold over one million copies worldwide.[10] Use of Freire's work has become its own subfield within education, with numerous books, chapters, articles, and organizations being built around his name and ideals.[11] In the process Freire and his conception of critical pedagogy have become commodified and recontextualized in good and bad ways.[12] Further, despite important books on Freire's Marxist politics, his Marxist conception of consciousness, and the power of his legacy for teachers and activists,[13] the popularity of Freire among "respectable" progressive educators has meant that, much like Vygotsky's, Freire's foundation in Marxism is often left unsaid, unacknowledged, or spoken in hushed voices—as if we have to forgive him this trespass.

Here, my intention is to push in two directions with regard to Freire. Mainly I want to reclaim Freire's conception of critical pedagogy as part of the Marxist, dialectical materialist tradition. This is particularly important for Marxist educators because it is through Freire's Marxism that we can see a pedagogy for building critical consciousness—the *how* that is missing from both Vygotsky's and Lenin's analyses of individual and social development.[14] The secondary direction I push here is to defend Freire's critical pedagogy from several detractors, most of whom operated from deep misunderstandings of Freire's dialectical materialism—and therefore have propagated deeply misplaced criticisms of his pedagogy.

Dialectical Materialism and Freire's Epistemology

Before attending to the Marxist dialectical materialism at the core of Freire's pedagogy, let me offer a quick review of dialectical materialism as a paradigmatic worldview (explained in greater detail in chapter 2). A Marxist, dialectical view understands that all "things" are in fact processes in constant motion and development, where the movement and development is driven by the tension created by two interrelated opposites acting in contradiction with each other and which, as a unified whole, require each other to exist. Further, in dialectics the world is seen as a multilayered system, a totality, a chain of relationships and processes.[15] Relative to some of the specific arguments made against Freire (discussed later in this chapter), it is also important to highlight that dialectical philosophy is qualitatively distinct from, if not oppositional to, the individualist rational logic of Western Enlightenment—most notably the positivistic sciences, which presume that things exist in isolation of each other and are analyzed as if fixed in space and time.[16]

Additionally, to be "materialist" in terms of dialectical materialism means that the material world exists outside of our consciousness of it. Following both Vygotsky and Engels, then, in a materialist view our consciousness comes from and is a reflection of our interaction with a material world that exists objectively outside of our subjective perceptions, instead of the world emerging from human consciousness alone.[17] Dialectical thinking and materialism are united within Marxist theory because the point is to (1) understand the interrelated processes happening in the material world; and (2) to enable human intervention in those processes to change material conditions for the better. Within Freire's conception of critical pedagogy, dialectical materialism provides a framework for analyzing objectively existing conditions in the world (i.e., various forms of institutionalized and systemic oppression), for understanding that humans can become actively conscious of both the conditions themselves and their sources, and for changing these conditions through human (social) intervention and action.

There is significant evidence that Freire was a materialist in his conception of how humans understand and interact with the reality of our world. For instance, in multiple texts he expressed that the world existed objectively outside of human consciousness, often framing this in terms of objective social reality, objective conditions, and general references to human interaction and transformation of reality or the world.[18] Freire also explicitly critiqued nonmaterialist perspectives on reality while affirming his position that an objective reality does indeed exist, stating that "[subjectivity] starts by denying all concrete, objective reality and declares that the consciousness is the exclusive creator of its own concrete reality . . . Idealism errs in affirming ideas which are separate from reality govern the historical process."[19] This is not to assert that Freire believed we know the existing world in a completely objective manner. Rather, he posited a dialectical relationship between the objectively existing world and our subjective understanding of that world. For instance, Freire addressed the issue as follows: "Consciousness and the world cannot be understood separately, in a dichotomized fashion, but rather must be seen in their contradictory relations. Not even consciousness is an arbitrary producer of the world or of objectivity, nor is it a pure reflection of the world."[20]

> Despite his materialism, some have asserted that Freire did not believe that "reality can be directly understood 'in itself,'"[21] essentially aligning him with what Lenin and others have correctly argued is ultimately a nonmaterialist conception of reality[22]—because if you can't know material reality "in itself," then the creation of that reality is left completely to the subjective consciousness. Rather, Freire saw the world as "an objective reality, independent of oneself, capable of being known," and regularly refers to the "knowable object."[23] The evidence suggests that Freire did in fact see an objectively existing world outside of our consciousness (one that could be known and understood), but that he also recognized that we come to understand it through our subjective lenses as sociocultural human beings.[24]

This philosophical argument is important because Freire's conception of human consciousness is a direct extension of his materialism.[25] Freire suggests that we are conscious because we "are not only *in* the world, but *with* the world" and thus have "the capacity to adapt . . . to reality *plus* the critical capacity to make choices and transform that reality."[26] This point appears consistently from Freire's earlier work through his last writings,[27] and it remains firmly within a Marxist, dialectical materialist conception of human consciousness.[28] Further, this relationship between consciousness and our material environments must also be thought of *dialectically*—as an interconnection between humans and their social, cultural, and material environments that is characterized by interaction, relational unity, and dynamic fluidity. This dialectical materialist conception provides the foundation for Freire's own formulation of consciousness, or *conscientização*, where he explains that "[o]nly when we understand the 'dialecticity' between consciousness and the world—that is, when we know that we don't have a consciousness here and the world there but, on the contrary, when both of them, the objectivity and the subjectivity, are incarnating dialectically, is it possible to understand what *conscientização* is, and to understand the role of consciousness in the liberation of humanity."[29]

As such, and echoing both Vygotsky's and Lenin's conceptions of consciousness discussed in chapter 5 of this book,[30] Freire sees "consciousness as consciousness *of* consciousness," holding that "*[c]onsciousness is intentionality towards the world.*"[31]

Further, and once again echoing Vygotsky,[32] Freire's conception of consciousness acknowledges that because humans are part of the world, and because our consciousness arises from a dialectical interaction with that world (other humans included), ours is first and foremost a social consciousness.[33] For Freire, as people we therefore "cannot think alone," and there "is no longer an 'I think' but 'we think.'"[34] Further, within Freire's conception, critical reflection creates the potential capacity to change the material world and our relations because we are not totally "determined beings" and we can "reflect critically about [our] conditioning process and go beyond it."[35] Freire discusses the reciprocal, spiraling, dialectical relationship between reflection, action, and transformation as follows: "[H]uman beings . . . are beings of 'praxis': of action and of reflection. Humans find themselves marked by the results of their own actions in their relations with the world, and through the action on it. By acting they transform; by transforming they create a reality which conditions their manner of acting."[36] This process of critically reflecting on the world and taking conscious, purposeful transformative action defines Freire's conception of "praxis."[37]

Freire's critical pedagogy is also built upon a dialectical materialist presumption that we can know things as integrated totalities—to use the language of Vygotsky, generalizing them in more systematic and "scientific" ways.[38] Freire explains that

> what we do when we try to establish a cognitive or epistemological relationship with the object to be known, when we get it into our

> hands, grasp it, and begin to ask ourselves about it, what we really begin to do is to take it as a *totality*. We then begin to split it into its constituent parts. . . . In a certain moment, even though we may not have exhausted the process of splitting the object, we try to understand it now in its totality. We try to *retotalize* the totality which we split! . . . The moment of summarizing has to do with this effort of retotalizing of the totality we divided into parts.[39]

For Freire, learning and developing critical consciousness happens through a dialectical process of breaking things down into related parts and then "retotalizing" them yet again to arrive at more complex, systematic understandings.[40]

In essence, the summary of Freire's Marxist dialectical materialism that I have outlined here is also a summation of his humanism. For Freire, to be human is to be able to both understand the world and take action to change that world: we are humanized through praxis.[41] Freire's pedagogy extends directly from these same dialectical materialist underpinnings.

Freire's Critical, Liberatory Pedagogy

> *We need praxis or, in other words, we need to transform the reality in which we find ourselves.*
>
> —Paulo Freire, "Education for Awareness: A Talk with Paulo Freire"[42]

Freire's formulation of critical, liberatory pedagogy is built with three goals in mind. First, it must be a pedagogy that enables both teachers and students to develop more critically conscious, systematic understandings of their relationship with the world. This is what Freire refers to as "education for freedom" where we learn to better understand our "concrete situation" by seeing the relationships that impact that situation.[43] Classroom examples of this abound, as documented by both Rethinking Schools and the Zinn Education Project.[44] One such example can be found in New Orleans third-grade teacher Rowan Shafer's lesson on global warming.[45] Using the students' concrete experiences with climate change as a starting point (i.e., Hurricane Katrina, coastal erosion, sea level changes, and shifts in weather patterns), Shafer helps them understand how what is happening in New Orleans is connected to larger, global shifts in climate, as well as how human actions like burning fossil fuels are contributing to these changes. In a Freirian sense, Shafer is getting his students to understand their concrete situation better through the ways it is connected to a larger system of relationships. This is also entirely consistent with a Vygotskian conception of moving from an everyday understanding of climate change to a more scientific one.

The second goal of Freire's critical, liberatory pedagogy, interrelated with the first, is for students and teachers to become "consciously aware of [their] context and [their] condition as a human being," thus becoming "an instrument of choice."[46] In this way teachers and students are positioned as *cognitive* subjects, and as "critical agents in the act of knowing."[47] In Vygotsky's terms from the previous chapter, this is "conscious awareness." In terms of classroom practice, we can return to the above example from Shafer's classroom.[48] Shafer's third graders are literally becoming more consciously aware of their contexts. This is important for Freire and for Shafer's students because, once you develop this kind of conscious awareness of how we fit into our contexts, it creates the capacity for choice—either to choose to take action about those conditions, or to choose to do nothing and perpetuate those conditions. In this case, Shaver's students, in learning about global warming and climate change and in connecting that learning with their local/personal experiences, are then positioned to decide whether they want to do anything to address this problem facing their own community and the world.

The development of conscious awareness, and being put in a cognitive position to decide whether or not to take action, leads to the third goal of Freire's pedagogy: transformation. For Freire it is not enough to merely reflect on the world in a critical manner as part of the development of consciousness. Rather, the point of critically understanding our relations is to take action to change the world around us because, as Freire explains, once we discover our "own presence within a totality, within a structure," we are "not as 'imprisoned' or 'stuck to' the structure or its parts."[49] The very act of seeing the structure helps us break from it. Shafer's work with third-grade students on climate change also illustrates this aspect of Freirian pedagogy.[50] Once students learned about global warming, how it connected to their community, and how it was impacting other people around the world, they very much wanted to take action. They deliberated on whether to focus action at the local, state, or national levels, and which action could potentially have the most impact. In the end, his students decided to write letters to the president of the United States, expressing their concern about climate change and their thoughts on how the United States should engage with the 2015 Paris Climate Conference.

Fundamentally, then, Freire's critical, liberatory pedagogy revolves around theory-in-action, also referred to as "praxis," and aims for students and teachers to critically reflect upon that reality and take transformative action to change that reality. To do this, Freire suggests a pedagogical process of problem posing, coding/decoding, and dialogue as ways to develop critical consciousness to transform both the classroom and the world.

Problem Posing and Decoding

In *Pedagogy of the Oppressed*, Freire offers a clear summary of how problem-posing education works as a form of liberatory pedagogy:

> In problem-posing education, [humans] develop their power to perceive critically *the way they exist* in the world *with which* and *in which* they find themselves; they come to see the world not as a static reality, but as a reality in process, in transformation. Although the dialectical relations of [humans] with the world exist independently of how these relations are perceived (or whether or not they are perceived at all), it is also true that the form of action [humans] adopt is to a large extent a function of how they perceive themselves in the world.[51]

Problem posing, then, is based on the idea that both material reality and our knowledge of that reality are neither static nor fixed—a core concept of dialectical materialism. This is fundamental to praxis because if reality were fixed and unchanging, then we could do nothing to alter it, with or without critical reflection: our lives would be completely determined, and we would no longer be subjects of our own existences. Hence, Freire grounds problem posing in action itself:

> The process of problematization implies a critical return to action. It starts from action and returns to it. The process of problematization is basically someone's reflection on a content which results from an act, or reflection on the act itself in order to act better together with others within the framework of reality. There can be no problematization without reality. Discussion about *transcendence* must take its point of departure from discussion on the *here*, which for humans is always a *now* too.[52]

Pedagogically, the process of coding and decoding reality is at the root of problem posing, where the learner focuses on a "problem situation," codifies it, and attempts to understand it through dialogue with others.[53] This corresponds with the way that Freire explains how we develop consciousness by breaking down reality and retotalizing it through analysis and critical reflection. With problem posing, a problem situation is presented to or raised by the students. In this moment the problem situation represents a perceived totality, and in the next movement the teacher and students move through a process of decoding the problem situation—breaking it down, critically analyzing, picking it apart. The decoded problem situation is then reconstructed through making more systematic connections—making new sense of the problem within a new relational context.

Again, there are many good examples of this process to be found in the pages of *Rethinking Schools* and elsewhere. In my own practice, one example would be the critical teaching of the concept of race in the United States. My students generally come to me with uncritical, very commonsense understandings of race—they arrive in my classroom with a conception of race that exists as a totality for them. I then problematize their existing understandings (their commonsense totalities) of race in a few ways. For instance, I ask them to consider what physical attributes (phenotypes) are supposed to define any one race, which allows us as a class to become conscious of the inconsistencies and relative arbitrariness of racial categories defined by physical traits. I also ask students to consider the lack of genetic evidence for biologically defined races (genotypes). Additionally, I review racial terminology with my students. I ask them if they know the origins of specific racial terms, like "Caucasian." (For the record, it was created by a single German scientist—Johann Friedrich Blumenbach—who though that the most beautiful people came from the Caucasus Mountain region, and that, by reason, Europeans must have descended from them; hence, "Caucasian.")[54] I also discuss the evolution of the names for racial groups, highlighting, for instance, how certain groups are named for color at some times (i.e., "white" and "Black") but named for geographic heritage at other times (i.e., "Oriental," "Asian American," "Latin American" or "Hispanic," and "African American").

Perhaps most importantly, I help my students reflect on how legal definitions of different racial groups function in different ways and toward different ends. In this regard we talk about, for instance, the "one-drop rule" for African Americans, which historically has been connected to chattel slavery and maintaining white ownership of land and enslaved Africans (as property). Simply put, the one-drop rule meant that when white masters raped female slaves, all offspring would become property and have no rights to land ownership. The one-drop rule also functionally meant that there were more slaves, not less. Conversely, because of settler colonialism, the white elites who founded the United States required the dispossession of Native land. Beyond the violent and forceful removal of indigenous peoples, one tactic of the US government was to try and define tribal nations out of existence. To do so, elaborate blood quantum systems were developed, such that, if you didn't have enough percentage of heritage from a particular nation, you did not officially count on the register. If a nation's official register became too small, then the tribe could cease to officially exist in the eyes of the federal government—essentially disqualifying the now-disappeared tribe from being eligible for needed economic resources.[55]

I engage my students in similar discussions about Asian Americans and whites. Specifically, I point to the historical construction of "Orientals," as well as the ludicrousness of lumping people as diverse as those from South India, the Philippines, and Korea into a single racial category. We also discuss who legally counts as "Caucasian," drawing on the case history of Syrians and Asian Indians—who are technically "Caucasian"—and their challenges to laws granting citizenship only to white people. Finally, we also discuss the historical construction of whiteness, reviewing how white people in the United States weren't really seen as one European racial group until after the official end of slavery.[56]

By decoding racial categories, pointing to the inconsistencies in using phenotype and genotype in the development of those categories, as well as dissecting the ways that language we use to name different races has changed and developed, my students and I have taken up these original concepts of race and decoded them. In a Vygotskian sense I have initiated the development of my students' spontaneous racial concepts toward more scientific concepts of race. By placing the US racial categories in social, historical, and economic contexts, my students begin to understand race *relationally*, with the ultimate goal of them developing more meta and systematic understandings of themselves and their own conceptions of race. But I don't just didactically tell my students about these problems. Instead, we pose questions, discuss them, and work toward a dialogue about these issues. Perhaps most central to Freire's critical pedagogy is that these kinds of problem posing and coding/decoding happen through such a process of dialogue.

Dialogue

It would be difficult overemphasize the importance of dialogue in Freire's conception of critical, liberatory pedagogy, as he sees it as a general part of the development of human consciousness historically. He writes, "Dialogue must be understood as something taking part in the very historical nature of human beings. It is part of our historical progress in becoming human beings. That is, dialogue is a kind of necessary posture to the extent that humans have become more and more critically communicative beings. Dialogue is a moment where humans meet to reflect on the reality as they make and remake it."[57] As human beings we know what we know (and what we don't know) through dialogue—testament to the social nature of language itself. It is through reflection of this imperfect knowledge that we can then improve our understanding and increase our capacities to transform reality.

Additionally, the act of dialogue automatically requires active reflection in relation to other human beings (as we "read" each other, think, ask questions, respond, etc.), grounding it in the material world (society and culture included) and necessitating critical thinking. According to Freire, this is a type of critical thinking that "discerns an indivisible solidarity between the world and [humans] and admits of no dichotomy between them—thinking which perceives reality as process, as transformation, rather than as a static entity—thinking which does not separate itself from action."[58] Freire's dialectics are readily apparent in his explanation of this critical thinking as never-ending due to the movement and constant transformation of reality itself. As such, humans are constantly taking part in this process and moving to action through dialogue with each other and in their interactions with the world.

In Freire's critical, liberatory pedagogy, the goal of dialogue about an object of study is to "try to reveal it, unveil it, see its reasons for being like it is, the political and historical context of the material. This . . . is the act of knowing."[59] This in turn becomes the pedagogical foundation of dialogue, as Freire explains:

> [S]ince dialogue is the encounter in which the united reflection and action of the dialoguers are addressed to the world which is to be transformed and humanized, this dialogue cannot be reduced to the act of one person's 'depositing' ideas in another, nor can it

> become a simple exchange of ideas to be 'consumed' by the discussants . . . Because dialogue is an encounter among [humans] who name the world, it must not be a situation where some [humans] name it on behalf of others.[60]

Hence, if we are in dialogue, we cannot "deposit" our ideas into other people—a form of teaching Freire famously and aptly called the "banking" method of education. Dialogue requires the social act of naming the world together in a process which also helps you understand it for yourself. Consequently, Freire posits, "I cannot think *for* others or *without* others, no one can think *for me* . . . Producing and acting upon [our] own ideas—not consuming those of others—must constitute [this] process."[61] Thus, students and teachers both exist in a dialogical relationship as subjects where both learn from each other, where "the flow is in both directions."[62]

Freirian Authority

Importantly, in this relationship, even if the teacher may "know" more or differently about an object of study, the teacher also comes to re-know the object through the process of the student knowing the object as well. As Freire explains, teachers and students are thus remade:

> Through dialogue, the teacher-of-the-students and the students-of-the-teacher cease to exist and a new term emerges: teacher-student with students-teachers. The teacher is no longer merely the one-who-teaches, but one who is [themselves] taught in dialogue with the students, who in turn while being taught also teach. They become jointly responsible for a process in which all grow.[63]

However, being remade as "teacher-student with students-teachers" does not automatically establish a nonhierarchical relationship of total equality between teachers and students. Both still maintain their individual identities as dialectical opposites in the process of education. In Freire's words,

> Dialogue between teachers and students does not place them on the same footing professionally . . . Teachers and students are not

> identical. . . . After all, it is a *difference* between them that makes them precisely students or teachers. Were they simply identical, each could be the other. Dialogue is meaningful precisely because the dialogical subjects, the agents in the dialogue, not only retain their identity, but actively defend it, and thus grow together. Precisely on this account, dialogue does not *level* them, does not "even them out," reduce them to each other.[64]

For Freire, the liberatory teacher is "[*n*]*ot* directive of the *students*"; rather, they are "directive of the process."[65] As such the liberatory teacher knows both the starting point for the learning process (knowledge of the object of study) and the "the horizon that she or he wants to get to" in that process.[66] This means that while teachers may be an authority on the process of learning, or perhaps even an authority on a particular subject, they should not be *authoritarian* in that position. Freire explains, "[T]he moment the educator's 'directivity' interferes with the creative, formulative, investigative capacity of the educands . . . the necessary directivity is transformed into manipulation, into authoritarianism."[67] To be authoritarian would mean treating students as objects, essentially dehumanizing them. Liberatory pedagogy instead requires teachers to negotiate the relationship between freedom and authority in their classroom, and understand that "authority . . . has its foundation in the freedom of others."[68] Such a position requires that the teacher is neither completely hands off ("laissez-faire"), nor authoritarian and dictatorial. Rather, liberatory educators are "radically democratic" in their pedagogy, which includes being "responsible and directive" while also respecting students' fundamental rights to come to their own conclusions.[69]

Examples of this kind of Freirian authority can be found in many of the role plays published in *Rethinking Schools*, at the Zinn Education Project, and elsewhere. These role plays represent practiced classroom lessons that present multiple positions on an issue, asking students to first play a role that holds a firm position, and then come up with their own personal perspective in reflecting on the experience. For instance, for a curriculum book on Asian Americans, I developed and taught a role play about Japanese American redress and reparations in response to their community's illegal and unconstitutional incarceration by the US federal government during World War II.[70] In this exercise, students were asked to play one of six different roles, all of which were real, and all of which held a variety of views on the issue of reparations for the Japanese American community. The roles included the white racist group Americans for Historical Accuracy—who at worst denied that the incarceration happened, and at best argued that the camps were fun; S. I. Hayakawa—a conservative Japanese American senator who strongly opposed reparations; the national Japanese American Citizens League, which struggled with endorsing the idea of reparations, but eventually came around; the Seattle chapter of the Japanese American Citizens League, which, early on, spearheaded efforts for reparations; Washington state congressman Mike Lowry, who very strongly supported reparations; and the Commission on Wartime Relocation and Internment of Civilians (CWRIC), which was a government commission making recommendations to the government regarding reparation. In this lesson, students, playing their roles, needed to come up with arguments either for or against reparations and present their arguments to the CWRIC. In the process, role-playing students also playfully argue with each other, trying to build alliances and/or debunk other groups' arguments. Once the role play runs its course and the CWRIC makes its recommendation, students step out of their roles to read about what really happened historically, as well as to consider some reflective prompts to spur their own thinking and opinions on the issue, which they write about and discuss as a class.

Role plays like this one operate very much within the framework of Freirian authority. As the teacher and curriculum designer, I researched and created the roles, designed the overall process, suggested the reflective prompts, and facilitated the post–role play debrief and discussion activities. I had a horizon in mind—a few basic objectives—and I served as the organizer and facilitator of the process of the role play. However, within that loose framework students are given a tremendous amount of leeway to make sense of the various roles, act out their roles, and, eventually, come to their own conclusions about the content and experience provided in the process. In many ways, role plays like this one embody a dialectical relationship between chaos and order: there are some broad limits set, but within those limits, students are very much invited to take initiative, be creative, and be relatively chaotic as they argue (in their roles) and discuss (outside of their roles). Similarly, within this structure, students are also invited—using Freire's above words—to "develop their own conclusions," even if I, as their teacher, was "responsible and directive" of the process. Of course, as was the case in my role play on Japanese American redress and reparations, the point is to consider injustice and how to act in response to injustice, which points to ways that Freirian pedagogy is interested in social justice and social transformation.

A Pedagogy of Social Transformation

Finally, it is critical to recognize that Freire's liberatory pedagogy is enacted in the material, already-existing world. Because of this, like everything else, Freire's pedagogy is inherently ideological, political, and non-neutral. Similarly, liberatory pedagogy cannot be disentangled from a broader project of social change, because its goal of developing critical consciousness is operationalized through students, teachers, and knowledge itself, all of which are dialectically interrelated with the world. If the point of liberatory pedagogy is to *be* praxis, to embody critical reflection in action, then conscious knowledge of the world cannot be decoupled from taking action in the world.

One example of this can be found in the work of my dear friend, education activist and Seattle teacher Jesse Hagopian. After his own arrest at the Washington State Capitol for attempting a citizen's arrest of state legislators who failed to fully fund public education, his students organized a mass protest—at first in support of him. Once he got released, they shifted the focus of their walkout and demonstration to support education funding more generally. Jesse saw a direct link between the kinds of teaching he was doing and student activism. He reflected,

> I have often hoped that my students would one day learn the lessons of history I had taught them—from the struggles of the abolitionists and women's rights advocates in antebellum America, to student movements against the Vietnam War, to the Freedom Riders of the Civil Rights Movement—and use them to start their own revolution.
>
> The moment my students lost their contentedness with studying history and started making their own—that was the most gratifying day of my career.[71]

In this way we see that liberatory pedagogy is not a pedagogy contained in the classroom alone, because it is also inextricably linked to social action. In an excellent discussion in *A Pedagogy for Liberation*, perhaps echoing Bowles and Gintis's *Schooling in Capitalist America*, Freire is clear that while schools are not powerful enough to be a totalizing driving force for social transformation, because of the key role that they play in the development of critical consciousness in the world, they are absolutely essential in building mass movements.

Critics of Freire's Critical Pedagogy

Thus far I have demonstrated how Freire's conception of critical, liberatory pedagogy flows directly from Marxist dialectical materialism. My intent has been to show how grasping Freire's Marxism allows for a deeper understanding of Freire's pedagogy.[72] The importance of this connection between Freire's pedagogy and Marxist dialectical materialism cannot be overstated, because Freire's pedagogy does not make sense without it. As one of the most influential educational thinkers of the twentieth century, Freire's books, words, and ideas have traveled the world, moved through time, and have been used in a wide variety of contexts outside of Brazil. Such widespread exposure has inevitably—and rightfully—pushed the limits of Freire's critical, liberatory pedagogy, leading to several scholarly and conceptual critiques. The natures of these critiques have differed dramatically. Some have arisen out of a serious engagement with Freire's political project and growing social and pedagogical movements, while others have been built upon overly simplistic reads of Freire's politics and pedagogy.

One such example of an overly simplistic read of Freire's politics and pedagogy can be found in the collection *Rethinking Freire*.[73] In it, under the leadership of Chet Bowers (a constant critic of Freire), several indigenous scholars launch a series of critiques of Freirian pedagogy aimed at completely undermining its validity. These critiques include assertions that Freire and his pedagogy are fundamentally individualist and based in Enlightenment philosophy, philosophically committed to a linear development of culture, conceive of teacher–student relations in an elitist manner, disregard the role schools play in social reproduction and maintaining oppression, colonize indigenous cultures, devalue indigenous knowledge, and promote an anthropocentric disregard for environmentalism.[74]

If we look at the depth and breadth of Freire's work, it is clear these critiques are largely misplaced and based on a very limited, and perhaps mistaken, reading of Freire and the dialectical materialist basis for his pedagogy.[75] For instance, take the claims that Freire's pedagogy promotes individualism.[76] This assertion about Freire's work is not new,[77] and it is based on an understanding of Freire as the ideological descendant of the Western rationalism associated with the European Enlightenment. By extension, these critics argue, Freire's critical, liberatory pedagogy is colonizing toward indigeneity, imperialistic, and dismissive of environmental issues. Not only does this critique completely miss the parallels between Freire's conception and indigenous models of learning—such as, in the Nahua (Aztec) tradition, the "Four Movements," concepts corresponding to the deities Tezcatlipoca (self-reflection), Quetzalcoatl (precious and beautiful knowledge), Huitzilopochtli (the will to act), and Xipe Totec (transformation), that make up the Nahui Ollin used pedagogically in Tucson's Mexican American Studies[78]—

it also misses Marxist dialectical materialism in Freire's approach altogether.

As I have explained previously in this chapter, Freire's conception of consciousness and transformation is entirely social, not individual. He was very clear in his pedagogy and analysis that he saw no dichotomy between humans and the world around them—other humans included.[79] Freire's conception of consciousness is built upon the idea that there is an ongoing, dialectical, and reflexive relationship between individuals and the world—a social consciousness—such that there is no "I think" and only a "we think."[80] Or, if we put this in terms of Vygotsky: we use language to think, and since language is fundamentally social, our individual thinking is also always social in nature. Further, harking back to Engels, such a conception is also the basis for seeing strong dialectical connections between humans and their environments, a point that speaks to environmental and ecological possibilities within Freire's pedagogy as well.[81] To suggest that Freire's pedagogy inherently promotes individualism as part of the lineage of Western rationality simply fails to grasp Freire's dialectical materialist conception of consciousness as fundamentally based in human collectivity in interaction with our environments.

Rethinking Freire offers other examples of how a failure to grasp Freire's dialectical materialism leads to other kinds of misreadings and misapplications of Freire's liberatory pedagogy.[82] For instance, several of these critics suggest that Freire's conception is fundamentally elitist, does not recognize or honor indigenous knowledge, and is based on an authoritarian relationship between teachers and students.[83] As I argued above, Freire's Marxist dialectical materialism essentially sees humans—both teachers and students—as being in constant interaction and in constant development, while also recognizing that individuals can only think for themselves as part of consciousness that arises socially. Further, Freire's dialectical, materialist conception of pedagogy does not allow for the teacher to be elitist or to disregard student/indigenous knowledge and perspective,[84] because, for Freire, developing critical consciousness is based on, and begins with, the input, experience, participation, and perspectives of students themselves. As Freire explains, "With progressive education, respect for the knowledge of living experience is inserted into the larger horizon against which it is generated. . . . Respect for popular knowledge, then, necessarily implies respect for cultural context. [Students'] concrete localization is the point of departure for the knowledge they create in the world. 'Their' world, in the last analysis, is the primary and inescapable face of the world itself."[85] To claim that Freire's conception of critical, liberatory pedagogy is based on the assumption that teachers are an elite vanguard that deliver the "correct" knowledge to the people is to claim that Freire advocates a "banking" form of education—a form which lies directly in opposition to Freire's pedagogy.[86]

Freire himself was cognizant of how partial understandings of his philosophy and pedagogy led some to view his work negatively. In reflecting on this issue he remarked,

> [O]ne of the reasons that many progressive and liberal educators in the United States have difficulty in comprehending [my] concept . . . is not necessarily because they are incapable of understanding the concept. It is perhaps because they have only absorbed the substance of my ideas to a certain degree, while remaining ideologically chained to a position that is anti-Freirian. Thus, by only partially accepting my ideological aspirations, they then develop doubts and questions with respect to specific methods and techniques. In this way they rationalize their total movement away from critically embracing what I represent in terms of theoretical proposals for change and for radical democracy and for history as possibility and for a less discriminatory society and a more humane world.[87]

It would appear that by not grasping the dialectical materialism of Freire's pedagogy, the contributors to *Rethinking Freire* have rationalized "their total movement away" from him, thereby positioning themselves as anti-Freirian via claims that his pedagogy is inherently oppressive.[88]

Another important example of an educator absorbing "the substance of [Freire's] ideas to a certain degree, while remaining ideologically chained to a position that is anti-Freirian" can be found in the work of Elizabeth Ellsworth, who sparked an academic controversy when she wrote about how her attempt at using critical pedagogy failed and ultimately strengthened the structures of oppression and dominance in her university classroom.[89] In the article Ellsworth recounts how her application of critical pedagogy (her version of Freirian pedagogy) was oppressive and damaging because of her positionality as a white woman teaching students of color, arriving at the conclusion that Freirian pedagogy upholds universal truths, is based in the rationality of Western logic, does not recognize subjectivity, does not recognize that knowledge is socially constructed, does not ask teachers to be critically reflexive of their own identities in relation to their students, upholds "repressive myths," and perpetuates "discourses of dominance" in the classroom.[90]

The critical piece here is that, in her article, Ellsworth declared that it was her position as a white woman that kept her from being able to understand the racism her students were facing. While I appreciate her recognition of her positionality relative to her students, in doing so Ellsworth functionally argues that we cannot understand the world outside of our subjective, individual experiences. Consequently, Ellsworth concluded that she could not develop any material knowledge or understanding of her students, their experiences, and their identities, which then caused her difficulties in implementing an anti-racist, critical pedagogy in her university class. This aspect of Ellsworth's article and difficulties is critical because it illustrates how, fundamentally, her orientation toward consciousness about the world stands in deep ideological opposition to the dialectical materialism that is at the base of Freire's conception of critical, liberatory pedagogy—which strongly asserts that we can understand the world around us, including the experiences of others.

Ellsworth's fundamental difference with Freirian epistemology and pedagogy thus ended up subverting her classroom dynamics in several ways. Ultimately it kept Ellsworth from being authoritative (in the Freirian sense) in the classroom because, as she asserts, she could not help her students learn about racism since as a white person she cannot know or understand it. In response she chose to take a hands-off, laissez-faire approach to classroom relations, pedagogy, and content because, from her own perspective, she was not in a position to direct the learning process. Not only have hands-off, lassez-faire approaches to teaching been found to actually increase existing inequalities, as in research conducted in elementary schools by Rachel Sharp and Anthony Green[91]; Freire himself has vehemently critiqued it as reproducing oppression in the classroom. Simply put, Ellsworth's failure to implement Freirian pedagogy arose because she was fundamentally "chained to a position that is anti-Freirian."[92]

Reclaiming Liberatory Pedagogy for Marxist Dialectical Materialism

The point here has not been to argue that Freire was somehow perfect in his conception of liberatory pedagogy. He was just as fallible and imperfect as any of us. However, part of my argument has been that some critiques are more substantial and warranted than others. To that end, there are critiques of his work that are much more in solidarity with the political project of education for social justice and social transformation. For instance, Freire has been rightly critiqued for using discriminatory language, including the "universal man" and overly general terms such as "oppressor" and "oppressed."[93] Freire has also been critiqued for not adequately addressing issues of race,[94] for not explicitly dealing with feminist and gender issues,[95] and for neglecting overlapping forms of oppression.[96] Others have pointed out that Freire assumed that critical consciousness automatically developed people in progressive ways.[97] Nevertheless, many critical scholars have upheld critiques of Freire while explicitly aligning themselves with him and his work. Several feminist scholars have maintained an affinity between Freire and feminism,[98] and critical race scholars in education have used his work to build robust theoretical frameworks for understanding the relationship between liberatory pedagogy and racial justice.[99] These efforts have pushed the boundaries of Freire's liberatory pedagogy, as well as suggest a fruitful route toward the growth of critical pedagogy more generally.

Regardless of their natures, these solidarity-based critiques of Freire's pedagogy point to a critical issue: the cultural, historical, political, and philosophical origins of Freire's work shape how his words are read and how his conceptualization is understood. In this regard Freire's intent was to provide "the possibility for the educator to use my discussions and theorizing about oppression and apply them to a specific context,"[100] which he felt could be applied to deal with racism and women's oppression in other contexts like the United States and Guinea-Bissau.[101]

Freire took up these solidarity-based critiques in his later books and essays. In *Pedagogy of Hope*, Freire admits that as soon as *Pedagogy of the Oppressed* was published in 1970, he received letters from women around the world criticizing his use of the "universal man" in his writing. Freire explained that he had not meant to alienate women in his writing, and that the issue had not occurred to him when he used the term "man" to mean all of humanity. Freire immediately committed himself to changing his language from then on. In response to other criticisms regarding race and gender, Freire has reflected,

> [W]hen I wrote *Pedagogy of the Oppressed*, I tried to understand and analyze the phenomenon of oppression with respect to its social, existential, and individual tendencies. In doing so, I did not focus specifically on oppression marked by specificities such as color, gender, race, and so forth. I was more preoccupied then with the oppressed as a social class. But this, in my view, does not at all mean that I was ignoring the many forms of racial oppression that I have denounced always and struggled against even as a child . . . Throughout my life I have worked against all forms of racial oppression, which is in keeping with my desire and need to maintain coherence in my political posture. I could not write in defense of the oppressed while being a racist, just as I could not be a machista either.[102]

Freire offers an incomplete defense, but he does at least show that the overall focus of his political and educational project was that of anti-oppression, in whatever forms oppression takes (race, class, gender, ability, sexuality, etc.). Further, he also highlights how he was interested in developing an overarching framework for understanding how education can contribute to liberation generally, even if he did not focus on the nuances of how, for instance, race or gender manifest in that process.

In general, these criticisms of Freire's critical, liberatory pedagogy should be welcomed. Indeed, as Freire himself noted, "Criticism creates the necessary intellectual discipline, asking questions to the reading, to the writing, to the book, to the text. We should not submit to the text or be submissive in front of the text. The thing is to fight with the text, even though loving it, no?"[103] His Marxist, dialectical materialist understanding of the development of consciousness, as well as the pedagogies he developed to move learners toward critical consciousness and action, are all based on the fundament of critical self-reflection. Criticism, especially the kind that both loves and fights with the text (that I would say is more akin to what it means to struggle over issues with friends, comrades, or family members), is central to the ongoing development of critical consciousness—which itself is central to Freire's broader political project of revolutionary social change. And that is the important thing to keep in mind, and what has been neglected as Freire's name has been co-opted by deregulated charter schools, neoliberal corporations, and even moved into the mainstream of progressive education: Freire's liberatory pedagogy is a part of the Marxist, dialectical materialist tradition, and as such, it is fundamentally anti-capitalist and has the goal of upending capitalist relations.[104] This is why Freire was jailed and exiled, why Freirian pedagogy is so powerful for teaching and organizing, and why right-wing conservatives remain bitter and fearful about his influence in US education.[105]

Freire's pedagogy also inherently articulated a curriculum of the oppressed, and taking up the standpoint of the oppressed in the curriculum is the focus of the next chapter.

Chapter 7

Curriculum to Change the World

Developing a Marxist-Feminist Standpoint in the Politics of Knowledge

There is a long history of struggle over the content of school curriculum in the United States,[1] and historically it has been dominated by the interests of capital as well as white men in universities.[2] Current examples litter the educational landscape, ranging from the attacks on—and fights for—ethnic studies,[3] to the constant battles over sex education,[4] the white-washing of history through racist content standards,[5] the annual resistance to teaching the truth about Columbus,[6] and the struggle over whether evolution (or, conversely, "intelligent design") should be taught in science classes.[7] Regardless of whether these fights are happening today or took place a century ago, the struggle over curriculum is ultimately based around a single question: What knowledge should our children learn in school?

On the surface this question seems innocuous. Kids should just learn how to read, write, and do calculations, right? However, in actuality the question of what children should learn carries very fundamental social, cultural, and political implications because we are also considering not only what counts as important knowledge to be learned, but also who has the power to determine its importance.[8] In this way, curriculum implicates choices about what should and should not be learned vis-à-vis the inclusion and exclusion of certain knowledge, and these choices are deeply connected to broader systems of power.[9] Thus, curriculum is also always an expression of social relations—just like consciousness, teaching, and learning—because it takes "particular social forms and embodies certain interests which are themselves the outcomes of continuous struggles within and among dominant and subordinate groups."[10] Curriculum always implies struggles about content, and it carries with it explicit and implicit messages about whose perspectives on the world are valuable, because some groups' perspectives are validated over others.[11] If the curriculum is an expression of social relations and struggle, then we have to acknowledge that there is no neutral or abstract curriculum. Rather, when it comes to curriculum, all we are left with is a struggle over whose knowledge is considered of worth, and whether or not that knowledge provides us a clearer, more truthful understanding of the world. This reality, that knowledge is inherently political and requires struggle for legitimacy within our given social, cultural, and economic relations, is the basis for this chapter.

As I've emphasized throughout this book, schooling and education can play important roles in challenging capitalist relations. In the previous chapter, I looked at the relationship between *how* we teach and the development of critical consciousness that favors equality and social justice—again showing how a dialectical materialist analysis of pedagogy can help us better understand the relationship between teaching and social transformation. Having looked at the *how*, here I turn to the importance of *what* we teach—the curriculum—in fostering critical consciousness and social change. Specifically, I make use of Marxist-feminist standpoint theory conceived by leading critical, feminist scholars Nancy Hartsock and Sandra Harding[12] as a framework for understanding the kind of orientation we need to take up in the curriculum in order to foster more revolutionary learning.

Standpoint Theory

Standpoint theory formally originated with Marxist philosopher Georg Lukács and his elaboration of the concept of "proletarian standpoint."[13] Lukács drew this conception of proletarian standpoint from Marx's discussion of how different economic classes experience alienation from labor and capitalist production in very different ways:[14] workers who produce commodities are not allowed control over their own labor, nor are they allowed to get the full value of what they produce; whereas conversely, capitalists control the labor process and profit from the workers' labor. These different relationships to capitalism would, as Lukács suggests, create very different experiences with and perspectives on capitalism itself. Thus, if we wanted to understand capitalism, we would need to take into account how these differences would produce very dissimilar interpretations of how it works.[15]

In the 1970s and '80s, critical and Marxist-feminist scholars drew on Lukács's concept of proletarian standpoint to challenge both masculinist norms and regressive gender politics found in scientific research.[16] Since then, standpoint theory—in parallel with feminism more broadly—has struggled with its own internal politics of difference and intersectionality surrounding issues of race, class, nationality, and sexuality. Feminists of color, for instance, have critiqued earlier manifestations of standpoint theory for upholding the notion of a "universal woman" and neglecting nonwhite, non-Western experiences.[17] Women of color have also contributed to standpoint theory, for instance, with Chela Sandoval's articulation of oppositional consciousness, and Patricia Hill Collins's Black feminist standpoint, providing foundational contributions in ways that challenge white, Western norms.[18]

Standpoint theory comes from the basic understanding that power and knowledge are inseparable, and that in fact "they co-constitute and co-maintain each other."[19] This happens because knowledge of the world always exists in social context, with knowledge being either validated or invalidated by those with power.[20] We see this process at work, for instance, in the realities that are constructed and validated with regard to the killing of Black women and men by the police, relative to crime suspects who are white. Black victims of police violence are too-often portrayed by media and government officials as threatening, deserving of punishment, dangerous, or unstable through messy mug shots or other images, as well as headlines and stories emphasizing criminal histories or poverty—all used to visually reinforce the constructed narrative. Conversely, white perpetrators of crime and violence are often portrayed as more human, more stable, and less dangerous, and the crime sometimes portrayed as atypical, rather than typical, behavior.[21] An example can be found in the initial coverage of Stephen Paddock, the white gunman who killed fifty-eight people and injured over five hundred in the October 2017 shooting spree in Las Vegas. Rather than painting him as the white male terrorist that he was, some major news outlets like the *Washington Post* instead published headlines that read, "Las Vegas gunman, Stephen Paddock, liked to gamble, listened to country music, lived quiet retired life before massacre"; elsewhere he was repeatedly described as not meeting the profile of a mass shooter.[22]

Because of differences in social, economic, and cultural power in the United States (really, because of racism and white supremacy), the media and other institutions ultimately produce narratives and construct a reality that portrays Black people in particularly racist ways, often projecting guilt when there is none, while also projecting white innocence—even when there is clear evidence of guilt. So, when we think about how we know and understand the world, our epistemology, we have to recognize that "there are some perspectives on society from which . . . the real relations of humans with each other and with the natural world are not visible,"[23] because differences in power mean that the perspectives of some positions in society are favored and protected while others are demeaned and villainized. Put differently, because some groups have more power than others, some realities are constructed as "real" while others are "fake." This is foundational for standpoint theory.

Through their respective works, both Nancy Hartsock and Sandra Harding have articulated five central themes that guide standpoint theory as a way of understanding and researching the world.[24] First, standpoint theory asserts that our experiences with material reality—which includes our social relations—structure how we understand the world in ways that both limit and enable what we learn and come to "know" about that world. That is, our social location enables us to see and understand the world more clearly with respect to our positions *and* places limits on our ability to immediately understand the world beyond that same position.

Second, because our experiences and material conditions are structured by, and embedded in, power relations of race, class, gender, sexuality, nationality, and other categories of difference, the worldviews and understandings of groups in power generally contradict and run counter to the worldviews and understandings of less powerful groups.[25] Put in more straightforward terms, the ruler's view of the world will in many ways be oppositional to that of the ruled because of their different experiences.

Third, differences in power mean that the perspectives of those in power are made functional in the lives of everyone regardless of social location, because "the ruling group can be expected to structure the material relations in which all people are forced to participate"[26] as "all are forced to live in social structures and institutions designed to serve the oppressors' understandings of self and society."[27] This point speaks directly to Gramsci's conception of hegemony and how the ruling capitalist class maintains control: their skewed understanding of the world is imposed institutionally and constructs a view of reality that may contradict the reality facing the oppressed.[28] We might say that the unequal distribution of power leads to the unequal distribution of worldviews, where those with more power can exert stronger influence on our commonsense understandings of the world, even if such commonsense understandings fundamentally operate as distorted conceptions of material reality.

Fourth, and as an extension of the previous, a standpoint always comes out of a struggle against the commonsense, hegemonic worldviews of those in power. In this sense, a standpoint is an achievement that arises from active, conscious work against the reigning, institutionalized commonsense understandings that generally justify and support status quo inequalities. Subsequently, a standpoint "must be struggled for against the apparent realities made 'natural' and 'obvious' by dominant institutions,"[29] the activity of which "requires both systematic analysis and the education that can only grow from political struggle to change those relations."[30] This is in completely alignment with both Vygotsky's and Freire's discussion of consciousness from the previous chapters.

An important outgrowth of this is that we can never assume that a standpoint is simply given by one's social location. Just because someone comes from a marginalized social location does not mean that they have automatically taken up a specific standpoint; people from marginalized or less powerful groups can and do maintain forms of consciousness that are regressive and function to support their own oppression, just as people from dominant groups can also develop forms of consciousness that are progressive and openly challenge their own power and privilege. Rather, a standpoint arises from conscious, resistant struggle against the prevailing and hegemonic forms of consciousness that are aligned with status quo inequalities.

Fifth and finally, the taking up of a standpoint by the less powerful carries the potential for liberation because it "makes visible the inhumanity of relations among human beings,"[31] emphasizing that, in a very Marxist sense, "an oppressed group must become a group 'for itself,' not just 'in itself' in order for it to see the importance of engaging in political and scientific struggles to see the world from the perspective of its own lives."[32] In this way the development of a standpoint requires the development of "oppositional consciousness,"[33] since those with less power create transformative ways of knowing as part of their struggle against the power relations responsible for their own oppression. Indeed, this liberatory potential of standpoint makes it dangerous to the prevailing social order—as we saw with Freire and his treatment by the Brazilian government, for instance—and therefore gives cause for the more powerful to actively seek to discredit such positions.[34]

Standpoint and "Strong Objectivity"

Because of its focus on positionality and social location, standpoint theory provides a foundation for understanding how the world works. From the perspective of standpoint theory, the experiences of systematically oppressed or marginalized groups can provide the best "starting off thought" for generating "illuminating critical questions that do not arise in thought that begins from the dominant group lives."[35] As Hartsock explains,

> [T]he criteria for privileging some knowledges over others are ethical and political as well as purely "epistemological." . . . Marx made an important claim that knowledge that takes its starting point from the lives of those who have suffered from exploitation produces better accounts of the world than that starting from the lives of dominant groups. . . . [T]he view from the margins (defined in more heterogeneous terms) is clearer and better.[36]

As an orientation on understanding the world, standpoint thus openly acknowledges that the social location of the oppressed and marginalized (as defined by historical, social, cultural, and institutional contexts) is the best vantage point for understanding society because it can provide a clearer, more truthful view of how a society functions. Additionally, it is important to note that standpoint theory does not singularly focus on women or gender to the exclusion of other aspects of power and identity. Rather, Harding explains that standpoint theory thus invites a recognition of personhood and one's equality, which means that by definition it must contend with issues of power and oppression in ways that recognize how, for instance, class is expressed in material ways that are raced and gendered.[37]

However, we have to be clear that, despite its focus on positionality and social location, standpoint theory does not argue for total relativity of viewpoints; every individual, socially located standpoint is equally strong for understanding reality. Rather, consistent with Marxist dialectical materialism, standpoint embraces the fact that we, as individuals, are expressions of social relations, and that, as such, we are tied historically, culturally, politically, and materially to institutions. Thus, the point isn't to say that "all standpoints are equal," but instead that the position of the oppressed creates a stronger standpoint for better understanding the material reality of society.[38]

The movement to make #BlackLivesMatter in the face of white supremacy, anti-Blackness, and police violence provides a perfect example of this. Many liberals and conservatives have argued that "all lives matter," out of fundamentally racist feelings that somehow their views and experiences are being excluded or demeaned—that all experiences and viewpoints should matter equally, and that we shouldn't be focusing on Black people specifically. Conversely, and consistent with standpoint theory, #BlackLivesMatter activists and supporters argue that, because the police seem to get away with killing Black people with little to no provocation or accountability, and because this is an issue that affects Black people disproportionally, the best way to understand how racism and white supremacy function in the United States is through the standpoint of Black people and Blackness.

The movement to make Black lives matter does not deny that racism exists for other nonwhite peoples, nor does it say that white people don't matter. Rather, the #BlackLivesMatter movement points out that the experiences of Black people with the police in the United States provides the sharpest and clearest view for understanding how racism and white supremacy operate institutionally and in our day-to-day experiences. To put it a bit differently, if we want to understand the realities of racism and police violence, the relatively privileged and shielded perspectives of white people will yield us less sharp, less clear, and less truthful perspectives on how the police operate to support institutionalized racism and white supremacy. In this way, rather than a call for a form of relativism, a standpoint is perhaps better conceived as a tool that allows, following Hartsock, for "the creation of better (more objective, more liberatory) accounts of the world."[39]

I want to highlight the specific language here. Both Hartsock and Harding refer to "objectivity" in their analyses, and elsewhere Harding and noted feminist theorist Donna Haraway both talk about "strong objectivity" as well.[40] It might seem contradictory that standpoint theory and its basis in feminism and feminist theory relies so heavily on an idea of objectivity, especially given that it emphasizes the subjectivity of social location and is grounded in the historical rejection of Western, male notions of objectivity perpetuated within the sciences. What is critical to understanding their use of "objectivity" is that, consistent with Marxist dialectical materialism, these scholars acknowledge that a world exists outside of the human subjective perception of it, and that it is a world that can in fact be understood. Further, their recognition of social location illustrates the dialectical interaction and mutual reaction between people and their environments. This conception of standpoint argues that we can achieve *more* objective knowledge of the world not only by recognizing how our social location shapes our understanding of the world, but also by explicitly reflecting on that location in the process of learning. Harding calls this "strong objectivity," explaining,

> Strong objectivity requires that the subject of knowledge be placed on the same critical, causal plane as the objects of knowledge. Thus, strong objectivity requires what we can think of as "strong reflexivity." This is because culturewide (or nearly culturewide) beliefs function as evidence at every stage of scientific inquiry: in the selection of problems, the formation of hypotheses, the design of research (including the organization of research communities), the collection of data, the interpretation and sorting of data, decisions about when to stop research, the way results of research are reported, and so on. The subject of knowledge—the individual and the historically located social community whose unexamined beliefs its members are likely to hold "unknowingly," so to speak—must be considered as part of the object of knowledge from the perspective of scientific method.[41]

By employing strong objectivity we gain better, clearer, and more truthful—more strongly objective—knowledge of social and material realities of the world from the achievement of a standpoint because we critically examine the process of understanding something as much as we critically examine the thing itself.[42] Again, taking the same #BlackLivesMatter example as discussed above: if we are trying to understand how racism, white supremacy, and police violence function in the United States, then to be strongly objective in that context means to critically analyze how we approach our learning about racism, white supremacy, and police violence—being conscious of the process of learning as much as the thing we are learning about. In this view, where we look for information, who we ask for information, who is asking or looking for information, and what kinds of questions we decide to ask to get information are just as important as the information itself—again, working under the presumption that asking white people about police violence would yield very different information than asking Black people (just as it would generate different information between rich and poor people).

Curriculum Standpoint to Change the World

Standpoint theory has been little used in educational theorizing and practice, and elsewhere I have discussed its use (and lack thereof) in more depth.[43] What is critical to understand in this context is that when applied to curriculum, standpoint theory offers us a concrete tool for developing forms of critical consciousness to change the world. Here I map standpoint theory into curriculum to form *curriculum standpoint*.

First, we have to recognize that curriculum is an extension and expression of material and social relations. Textbook companies, nonprofit organizations, parents, business groups, school boards, state and federal education committees, politicians, school principals, school departments, and individual teachers all have differing levels of interest in, and control over, curriculum. This means that whatever knowledge is taught in schools is fraught with every aspect of power and politics we see in society. In this same sense, those with more resources and power are positioned to try and influence what curriculum is taught in schools. Curriculum standpoint embraces this reality, understanding that curriculum itself is imbued with the social locations of its authors, designers, or sponsors (e.g., major corporations), and as such curriculum creates potentialities for understanding the world more clearly or in more obscurity relative to such locations.

A brief example of this can be found in a Rethinking Schools campaign against fossil fuel propaganda. In 2011, Rethinking Schools editor and author Bill Bigelow worked with his students to analyze a curriculum about coal that was published by *Scholastic Magazine*, and that was distributed freely to upwards of one hundred thousand teachers in the United States.[44] He and his students found that not only was the curriculum funded by the coal industry, but that it also completely neglected all of the negative effects of coal mining, like mountain top removal, erosion and flooding, the poisoning of water, the production of toxic waste from burning coal, and how coal burning contributes to greenhouse gases. Fortunately, in conjunction with the Campaign for a Commercial-Free Childhood, Rethinking Schools led a successful resistance movement, where *Scholastic* eventually stopped distribution of the curriculum, cut its ties to the coal industry, and established a formal review process for the development of future curriculum.[45] Despite the victory, what this example shows is how those with power—like the coal industry and *Scholastic Magazine*—can leverage their resources to try and influence what is taught in schools. By taking up a curriculum standpoint in their critical analysis, Bigelow, along with his students, was able to cut through the political agenda of the coal industry, uncovering the reality of both coal as a fossil fuel, and the coal industry as a producer of curriculum.

A second aspect of curriculum standpoint is that it recognizes how schools and school knowledge exist within institutional and social contexts, and that these contexts are themselves structured by systems of domination and rule organized hierarchically around power relations of race, class, gender, sexuality, nationality, and other forms of socially determined difference. In this way, the curriculum knowledge asserted by groups in power generally supports status quo, hegemonic social relations and worldviews, and runs counter to the worldviews, experiences, and curriculum knowledge advanced by oppressed groups. Put differently, the curriculum of the ruler will in many ways be oppositional to the curriculum of the ruled. Again, following the above example of how the coal industry influenced the *Scholastic* coal curriculum, those with power in that instance used their influence to create a curriculum that obscured the reality of coal production and burning, and supported the status quo of capitalist exploitation and degradation of people and the planet: it was the worldview of the coal industry, and not the view of those immediately and negatively affected by the extraction and burning of coal.

A third aspect of curriculum standpoint is that the perspectives of those in power are made universally operational in curriculum knowledge for everyone, regardless of social location and regardless of whether or not such perspectives are complimentary (or contradictory) to the material and social realities of students, teachers, and their communities. Put differently, the unequal distribution of power leads to the unequal distribution of curricular knowledge, where those with more power can exert stronger influence on our commonsense understandings of the world vis-à-vis the curriculum, even if such commonsense understandings fundamentally operate as distorted conceptions of how the world works. Again, we can return to the above example of the coal industry's influence on *Scholastic*'s curriculum. Even though in this specific case the curriculum was effectively stopped, it is important to remember that—as I discussed in chapter 4—corporations are deeply involved in both the development and implementation of school policy, including curriculum. In this regard, they have disproportionate power in trying to make their viewpoint on the world *the* legitimate viewpoint. So even though in this one instance a campaign led by Rethinking Schools did stop the corporations, that was an anomaly. In general, corporate influence over curriculum seeks to validate a view of the world that operates in their interests, as was the case before *Scholastic* and the coal industry were caught.

Fourth, because school knowledge is always embedded within dominant power relations, curriculum standpoint is more than just a "perspective." Rather, curriculum standpoint is produced in the struggle against those very same power relations and their manifestations in curriculum knowledge. In this sense, curriculum standpoint is achieved, not received, because it arises from active, systematic, and conscious reflection on—and consideration of—the reigning, hegemonic, institutionalized forms of curricular knowledge. In the case of *Scholastic*'s coal curriculum, Bigelow and his students achieved a curriculum standpoint in struggle against the hegemonic perspective on coal advanced in the curriculum.

A fifth aspect of curriculum standpoint is that because it works to reveal unequal social and material relations, it carries the potential for liberation. In bringing those inequalities to light, curriculum standpoint can be part of a process of actively challenging those same unequal social and material relations. Further, curriculum standpoint helps in the development of "oppositional consciousness," or critical consciousness, as I discussed in chapters 5 and 6. This is because curriculum standpoint creates the potential for students, teachers, and researchers to develop ways of understanding that invoke and bolster their own resistance to status quo knowledge and relations, in turn building capacity to individually, institutionally, and socially take transformational action. In this way, the potential of human liberation embedded in curriculum standpoint moves us beyond simple critique, as it also calls upon us to reconstruct not just our knowledge of the world, but the world itself. In this sense, curriculum standpoint requires a commitment not only to critique, but also to vision and creativity.

The important work of Bill Bigelow and his students, as well as Rethinking Schools's challenge to *Scholastic* and the coal industry's influence on curriculum and the Campaign for a Commercial-Free Childhood, clearly illustrate this critical dimension of curriculum standpoint. For Bigelow and the students, it was their systemic analysis that helped develop critical consciousness about coal, the coal industry, and the politics of *Scholastic* and their coal curriculum. This work also laid the groundwork for Bigelow to write about his teaching and what he learned about the *Scholastic* curriculum, which in turn became the basis for the successful campaign challenging *Scholastic* and its materials. The act of curriculum standpoint helped create the possibility of action to stop an injustice.

Sixth, and finally, curriculum standpoint requires that we seek to develop strong objectivity relative to curriculum knowledge. This requires that we reflect not only upon the standpoint of knowledge itself, but also upon the origins, politics, and process that determine how knowledge makes its way into the curriculum. Indeed, curriculum standpoint is a product of strong objectivity because it recognizes the politics of school knowledge in a way that makes the curriculum *itself* an object for analysis in the same way we need to analyze the knowledge contained *within* the curriculum. In this way, curriculum standpoint is complimentary to the Marxist, dialectical materialist conception of critical consciousness because it invites us to develop meta-understandings of curriculum. Bigelow and his students' analysis of *Scholastic*'s coal curriculum exemplified strong objectivity because they analyzed the curriculum itself, the process of the development of the curriculum, and their own relation to it. The result was a critically conscious engagement in the politics of the coal industry and a strongly objective meta-analysis of the politics of curriculum itself.

Curriculum Standpoint in Practice

While Bill Bigelow's curriculum about coal offers a singular and powerful example of teaching and organizing extending from curriculum standpoint, it also exists in other practices, even if it hasn't been named as such. For instance, Linda Christensen's "Putting Out the Linguistic Welcome Mat" provides a brief, concrete example of curriculum standpoint in practice.[46] In this piece, Christensen talks about her curriculum on the politics of language and discusses classroom strategies she uses with her high school language arts students. She reflects,

> During 30 years as a language arts classroom teacher, I realized that if I wanted my students to open up in their writing, to take risks and engage in intellectually demanding work, I needed to challenge assumptions about the superiority of Standard English and the inferiority of the home language of many of my black students: African American Vernacular English. . . . When students feel attacked by the red pen or the tongue for the way they write or speak, they either make themselves small—turning in short papers—or don't turn papers in at all. To build an engaging classroom where students from different backgrounds felt safe enough to dare to be big and bold in their writing, I had to build a curricular platform for them to stand on. . . . I finally realized that I needed to create a curriculum on language and power that examined the roots of language supremacy and analyzed how schools perpetuate the myths of the inferiority of some languages.[47]

Using a variety of resources and writing activities, Christensen introduced her students to the origins and grammatical rules of African American Vernacular English (AAVE). As her African American students learned that AAVE has linguistic roots in West African languages and cultures, they began to understand and challenge forms of racism they had internalized relative to their home languages. Christensen also highlights the way learning about AAVE aided students in developing a meta-cognitive understanding of not only the structures of their own spoken English, but also the relationship between AAVE and the Standard English taught and enforced in racist ways in schools. This created the potential for these students to take conscious action in their own educational futures because they were able to apply awareness of linguistic tools such as code switching, code meshing, and meta-awareness of Standard English itself as they navigated their schooling.

While not naming it as such, Christensen takes up curriculum standpoint here. Her teaching explicitly seeks to expose the ways in which systems of domination exist within classroom knowledge and linguistic practices through the exploration of the relationship between AAVE and Standard English, and by examining the systemic denigration of non-standard forms of English. Christensen's curriculum essentially takes up the standpoint of a marginalized form of the English language, acknowledging the ways that language and culture are intertwined and recognizing the concrete experiences of her African American students. Along the way, Christensen also helps students uncover linguistic relationships that may have been previously obscured from their commonsense understandings of culture and language. Christensen's curriculum standpoint is also clearly a conscious act as a teacher, making it an achievement she has struggled to achieve as her curriculum and instruction have developed over time. Finally, although Christensen uses AAVE as her starting point, she is quick to point out that the resources she uses speak to a wide range of non-standard forms of the English language. Thus, the issue for Christensen is the validation of "home language," regardless of the cultural specifics of social location of one's home.

Another example of curriculum standpoint in practice can be found in Eric Gutstein's "Math, SATs, and Racial Profiling."[48] There, Gutstein writes about using race and class as a standpoint to connect students with basic mathematics content. For instance, Gutstein explains how he connects mathematics and racial profiling through a lesson on proportion and statistical probability: "The essence of profiling is proportion and expected value: A higher proportion of African Americans (or Arabs/Arab Americans today) are stopped and searched than would be expected given their percentage in the population—assuming random (i.e., fair) searches or stops."[49] Gutstein leads students through activities that illustrate the concept of theoretical probability using graphing calculators and dice. Students then use their knowledge about theoretical probability to analyze statistics on traffic stops, including clear patterns of racial profiling by police officers.

Gutstein does similar mathematics work with class and race in relation to the SAT college-entrance exam. Here Gutstein's students use raw (disaggregated) SAT data to look for correlations between scores and data sets on race and class, as part of a unit on data analysis and creating scatter plots (a type of graph that can be used to look at correlations between two variables). In their mathematical analyses, students found strong correlations between SAT scores and family income. They also found that specific racial groups, such as working-class Mexican Americans (the predominant racial group at Gutstein's school), were clustered close to the bottom in terms of SAT scores. This statistical analysis raised a lot of questions for the students, mostly revolving around race, class, and school achievement. In response to those questions, Gutstein's students wrote letters to the Educational Testing Service (the institutional body responsible for creating and administering the SAT), explaining what their statistical analysis found and requesting that changes be made to this gatekeeper college entrance exam.

Like Christensen's curriculum on the politics of language, Gutstein's mathematics teaching also demonstrates curriculum standpoint. Gutstein uses the social location of his students and other marginalized communities as a starting point for classroom knowledge projects on race and class inequality; in so doing, he pushes students to confront and reflect upon their social and material reality in a way that not only identifies critical issues they face in their lives, but also creates a potential for them to take action on those issues. Gutstein's curriculum standpoint is also the product of conscious struggle—an achievement—in multiple ways. For one, this lesson required an active reckoning with the politics of knowledge in what is often incorrectly considered an apolitical subject area—mathematics. For the students, this was an achievement because they had to struggle with the political and educational realities this teaching brought to bear, on top of any struggles they already experienced in learning the mathematics concepts and putting them into practice. Additionally, we see curriculum standpoint here in that Gutstein and his students are using mathematics to gain a more strongly objective understanding of how the material and social world functions: the example illustrates a reach for understanding reality more objectively and in ways that run contradictory to hegemonic constructions of both the legal and education systems in the United States as unbiased and individually "fair" institutions. Such understanding is critical because it always carries with it the potential for reconstruction, revision, and transformation.

The two above examples illustrate a basic potential power of curriculum: it can be used to confront the material realities faced by students, particularly if we use their social locations as the starting point. This orientation is particularly important right now, given rising poverty, increasing inequality, white supremacist attacks and violence, government raids against immigrant communities, police violence against Black and Brown people, increasing anti-Muslim actions, and transphobic violence. These are the realities that our students face in their lives, schools, and communities every day,[50] and we need to marshal our resources in solidarity with their struggle. The key point here is to understand that curriculum is political and helps shape our understandings of the world. Given this reality, it is imperative that we continue to develop curriculum standpoint—a curriculum of the oppressed, if you will—in order to both help students understand reality more critically *and* lay a foundation for students to become the activist changemakers and leaders of mass movements of the present and future.[51] This is perhaps the most important reason for taking up curriculum standpoint: if Freirian pedagogy can provide the *how* we teach to change the world, curriculum standpoint can help us understand *what* we teach to change the world. But pedagogy and curriculum are about more than just what we do in schools or classrooms. Everyday, we teach ourselves and each other, learn from ourselves and each other, and make decisions about how we approach all of our relations. The ways we live our lives, engage with communities, be with our families, do our work, and navigate our institutions also embody a kind of pedagogy of being as we experience the curriculum of the world.

Chapter 8

A Dialectical Life

Working to Change the World

I love going to radical, leftist rallies and demonstrations. I revel in the energy of the gathering crowds, marvel at the creativity of the signs, and enjoy hearing the chants and songs people come up with. In October of 2017, I attended a rally in the city of Bellevue, just outside of Seattle. The occasion: Trump's Secretary of Education, Betsy DeVos, was keynoting a conservative fundraiser dinner there. I arrived carrying a sign that read "Choice = Charters 2.0" on one side and "White Supremacy 'hearts' School Choice" on the other.

A few hundred people showed up, and it proved to be a spirited rally against Secretary DeVos, her education agenda, and the political vulgarity of the Trump presidency. Despite the demonstration being co-opted by several mainstream organizations, there were still a lot of comrades and radicals in the crowd. I was able to catch up with friends, gauge the wide-ranging politics of the demonstrators, and be reminded of the feeling that none of us are alone in this work. And while I saw many teacher-activist friends and some former students of mine, I was once again struck by the lack of education professors in attendance. Perhaps I missed seeing them in the crowd, but in my experience, unless it is a very mainstream demonstration (like the January 2017 national Womxn's march), my colleagues in education generally don't show up to protests about education politics, even if they themselves agree with the protests.

Many people end up seeing me as *the* radical education professor here in the Seattle area: the one who speaks publicly against the power and education policy agenda of Bill Gates Jr. and the Gates Foundation (which is almost blasphemy here in Gates's backyard); the one who openly challenges charter schools—in local media and the courts—as part of a free market attack on public education and communities of color; the one who makes presentations to PTAs about why high-stakes testing is bad and how we should all be fighting for better assessments of our children; and the one who attends protests. In light of this, graduate students, colleagues in the academy, fellow activists, parents, and friends often ask me, how is it that I can be a college professor who speaks publicly about these things and still keep my job? I feel like they are asking me about my own praxis—about where my politics and practices meet. This is who I am in the world, and how I try to embody my political commitments of being a "critical" scholar, a professor, and an education activist—especially in the midst of navigating universities, school districts, and other institutions. So, by way of conclusion, I want to reflect on the questions: What does it mean to live a dialectical life? How do our politics live and breathe through us on a day-to-day basis? And, how does someone put their Marxism into operation, especially within this capitalist totality?

I face these questions on a daily basis because I am unavoidably dependent on chains of capitalist exploitation to survive, while also simultaneously working to break those chains in the interest of humanity and the planet. As a student and a teacher, I've lived this contradiction intimately, and I know that schools as institutions are rife with injustice. Colonization, nationalism, white supremacy, sexism, patriarchy, homophobia, class exploitation, and environmental degradation have historically been perpetuated within the halls of education at all levels. I know that schools exist as part of the settler-colonial state and have served the interests of whiteness and capitalism; this is the hard truth for all educators (including university professors) employed within them. Moreover, this legacy is present every day in our capacity to earn wages, build the futures of our families, eat, survive, and potentially thrive. For radical educators, this is the contradiction that we have to come to terms with—and to own, revel in, and sit deeply with—because we have no real choice in the matter: we're given these conditions and history. Indeed, thinking dialectically, the contradiction of schooling actually defines us as teachers and students: it drives our development as educators and learners.

However, even if I as an educator must come to terms with my own complicity in the oppressive structures of schools, I stay an educator because of the potential for liberation that also exists in schools. I see this potential in my students almost every day, especially as they develop more critical perspectives on the world and gather a wider vocabulary to give name to their realities. I see it in my own son as he learns about the world and develops as a young person. I see it in many of my son's teachers who, in the face of mounting attacks on public education, remain committed to loving their students. I see it in myself as I grow and strive to make a difference in the lives of the people around me, both inside of schools and within my community. To that end, I work hard to bring my work to the world, and I do so by playing a combination of overlapping roles. In what follows I articulate some of the ways I bring my Marxist politics to bear on my work as a professor, educator, activist, and parent.

Critical Scholar

When I began my PhD research, I was committed to bringing my politics with me. In a broad sense this meant that I always intended to do academic work *that mattered to people.* I wasn't interested in sitting in the ivory tower of the university, working on esoteric articles and books. If I was going to attend those classes, write those papers, accumulate those student loan debts, survive the strain on my family, write a dissertation, and get a PhD, then I was not going to waste it: my work had to take up radical politics and it had to be a political intervention wherever possible. For instance, this is why I chose to write about high-stakes standardized testing for my dissertation. No Child Left Behind and its federally mandated testing had just been established when I entered my program at the University of Wisconsin–Madison, and high-stakes tests were at the heart of that education policy. I made a political, strategic assessment of the educational landscape and chose to undertake a critical analysis of high-stakes testing as part of my contribution to the struggle against a particularly heinous educational policy. In addition to being the focus of my dissertation, this turned into my first academic book, *Unequal by Design: High-Stakes Testing and the Standardization of Inequality*, as well as a slew of articles that looked at testing through the lenses of Marxist political economy, critical sociology, gender studies, radical history, and empirical research.[1]

In the years since I became a professor, I've continued to think about my formal scholarship as a political intervention, letting my own political heart guide my research and writing. One of my favorite projects has been doing "social network analysis"—essentially mapping networks of power in neoliberal, corporate education policy. In conjunction with my dear friend and colleague Joe Ferrare, I analyzed the network of relations surrounding charter school education reform in Washington State.[2] Here in Washington it was clear to me that wealthy elites, like Bill Gates Jr. and other tech moguls, were heavily invested in making charter schools happen. My experience with this political struggle on the ground demonstrated that certain nonprofit organizations were operating as surrogates for this charter school push, and that the philanthropies associated with wealthy individuals like Gates were helping facilitate those nonprofits in that work. In our analysis, Ferrare and I identified a network of relations that clearly illustrated how unelected, unaccountable, wealthy elites essentially set education policy regarding charter schools in Washington State. This research, first published as an academic article, became the basis for the collection *Mapping Corporate Education Reform: Power and Policy*

Networks in the Neoliberal State, which took a more national and global look at the same issue.[3]

My work doing social network analysis also points to the ways that I've employed dialectical approaches to research. In particular I've been interested in understanding the relationship between the individual and the social/institutional: the micro and the macro. The above example—wealthy elites leveraging their capital to control public policy, using powerful networks to maintain and reproduce inequalities—is one instance. As another example, in my earlier work on high-stakes standardized testing I used something called "qualitative meta-synthesis"—a fancy term for gathering and combining the findings of a lot of classroom-based studies—to try and understand the ways that policies built around these tests were changing the day-to-day practices of classroom teachers and the day-to-day experiences of students.[4] In other work on high-stakes testing, I used the work of Basil Bernstein and critical sociology to examine how the tests transmit broader social relations into the classroom, again trying to understand how larger, structural, capitalist inequalities were reproduced at the level of the individual student.[5] This same impulse to understand the connection between the individual and the social was directly behind my study of Vygotsky,[6] and it has also reached into my teaching about multiculturalism and identity: I regularly ask my graduate students to produce autoethnographies, where they tell stories of their own experiences and then connect those stories to social science research, in an effort to see whether their lives fit into the patterns of others, or if they have beat the odds in one way or another.[7] In creating these autoethnographies, my students have explored issues related to sex education, drug use, racial identity development in schools, the preponderance of white teachers, and the ways race impacts their encounters with the police, among other topics. Again, the focus has been to elucidate the ways we as individuals become transmitters, carriers, or bearers of broader social and institutional relations and processes.

I've also been very purposeful about where I publish, because I know how the academic game is played: radical scholars, scholars of color, female scholars, and especially radical female or radical scholars of color have to publish more, and in more "elite" journals, just to prove, beyond a shadow of a doubt, that they legitimately belong in the conversation.[8] I've done this less for my own ego and more because I know that as a radical, critical, Marxist scholar, my work is much less likely to be taken seriously than that of mainstream researchers and academics. Radicals are typically and easily brushed aside as not doing "real" work. This is a living example of why we need standpoint theory: power relations external to the academy are clearly reflected within it, essentially controlling whose knowledge and perspectives are legitimized. Living with this contradiction means being drawn into an oppressive game (often despite our own disgust with it) in order to legitimize doing radical work in support of anti-oppressive, liberatory struggles. And yes, there are politics of respectability at play here too, because we are essentially proving that we are as good as those with power, and doing so on their terms. However, excelling at that game has allowed me to fend off attempts by conservatives and liberals to defame me as a scholar,[9] and it has also enabled me to feel free to publish in critical/radical open-access journals, as well as in magazines and blogs with more popular reach.[10]

Fundamentally, my scholarship has always focused on power, particularly on race, class, culture, economy, and labor, and I have tried to bring to light the ways these inequalities of power are inflected by and transmitted through education policy, curriculum, and teaching. In a very Gramscian sense, I've looked at education and constantly asked, who benefits, and who doesn't?[11] Also, because I am a Marxist dialectical materialist, I am committed to continually highlighting the material realities experienced by students, their communities, and their teachers within the context of educational reform. By extension, this has included exposing the lies and spin used to justify damaging policies—like the arguments for charter schools and high-stakes testing that I punctured in chapter 4. This exposure has also been the basis of my work as a professor who speaks publicly about power and inequality in education.

Activist, Public Scholar

To me, being a professor and scholar does not mean all that much if my work stays in the ivory tower of the academy. It isn't that I think conversations purely among academics are useless. I believe in employing deep thinking and theory in our attempts to understand the world. But, I also know two things: (1) if we are not grounded in the material world, then our theory is untested and likely wrong (philosophically this would be an idealist, not materialist, approach); and (2) there is a dangerous level of privilege and entitlement in academics' perception that they are somehow above the fray of the struggles that the masses of people face daily. Personally, I feel it would be an utter waste of privilege and resources if I didn't bring my PhD, and whatever prestige comes with my position as a professor of education, to bear on public issues and in very public ways. This feeling, combined with my political commitments as a Marxist, shapes my vision and actions as an activist, public scholar.

Concretely, my scholar-activism manifests in a few key ways. I am perhaps best known for my work with Rethinking Schools, a small, thirty-year-old nonprofit publishing house that focuses on teaching for social and environmental justice.[12] Rethinking Schools has a wide reach among practicing teachers and community educators, and, as one of the earliest practicioner-based social justice education magazines and book publishers, it has become a standard-bearing example of how to put a politics of justice into classroom curriculum and teaching on a daily basis. I have written for the magazine since 1996, and I have been an editorial board member since 2004. For me, working with Rethinking Schools has been a way to translate my theory into practice in a way that I know is making a difference—because practicing teachers read the pages of *Rethinking Schools*.

My scholar-activism also manifests in my efforts to use my PhD and reputation as a scholar to support local activists in their struggles for educational justice. To return to an example I discussed in chapter 4, when the teachers at Garfield High School in Seattle, Washington, decided to boycott the standardized MAP test, they came under significant fire from the district, becoming a focus for the struggle over high-stakes testing nationally.[13] My reputation as a scholar afforded me the capacity to support the Garfield teachers in several ways. I came out publicly in support of their boycott by talking to media and by publishing a supportive piece in a local blog.[14] I also organized, with Brian Jones, a national petition in support of the Garfield teachers, which was signed by over 220 professors from around the United States.[15] This petition was important not only because it demonstrated to the Seattle School Board and the Seattle Public Schools administration that respected professors from around the country were watching very closely, but also because it showed a broad base of scholarly support for the teachers' action. Additionally, after they approached me based on their interest in my research and my local reputation, I advised the Garfield teachers regarding the body of research on testing, alerting them to the various and well-known problems with high-stakes testing. I also attended press conferences and made sure I showed up when needed for interviews of consultation. Since then, through speaking engagements with local schools and teachers, I have also worked to improve community literacy around the problems with high-stakes standardized testing.

I've also put my role as an activist, public scholar to work in the struggle over charter schools in Washington State. Again, as during the struggle over Seattle's MAP testing, I was able to bring my degree, formal research on the networks of power surrounding charter school policy, and political commitments to bear in the fight about charter schools. For instance, in 2012 I entered a very public conversation about whether or not Washington State should get charter schools. I debated charter school supporters in a forum hosted by the Washington State Parent Teacher Association, exposing how their pro-charter arguments were based on willful ignorance of the research and the many examples of unethical charter school practices.[16] I also published op-eds in the *Seattle Times* and the *Spokesman-Review* explaining how the research on charters showed they were not as successful as charter supporters claimed.[17] Additionally, I did local and national media spots on the charter school struggle here, and I published a detailed analysis of the proposed charter school law in a local blog, highlighting how it worked in the interests of deregulation, privatization, and de-democratization of public schools.[18]

While the charter school law eventually passed here in Washington, I have continued as an activist, public scholar to struggle against its implementation. I have published chapters and articles highlighting the anti-democratic nature, the failure, the lack of transparency, and overblown claims of success of charter schools in Washington State. These include an opinion piece in our local Asian American community newspaper, the *International Examiner*.[19] Perhaps most significantly, I became a coplaintiff in a lawsuit that successfully challenged the constitutionality of Washington's charter schools. In that role I advised the legal team regarding charter school research for use in their legal briefs and arguments, provided my own charter school policy statements, and used my PhD and position as a local professor to provide added authority to my status as a plaintiff. The Washington State Supreme Court's finding that charter schools were unconstitutional was a monumental victory in the fight against privatization and corporate education reform.[20] Although the state legislature kept the charter schools open through a revised bill, the struggle continues, and I am once again a coplaintiff on yet another legal challenge to the constitutionality of our charter schools.

An unfortunate truth is that, even as I personally challenge and fight elitism in the academy, in the terrain of public conversations it does make a difference that *Dr.* Wayne Au, a book author and professor at the University of Washington Bothell, thought that the Garfield teachers were right to oppose high-stakes testing, and thinks that we should be opposing charter schools as part of a broader project seeking to privatize and deregulate public education. Given that reality, as a committed activist, public scholar, it is imperative that I continue to lend the weight of my PhD and position as a professor to struggles for educational justice, that I continue to stay grounded with local and national educational activists, and that I continue to build critical community literacy around education policy and practice. This has also meant doing this work at my son's school as a radical parent and professor.

Critical Scholar-Parent

As of this writing, my son is in the second grade. This means that, including kindergarten, I am in my third year of being part of his school's community. Over the last two-plus years, I have been very intentional about building relationships and being involved at the school, but also about remaining conscious of my presence in the school space. At first, only a few teachers at my son's school had read my essays or knew about my work with Rethinking Schools. After a while, more learned that I was Dr. Au, professor of education at UW Bothell. I have often worried that the staff at my son's school would be intimidated by my presence—not because I have delusions of grandeur, but because my job is to be an "expert" in education and teach teachers, and I was worried that the school staff would think I was standing around and judging them all of the time.

So, I was careful and moved slowly. I chatted with teachers and support staff as often as possible. I volunteered where I could, and our family joined the school's teachers on the picket line when the union went on strike.[21] I started figuring out where my community connections intersected with theirs, and I joined the parent-teacher association, which included some parents who were also teachers there. Specifically, I got involved directly with the PTA committee on race and social justice, and started helping the school with its race justice work. I also started offering some resources to a few teachers and the principal. I gave my son's kindergarten and first-grade teachers copies of *Rethinking Early Childhood Education*, *Rethinking*

Elementary Education, and *Rethinking Multicultural Education*—all books grounded in classroom practice and aimed at doing social justice work in schools.[22] When Columbus Day rolled around, I passed along a few copies of *Rethinking Columbus* as well.[23] As our relationships continued to build and we all got to know each other better, I eventually joined the school's race and equity team, offering my expertise and experience in multicultural education and teaching for social justice. As part of the RET, I was also asked to facilitate some race equity professional development with the school staff.

To be clear, I was entering an institution with an existing culture that prioritized equity and social justice: my son's school already had an institutional history of working on race issues, and the administration was committed to carrying that work forward. So, I did not initiate any racial justice work, nor was I a driving force. However, I was (and continue to be) a resource for my son's school, and I am known to them. We have built up a solid relationship, and the school staff know that they can look to me for support as they continue their work on educational justice.

Marxist Partner and Parent

Once, about twenty-five years ago, my spouse (then girlfriend), Mira Shimabukuro, jokingly demanded, "No dialectics in bed!" It was not because Mira was opposed to Marxism, but rather, at the time it was a jab about how much I was talking Marxist politics and theory (which was always). Throughout this book, I've argued over and over again for a social conception of our human nature: we are our relations. Our consciousness—the very way we think—is social; and our actions in the world, based on our consciousness, carry the weight of politics, power, and society too. As such, Mira and I now agree that Marxism certainly belongs in every part of our relationship (bedroom included) because we always bring our social relations with us everywhere we go. For those socialized male under capitalist patriarchy, this gendered conditioning affects all of our social relations, including our most intimate ones. For instance, in my relationship with my partner I have to constantly check myself for potential sexism, since we essentially breathe patriarchy in this society all of the time.

It helps that Mira and I share much of the same politics, including a commitment to challenging sexism, racism and white supremacy, capitalism, patriarchy, imperialism, colonization, homophobia, exploitation, and, broadly, injustice. This close alignment enables our relationship to be, at times, a greenhouse of political thinking and engagement. We each have different networks and connections, different areas of research and expertise, and different takes on what is happening in the world, and so together we very much help each other grow, learn, and develop, as—in a very dialectical way—parts of our individual selves also become parts of each other. In the words of Vygotsky, "[I]t is through others that we develop into ourselves."[24] And so, in a very Marxist, dialectical materialist sense, I see our relationship *as an ongoing process*, one where we are both committed not just to struggling with the world we live in, but also to struggling with one another: critically reflecting on our own and each other's thinking and actions as we develop spirally toward sharper consciousness about ourselves, our relationship, and our world. It is a process that requires great humility, love, vulnerability, and strength.

We try and bring all of this to bear into our parenting as well. In terms of our relationship as co-parents (again, in the midst of a capitalist patriarchy), I work hard to keep Mira and my son Makoto in mind relative to all of the activism and travel that I do. Mira and Mako also both keep me in check about getting too busy and making sure that I maintain my commitment to them throughout my work. While it is never really enough and never fully equal—since I do a lot more activism and travel than Mira—I recognize that my capacity to do what I do locally and nationally is entirely enabled by her emotional and physical labor as a single parent while I am away at a meeting, keynoting a conference, or speaking at a university (we do, however, try and attend as many protests together as a family as we can). Because of this, I see my decisions to speak or travel as collective family decisions. In very much the same way, I see any honorarium or speaking fees I get as not just paying for my labor and experience, but also paying for the extra labor I leave behind for Mira. And, to be clear, oftentimes the "payoff" for my work is entirely of political value, and Mira and I also weigh our labor and efforts relative to political importance. It is a dance for us, and it sometimes causes stress, but our commitment to struggling things out with each and our commitment to political struggle with the world help guide us.

My Marxist politics also carry through to how I understand and relate with my son, Makoto. For instance, I understand that, just like the rest of us, Mako is a fully social being. He is with and within the world, all of the time. He carries us with him everywhere, just as he carries his friends, other family, and all of his other relations with him too. I know that he is developing as his own person, both apart from us and as a part of us. And so our parenting is similarly a dialectical mix of constantly processing Mako's immediate experiences, reactions, and behaviors, but with an eye toward his long-term growth and development in this society. In this way, parenting is very much like working toward the long revolution, because the teaching and learning we do with Mako on a daily basis may end up contributing to who he is over the long haul, whether or not we see immediate results.

More concretely speaking, Mira and I are cognizant of Mako's maleness in a sexist and patriarchal world, and in that context we want him to think actively about how he sees and treats women. It is important to us, for instance, that Mako sees women as strong. One way we are fortunate in this area is that Mako's martial arts *sifu* (master) is a woman, and he knows her as a strong and accomplished fighter and teacher. I still remember when we showed Mako the documentary *The Eagle Huntress*, about a young woman who was to become the first female eagle hunter in twelve generations of her Kazakh family.[25] In the film some of the elder men in her community say that she can't become an eagle huntress because girls are too weak and can't handle the stress of the conditions. Completely unprovoked by us, Mako declared, in response, "That's so rude! My sifu is strong, and she could totally kick their butts!" To be clear, Mako is surrounded by many strong women in his family life, but none kick butt quite like his sifu, who has trained in wushu since she was a little girl and was a national champion in China. Mira and I considered Mako's declaration a victory, because in the face of the onslaught of patriarchal images of men, women, and gender relations we all are subjected to daily, we saw this as part of Mako's budding critical consciousness about gender and power.

We are also cognizant of Mako as a racialized being—one who physically presents as "more Asian" than either Mira and I, despite all of us being "mixed" (I'm Chinese and white, while Mira is Okinawan and white, making Mako Okinawan, Chinese, and white). To that end it is important to us that he be grounded culturally in our family, and grounded racially in the world. It is one of the reasons we value Mako taking martial arts in a Chinese-centered space, and reinforce small but important Japanese American cultural practices at home. Given the times, Mako's racialization has included explicit conversations about police killings of Black people relative to the #BlackLivesMatter movement, as well as about attacks on immigrants and rampant homelessness in Seattle, among other issues. In all cases, we work hard to make these issues "real" for him by helping him understand his connections to the people in his community: his Black friends and family members, his immigrant classmates and family friends, and the homeless encampments we see along the highways and exit ramps all figure prominently in our reflective landscapes.

Our politics also inform how we view Mako's schooling. We know that almost all of the official markers of what counts as a "good" school are bogus, and that test scores are a meaningless measure of quality, mainly serving as a proxy for poverty and whiteness. Instead we value other things, like whether or not the school culture is supportive of kids, teachers, staff, and parents; whether or not Mako feels heard and cared for by his peers and the adults around him; how conscious the school staff are of the inequalities and material conditions faced by their students—and whether they are actively working to shift policy and daily practices to address these issues; whether or not there are explicit discussions about race and racism at the school; whether or not kids feel safe in the environment.

We also value the racial and socioeconomic diversity of the school above all else, because Mako will know and experience the world through his classmates' eyes as well as his own. For instance, in the midst of the stark anti-Black, anti-immigrant, and anti-Muslim tenor of our times, it is particularly important to us that he has Black, immigrant, and Muslim friends that he knows and loves. And this is not to simply make the case that "I like diversity because it benefits my kid" (as we stereotypically see in the attitudes among many white, middle-class families). It is true that Mako does "benefit" in that, as part of his development, we want Mako to understand how the world works inequitably and to reflect on his own position as a middle-class, mixed Asian American kid with two professors as parents. His attending a school with a fairly high poverty rate filled with immigrant, Muslim, and mostly nonwhite children certainly affords us opportunities to push his consciousness in those directions. However, we are more driven toward diversity out of a collective interest: we want Mako to implicitly understand that he and his classmates are in the world together, that they are in a community together, that their lives are connected, and that the interests of their communities are his interests as well. In this sense, we are concerned with the development of collectivity and mutual solidarity as much as anything else, as well as for him to know that people in his family, classroom, and community (and even he, himself) are adversely impacted by the injustices in the world.

Ultimately, a dialectical understanding defines how I approach my intimate family relationships. Like Mako is developing as a child, we are all in a process of development as well. Fundamentally, this means a commitment to critical self-reflection and a commitment to constant, comradely struggle with myself, my partner and son, the rest of my family, and my community.

Marxist Professor

As a professor at my university, I teach both graduate and undergraduate courses in education policy, multicultural education, educational research, and teaching methods—both inside and outside of our teacher-credentialing programs. A truth that I've felt and understood since my early days as a public school teacher is that there are no neutral classrooms and that there is no neutral knowledge. My students are bombarded daily with commonsense, hegemonic views of education, culture, and politics through social media, the news, each other, and even other professors. In this context, I see my courses as my chance (perhaps my only chance) to introduce them to ideas, concepts, and realities that might contradict their commonsense understandings of the world generally and, hopefully, develop some critical consciousness about the politics of education policy and practice specifically. In that regard, I continually try to employ curriculum standpoint in all of my courses because I want them to see through the falsities about meritocracy, individual freedom and equality, and free market education reform that the media, politicians, and wealthy elites continually feed us. Instead, I aim for my students to develop an awareness of how, even if they weren't conscious of it, their lives and opportunities have been structured powerfully and in different ways based on their race, class, gender, nationality, religion, ethnicity, home language, culture, and sexual identity.

Integrating my politics into being a professor has meant embracing dialectics not just as theory, but, following Vygotsky and Freire, using social, interactive forms of learning in my teaching. To that end, I work hard at making my classes engaging. I do lecture some, but I mainly rely on group work, presentations, seminars, and other interactive pedagogies in my college classes. Further, although I am tied to the grading system of my university, I very actively push the idea that the grades are not equivalent to learning and that the points they earn are not the goal of the class. It is a hard push since all of my students are so inured to an educational system that only focuses on grades and points that they come to my classes with this model deeply ingrained in their understanding of what counts as learning.

Personally, I think my students' constrained views of education have been worsened by high-stakes testing, because my students were all raised under the testing mandates of No Child Left Behind. This is all they know, and the idea that the value of their education rests on the final grade or evaluation is something they take for granted. In my courses, through both content and pedagogy, I am actively trying to break most of my students of the constraints from their previous educational training and help them rebuild an educational view that is more connected to active learning. This means that in my courses we talk explicitly about what is important about learning and the fallacy and relative arbitrariness of grades. We then also think together about why we have grades to begin with, as well as why I use the kinds of assessments that I do. In Vygotsky's terms you could say that I try to help my students move from a more spontaneous concept of education to a more scientific one, or in Freire's terms, that I try to get my students to decode their educational understandings and then help them recode those understandings within the context of a larger totality.

My critical, Marxist politics find their way into my role as a professor in other ways as well. While I spend time mentoring my radical students of all races, many of my students of color look to me for leadership and advice. I work on my campus to build solidarity with the activist students, and I fight to maintain programs that support marginalized students and build campus culture. I also work with campus leadership on issues related to diversity, helping them shape policy, pushing them to concretely support marginalized students, faculty, and staff, and advising them on how to respond to racist, homophobic, and other campus incidences. Additionally, I take my work supporting other faculty very seriously. I mentor junior faculty, especially junior faculty of color, coauthoring with them when I can. I anonymously perform tenure file reviews for other institutions, most of them from women of color faculty who do "critical" scholarship of some form or another; since I both understand how academia functions and I can relate to their forms of research, I know that as a radical senior faculty of color I'm in a position to support these scholars as they navigate their institutions' tenure processes.

However, truth be told, being a critical, Marxist education professor can be alienating, especially in the context of the university. While I have many colleagues who are progressive—some whom I consider to be close friends and allies, and who actively support my scholarship and activism—in reality I am the lone Marxist education professor at my institution. All of which means that, to survive as a Marxist educator, I've had to make sure that I'm connected to other Marxist, socialist, and communist educators and activists regionally, around the country, and internationally. For instance, I can't emphasize enough how important my relationship with socialist educator and activist Jesse Hagopian and his family has been in this regard. The first time Jesse came to my house to visit, I remember how he shook my hand and said, "So glad to meet another Marxist educator." I received Jesse's comment with both a little shock and a lot of relief: shock because my radical childhood training to be quiet about my Marxism has been so deeply ingrained that I am still careful about where, when, and how loud I am about it; relief because Jesse was so natural, welcoming, and carefree about it that I realized I had found a true comrade and friend.

And that is the crux of it: we need to understand that, even if one might be the only Marxist teacher, the only Marxist professor, the only Marxist parent, or the only Marxist researcher, being the only Marxist does not have to mean being the *lonely* Marxist.[26] We need to build relationships with other radicals, both to survive and to be effective activists, teachers, and humans. We need community and comradeship. We need to know we are not alone, and to find safe harbors where we can relax, joke, talk serious politics, party with, organize with, love and struggle with, other Marxists. To that end I make sure to build community wherever I can: through various Teaching for Social Justice Conferences, through my teaching, through organizing efforts, through personal networks, through scholarship, at the annual Socialism Conference in Chicago, through music and art, on social media. In a way, there is a social cartography to being a Marxist educator, where we are constantly mapping out new and old radical spaces, connecting with new and old friends, as we organize toward a better and more sustainable future.

Learning to Change the World

Of course, what I've shared here is probably an idealized and romanticized version of what really happens in my life, and in relaying all of the work I do, I'm not saying I'm perfect. I make plenty of mistakes, and I've worked hard to learn from those, grow, and keep fighting. What I am saying, though, is that I have strived to bring my whole self to everything I do—that my politics is embodied, that I try to live a dialectical life in all aspects of my identity. I am a father; partner; parent of a child in public school; former public school teacher; PhD; scholar; professor; cisgendered, heterosexual male; Chinese American, "mixed" with some roots in Hawai'i; Marxist, public intellectual; scholar-activist; education activist; person of color; hip hop head and retired deejay; author, speaker, mentor, student, and teacher. These overlapping identities certainly do not all play equally important roles, but I list them because they illustrate how I, like everyone, am an intersectional being. All these aspects of who I am play roles in how I engage with capitalism and how I live my class position. Conversely, analyzing my intersectional identity does not preclude me from understanding that capitalism is completely unsustainable, is entirely exploitative of humans and the earth, and needs to be replaced with an economic system that can meet everyone's needs—especially because we have the means and capacity to do so. Indeed, our existence as a species likely relies on our ability to make this change happen.

Given the fierce debates among Marxists and other leftists about identity politics and intersectionality, the very act of bringing our whole selves to our political work, and vice versa, is at once a radical act and an unremarkable one:[27] radical, because it requires us to complicate how we understand the lived realities of class under capitalism; and unremarkable, because the simple reality has been that we all live our lives intersectionally—something radical Black feminists (including the Combahee River Collective), among others, have been telling us for quite some time.[28] Indeed, the concept of intersectionality, as noted by Keeanga-Yamahtta Taylor and previously quoted, reflects the layered and complex reality of class dynamics in this country and around the world:

> No serious socialist current in the last hundred years has ever demanded that Black or Latino/a workers put their struggles on the back burner while some other class struggle is waged first. This assumption rests on the mistaken idea that the working class is white and male, and therefore incapable of taking up issues of race, class, and gender. In fact, the American working class is female, immigrant, Black, white, Latino/a, and more. Immigrant issues, gender issues, and antiracism *are* working class issues.[29]

This perspective on the intersectional nature of class runs throughout the arguments I've laid out in this book and is essential to a politically effective apprehension of the struggle that lies before us—in a world where the expectations and discourses produced by the Far Right appear stronger and more unpredictable than in recent memory. We need to see each other for all of our complexities too, and to try to understand the ways that we are all dialectically connected to one other, just as we are dialectically connected to our institutions, economy, and society writ large. This is the value of Marxist dialectical materialism: it allows us to engage with the complex dynamics of our material reality, and to do so in ways that do not flatten our humanity, nor alienate us from our lived experiences. And, in the interests of liberation from capitalist exploitation and inequality, a Marxist education can help us understand how schools, teaching, learning, and curriculum can all play a role in the process of learning to change the world.

Acknowledgments

Nothing I do would be possible without the love and support of my partner, spouse, comrade, and co-parent, Mira Shimabukuro. My love for my son, Makoto, also drives much of what I do in the world. My father, Wilson Au, was foundational in my political development; and my academic advisor, Michael Apple, has been a dear friend and colleague, and a wonderful mentor in my political development as a scholar and professor. I also want to acknowledge the loving support of my other immediate family members, especially Kendal Au, J. C. McFadden, and Adisa Au.

I cannot thank the team at Haymarket enough, particularly Julie Fain, Dana Blanchard, and Nisha Bolsey. I'd also like to thank copyeditor Sam Smith. My friends and colleagues provided invaluable feedback on this book, and to this end I am indebted first and foremost to Adam Sanchez for doing such a close, critical read, as well as to Brian Jones, Curry Malott, Noah De Lissovoy, and my dear friend Jesse Hagopian for their feedback on various chapters.

I am lucky to have so many friends, colleagues, and mentors—education activists, professors, parents, and teachers—at Rethinking Schools, the University of Washington Bothell, and beyond. There are too many to name here, but suffice it to say I am indebted to all of them for their ongoing support and love, and for continually educating me about how to move forward in the world.

I would also like to acknowledge the University of Washington Bothell for granting me sabbatical while I wrote this book.

Notes

Chapter 1

1. See Wilson W. S. Au, *Reclaiming Communist Philosophy: Marx, Lenin, Mao, and the Dialectics of Nature* (Charlotte, NC: Information Age Publishing, 2017) for some of his work.
2. Wayne Au, *Unequal by Design: High-Stakes Testing and the Standardization of Inequality* (New York: Routledge, 2009).
3. Alicia Garza, "Our Cynicism Will Not Build a Movement. Collaboration Will.," *Mic*, January 26, 2017, https://mic.com/articles/166720/blm-co-founder-protesting-isnt-about-who-can-be-the-most-radical-its-about-winning#.JzNEW3kZQ; Keeanga-Yamahtta Taylor, "Don't Shame the First Steps of a Resistance," *Socialist Worker*, January 24, 2017, https://socialistworker.org/2017/01/24/dont-shame-the-first-steps-of-a-resistance.
4. Nancy C. M. Hartsock, *The Feminist Standpoint Revisited and Other Essays* (Boulder, CO: Westview Press, 1998); Sandra Harding, "Rethinking Standpoint Epistemology: What Is 'Strong Objectivity'?," in Sandra Harding, ed., *The Feminist Standpoint Reader* (New York: Routledge, 2004), 127–40.
5. Frank Chin and J. P. Chan, "Racist Love," in Richard Kostelanetz, ed., *Seeing through Shuck* (New York: Ballantine Books, 1972).
6. Jeff Chang, *Can't Stop Won't Stop: A History of the Hip Hop Generation* (New York: St. Martin's Press, 2005).
7. Ibid.
8. Wayne Au, "Decolonizing the Classroom: Lessons in Multicultural Education," *Rethinking Schools* 23, no. 2 (2009): 27–30.
9. Christine Choy and Renee Tajima-Pena, dirs., *Who Killed Vincent Chin?* (Public Broadcasting Service, 1987), 35 mm, 1 hr., 27 min.
10. It should be noted that I also met my partner and spouse, Mira Shimabukuro, while at TESC. We worked through much of our identity development around race, gender, sexuality, politics, and culture together and in parallel. Indeed, I wouldn't have become who I am today

without our partnership, allyship, and mutual commitment to struggle.

11. To be clear, I know that race is historically, institutionally, and socially constructed—and that it does not exist biologically. However, when it comes to identity, we're often stuck using the constructs and language that we are given, hence my use of the construct of race here.
12. Bill Bigelow and Bob Peterson, eds., *Rethinking Columbus: The next 500 Years*, 2nd ed. (Milwaukee, WI: Rethinking Schools, 1998).
13. H. K. Trask, *From a Native Daughter: Colonialism and Sovereignty in Hawaii*, rev. ed. (Honolulu: University of Hawaii Press, 1999).
14. For a useful summary of different philosophies of social sciences, including discussions of positivism and empiricism, see Ted Benton and Ian Craib, *Philosophy of Social Science: The Philosophical Foundations of Social Thought* (New York: Palgrave, 2001).
15. Fredric Jameson, *Postmodernism, or, The Cultural Logic of Late Capitalism* (Durham, NC: Duke University Press, 1999).
16. David Harvey, "Neoliberalism as Creative Destruction," *Annals of the American Academy of Political and Social Science* 610 (2007): 22–44.
17. Paulo Freire, *Pedagogy of the* Oppressed, Myra Bergman Ramos, trans. (New York: Seabury Press, 1974).
18. Wayne Au, "What the Tour Guide Didn't Tell Me: Paradise and the Politics of Tourist Hawai'i," in Bill Bigelow et al., eds., *Rethinking Our Classroom: Teaching for Equity and Justice*, vol. 2 (1998; repr., Milwaukee, WI: Rethinking Schools, 2001), 76–80.
19. Seattle Central Community College is now called Seattle Central College.
20. Howard Zinn, *A People's History of the United States: 1492–Present*, rev. ed. (New York: Harper Perennial, 1995).
21. South Seattle Community College is now called South Seattle College.
22. Zinn, *A People's History of the United States*; Eduardo Galeano, *Open Veins of Latin America: Five Centuries of the Pillage of a Continent* (New York: New York University Press, 1998).
23. Wayne Au, "Teaching about the WTO," *Rethinking Schools* 14, no. 3 (2000): 4–5.
24. Dr. Gloria Ladson-Billings is the Kellner Family Chair in Urban Education at the University of Wisconsin–Madison.
25. Karl Marx, "Preface to a Contribution to the Critique of Political Economy," in Karl Marx and Frederick Engels, *Selected Works* (New York: International Publishers, 1968), 181–85; Frederick Engels, "Engels to C. Schmidt in Berlin," in Marx and Engels, *Selected Works*, 694–99; Frederick Engels, "Engels to J. Bloch in Konigsberg," in

Marx and Engels, *Selected Works*, 692–93; Frederick Engels, "Ludwig Feuerbach and the End of Classical German Philosophy," in Marx and Engels, *Selected Works*, 596–618; Karl Marx, "The Eighteenth Brumaire of Louis Bonaparte," in Marx and Engels, *Selected Works*, 95–180; Louis Althusser, *Lenin and Philosophy and Other Essays*, B. Brewster, trans. (New York: Monthly Review Books, 1971).

26. Wayne Au and Michael W. Apple, "Rethinking Reproduction: Neo-Marxism in Critical Educational Theory," in Michael W. Apple, Wayne Au, and Luis Armando Gandin, eds., *The Routledge Handbook of Critical Education* (New York: Routledge, 2009), 83–95.
27. Wayne Au, "Devising Inequality: A Bernsteinian Analysis of High-Stakes Testing and Social Reproduction in Education," *British Journal of Sociology of Education* 29, no. 6 (2008): 639–51.
28. Wayne Au, "Between Education and the Economy: High-Stakes Testing and the Contradictory Location of the New Middle Class," *Journal of Education Policy* 23, no. 5 (2008): 501–13.
29. Wayne Au, "Techies, the Tea Party, and the Common Core: The Rise of the New Upper Middle Class and Tensions in the Rightist Politics of Federal Education Reform," *The Educational Forum* 80, no. 2 (2016), doi:10.1080/00131725.2016.1135378.
30. Peter McLaren and Ramin Farahmandpur, "Reconsidering Marx in Post-Marxist Times: A Requiem for Postmodernism?," *Educational Researcher* 29, no. 3 (2000): 25–33.
31. Wayne Au and Michael W. Apple, "Freire, Critical Education, and the Environmental Crisis," *Educational Policy* 21, no. 3 (2007): 457–70; Wayne Au, "Epistemology of the Oppressed: The Dialectics of Paulo Freire's Theory of Knowledge," *Journal for Critical Education Policy Studies* 5, no. 2 (2007), http://www.jceps.com/archives/551; Wayne Au, "Fighting with the Text: Critical Issues in the Development of Freirian Pedagogy," in Michael W. Apple, Wayne Au, and Luis Armando Gandin, eds., *The Routledge Handbook of Critical Education* (New York: Routledge, 2009), 83–95.
32. Lev S. Vygotsky, *Mind in Society: The Development of Higher Psychological Processes*, M. Cole, V. John-Steiner, S. Scribner, and E. Souberman, eds. (Cambridge, MA: Harvard University Press, 1978); Vygotsky, "Thinking and Speech," in Robert W. Rieber and Aaron Carton, eds., Norris Minick, trans., *The Collected Works of L. S. Vygotsky: Problems of General Psychology Including the Volume Thinking and Speech*, vol. 1 (New York: Plenum Press, 1987), 37–285.
33. Wayne Au, "Vygotsky and Lenin on Learning: The Parallel Structures

of Individual and Social Development," *Science and Society* 71, no. 3 (2007): 273–98.

34. David Levine and Wayne Au, "Rethinking Schools: Enacting a Vision for Social Justice within US Education," *Critical Studies in Education* 54, no. 1 (2013): 72–84, doi:http://dx.doi.org/10.1080/17508487.2013.738693.
35. Nancy C. M. Hartsock, "The Feminist Standpoint: Developing the Ground for a Specifically Feminist Historical Materialism," in Sandra Harding and M. B. Hintikka, eds., *Discovering Reality: Feminist Perspectives on Epistemology, Metaphysics, Methodology, and Philosophy of Science* (Dordrecht, Holland: D. Reidel, 1983), 283–310; ; Sandra Harding, "How Standpoint Methodology Informs Philosophy of Science," in Sharlene Nagy Hesse-Biber and Patricia Leavy, eds., *Approaches to Qualitative Research* (New York: Oxford University Press, 2004), 62–80; Georg Lukács, *History and Class Consciousness* (Cambridge, MA: MIT Press, 1971); Wayne Au, *Critical Curriculum Studies: Education, Consciousness, and the Politics of Knowing*, Critical Social Thought (New York: Routledge, 2011).
36. Hartsock, *The Feminist Standpoint Revisited*; Harding, "Rethinking Standpoint Epistemology?"
37. Wayne Au, "High-Stakes Testing: A Tool for White Supremacy for 100 Years," in Bree Picower and Edwin Mayorga, eds., *What's Race Got to Do with It?: How Current School Reform Policy Maintains Racial and Economic Inequality* (New York: Peter Lang, 2015), 21–44; Matthew Knoester and Wayne Au, "Standardized Testing and School Segregation: Like Tinder to Fire?," *Race Ethnicity and Education* 20, no. 1 (2015): 1–14, doi:10.1080/13613324.2015.1121474.
38. Anthony L. Brown and Wayne Au, "Race, Memory, and Master Narratives: A Critical Essay on U.S. Curriculum History," *Curriculum Inquiry* 44, no. 3 (2014): 358–89, doi:10.1111/curi.12049; Wayne Au, Anthony L. Brown, and Dolores Calderon, *Reclaiming the Multicultural Roots of U.S. Curriculum: Communities of Color and Official Knowledge in Education* (New York: Teachers College Press, 2016).
39. Wayne Au, "Proud to Be a Garfield Bulldog," *Rethinking Schools Blog*, January 12, 2013, http://rethinkingschoolsblog.wordpress.com/2013/01/12/proud-to-be-a-garfield-bulldog/.
40. Jesse Hagopian, ed., *More Than a Score: The New Uprising against High-Stakes Testing* (Chicago: Haymarket Books, 2014); Jesse Hagopian, "Seattle Test Boycott: Our Destination Is Not on the MAP," *Rethinking Schools* 27, no. 3 (2014), http://www.rethinkingschools.org/archive

/27_03/27_03_hagopian.shtml.

41. S. Bowles and H. Gintis, *Schooling in Capitalist America: Educational Reform and the Contradictions of Economic Life*, 1st ed. (New York: Basic Books, 1976).

Chapter 2

1. Wilson Au, *Reclaiming Communist Philosophy*, 26.
2. Bertell Ollman, *Dance of the Dialectic: Steps in Marx's Method*, 1st ed. (Chicago: University of Illinois Press, 2003), 13.
3. Au, *Reclaiming Communist Philosophy.*
4. Ibid., 203–204.
5. Ibid.
6. Robinson Meyer, "American Trees Are Moving West, and No One Knows Why: Climate Change Explains Only 20 Percent of the Movement," *Atlantic*, May, 17, 2017, https://www.theatlantic.com/science/archive/2017/05/go-west-my-sap/526899/.
7. Karl Marx, *Capital: A Critique of Political Economy*, S. Moore and E. Aveling, trans., vol. 1 (New York: International Publishers, 1967).
8. Engels, "Ludwig Feuerbach and the End of Classical German Philosophy"; V. I. Lenin, *Materialism and Empirio-Criticism*, 1st English ed. (Peking: Foreign Language Press, 1972); Au, *Reclaiming Communist Philosophy.*
9. Au, *Reclaiming Communist Philosophy*, 32.
10. See, e.g., Ward Churchill, ed., *Marxism and Native Americans* (Boston: South End Press, 1983); Edward W. Said, *Orientalism*, 1st ed. (New York: Pantheon Books, 1978).
11. Keeanga-Yamahtta Taylor, *From #Blacklivesmatter to Black Liberation* (Chicago: Haymarket Books, 2016); Tim Wise, "With Friends like These, Who Needs Glenn Beck?: Racism and White Privilege on the Liberal-Left," Tim Wise, official website, August 17, 2010, http://www.timwise.org/2010/08/with-friends-like-these-who-needs-glenn-beck-racism-and-white-privilege-on-the-liberal-left/.
12. Karl Marx and Frederick Engels, *Manifesto of the Communist Party* (Peking: Foreign Language Press, 1848).
13. Cheikh Anta Diop, *The African Origin of Civilization: Myth or Reality* (Chicago: Lawrence Hill, 1974); Curry S. Malott, "Social Class and Rebellion: The Role of Knowledge Production in Capitalist Society," in Ravi Kumar, ed., *Education and the Reproduction of Capital: Neoliberal Knowledge and Counterstrategies* (New York: Palgrave Macmillan, 2012), 23.

14. Kevin B. Anderson, *Marx at the Margins: On Nationalism, Ethnicity, and Non-Western Societies*, 2nd ed. (Chicago: University of Chicago Press, 2016).
15. Hartsock, *The Feminist Standpoint Revisited*; Harding, "How Standpoint Methodology Informs Philosophy of Science."
16. David Gilbert, "Is Marxism Relevant?: Some Uses and Misuses," *Abolition*, January 16, 2017, https://abolitionjournal.org/is-marxism-relevant-some-uses-and-misuses-by-david-gilbert-political-prisoner/.
17. Anderson, *Marx at the Margins*.
18. As quoted in ibid., 23.
19. Glen Sean Coulthard, *Red Skin, White Masks: Rejecting the Colonial Politics of Recognition* (Minneapolis: University of Minnesota Press, 2014), 11.
20. Anderson, *Marx at the Margins*.
21. Ibid.; Noah De Lissovoy, *Education and Emancipation in the Neoliberal Era: Being, Teaching, and Power* (New York: Palgrave Macmillan, 2015); Taylor, *From #Blacklivesmatter to Black Liberation*.
22. Marx, *Capital*, vol. 1, 751.
23. Ibid., 301.
24. Anderson, *Marx at the Margins*; Taylor, *From #Blacklivesmatter to Black Liberation*.
25. Benton and Craib, *Philosophy of Social Science*.
26. Au, *Reclaiming Communist Philosophy*.
27. Stephen Jay Gould, *The Mismeasure of Man*, rev. ed. (New York: Norton, 1996); Sandra Harding, ed., *The "Racial Economy of Science": Toward a Democratic Future* (Indianapolis: Indiana University Press, 1993); Benton and Craib, *Philosophy of Social Science*.
28. Benton and Craib, *Philosophy of Social Science*; Harding, "How Standpoint Methodology Informs Philosophy of Science."
29. Sydney Hook, "The Enlightenment and Marxism," *Journal of the History of Ideas* 29, no. 1 (1968): 93–108.
30. Au, *Reclaiming Communist Philosophy*.
31. Alan Woods and Ted Grant, *Reason in Revolt: Dialectical Philosophy and Modern Science*, vol. 1 (New York: Algora Publishing, 2002).
32. Alan Woods, "Chapter 2: The Early Dialecticians," *In Defence of Marxism*, July 9, 2006, http://www.marxist.com/history-philosophy-dialectics-materialism/page-2.htm.
33. Martin Bernal, *Black Athena: The Afroasiatic Roots of Classical Civilization*, 3 vols. (New Brunswick, NJ: Rutgers University Press, 1987); Diop, *The African Origin of Civilization*; Cheikh Anta Diop, *Civili-*

zation or Barbarism: An Authentic Anthropology* (Chicago: Chicago Review Press, 1991).

34. Diop, *Civilization or Barbarism*, 313.
35. Chenshan Tian, *Chinese Dialectics: From Yijing to Marxism* (New York: Lexington Books, 2005); Chenshan Tian, "Development of Dialectical Materialism in China," in Bo Mou, ed., *History of Chinese Philosophy* (New York: Routledge, 2009), 512–38.
36. Tian, "Development of Dialectical Materialism in China," 514.
37. Ibid., 515.
38. Ibid.; Arif Dirlik, "Mao Zedong and 'Chinese Marxism,'" in Saree Makdisi, Cesare Casarino, and Rebecca E. Karl, eds., *Marxism beyond Marxism* (New York: Routledge, 1996), 119–48.
39. James Maffie, *Aztec Philosophy: Understanding a World in Motion* (Boulder: University Press of Colorado, 2015); James Maffie, "Aztec Philosophy," *Internet Encyclopedia of Philosophy*, accessed February 6, 2017, http://www.iep.utm.edu/aztec/#SH2b.
40. Maffie, *Aztec Philosophy*, n.p.
41. Ibid.
42. For a discussion and application of dialectical materialism to the natural sciences and mathematics, see Au, *Reclaiming Communist Philosophy*.
43. Gilbert, "Is Marxism Relevant?"
44. De Lissovoy, *Education and Emancipation in the Neoliberal Era*; Peter McLaren and Nathalia E. Jaramillo, "Not Neo-Marxist, Not Post-Marxist, Not Marxian, Not Autonomist Marxism: Reflections on a Revolutionary (Marxist) Critical Pedagogy," *Cultural Studies—Critical Methodologies* 10, no. 3 (2010): 251–62, doi:10.1177/1532708609354317; Emir Sader, *The New Mole: Paths of the Latin American Left* (New York: Verso, 2011); Colin Mackerras and Nick Knight, *Marxism in Asia* (Sydney: Croom Helm, 1985); Robert A. Scalapino, *The Japanese Communist Movement, 1920–1966* (Los Angeles: University of California Press, 1967); Thomas Crowley, "The Many Faces of the Indian Left: In India, Even as Prominent Left Parties Falter, Radicalism Persists," *Jacobin*, May 12, 2014, https://www.jacobinmag.com/2014/05/the-many-faces-of-the-indian-left/; Michelle Williams, *The Roots of Participatory Democracy: Democratic Communists in South Africa and Kerala, India* (New York: Palgrave Macmillan, 2008); Alex de Jong, "The War Is Over: In the Philippines, One of the World's Longest Running Communist Insurgencies Is Being Worn down by the Passage of History," *Jacobin*, August 12, 2015, https://www.jacobinmag.com/2015/08/phillipines-maoists-communists

-marcos-aquino; Arnold Hughes, "The Appeal of Marxism to Africans," *Journal of Communist Studies* 8, no. 2 (1992): 4–20; Cedric J. Robinson, *Black Marxism: The Making of the Black Radical Tradition* (London: Zed Press, 1983); Williams, *Roots of Participatory Democracy.*

45. Robin D. G. Kelley, *Race Rebels: Culture, Politics, and the Black Working Class,* 1st ed. (New York: The Free Press, 1996); Mark Naison, *Communists in Harlem during the Depression* (New York: Grove Press, 1985); Taylor, *From #Blacklivesmatter to Black Liberation.*
46. As quoted in Taylor, *From #Blacklivesmatter to Black Liberation*, 203.
47. Robinson, *Black Marxism.*
48. Minkah Makalani, "An Apparatus for Negro Women: Black Women's Organizing, Communism, and the Institutional Spaces for Radical Pan-African Thought," *Women, Gender, and Families of Color* 4, no. 2 (2016): 250–73.
49. Harry Haywood, *A Black Communist in the Freedom Struggle: The Life of Harry Haywood*, Gwendolyn Midlo Hall, ed. (Minneapolis: University of Minnesota Press, 2012).
50. Yuji Ichioka, "A Buried Past: Early Issei Socialists and the Japanese Community," *Amerasia Journal* 1, no. 2 (1971): 1–25.
51. Minkah Makalani, "Internationalizing the Third International: The African Blood Brotherhood, Asian Radicals, and Race, 1919–1922," *Journal of African American History* 96, no. 2 (2011): 151–78.
52. Him Mark Lai, "A Historical Survey of Organization of the Left among Chinese in America," *Bulletin of Concerned Asian Scholars* 4, no. 3 (1972): 10–20.
53. Rick Baldoz, "'Comrade Carlos Bulosan': U.S. State Surveillance and the Cold War Suppression of Filipino Radicals," *Asia-Pacific Journal* 11, no. 33 (2014): 1–18; Michael Viola, "Toward a Filipino/a Critical (FilCrit) Pedagogy: A Study of United States Educational Exposure Programs to the Philippines" (PhD diss., Proquest Dissertations & Theses, 2012), http://gradworks.umi.com/35/08/3508951.html.
54. Fred Ho, "Fists for Revolution: The Revolutionary History of I Wor Kuen/League of Revolutionary Struggle," in Fred Ho, ed., *Legacy to Liberation: Politics and Culture of Revolutionary Asian Pacific America* (San Francisco: Big Red Media and AK Press, 2000), 3–14; Steve Yip, "Serve the People—Yesterday and Today: The Legacy of Wei Min She," in Ho, *Legacy to Liberation*, 15–30; Ray Tasaki, "New Dawn Rising: History and Summation of the Japan Town Collective," in Ho, *Legacy to Liberation*, 53–58; Laura Pulido, "Race, Class, and Political Activism: Black, Chicano/a, and Japanese-American Leftists

in Southern California, 1968–1978," *Antipode* 34, no. 4 (2002): 762–88; Helen C. Toribio, "Dare to Struggle: The KDP and Filipino American Politics," in Ho, *Legacy to Liberation*, 31–46; Viola, *Toward a Filipino/a Critical (FilCrit) Pedagogy*."

55. Zaragosa Vargas, *Labor Rights Are Civil Rights: Mexican American Workers in Twentieth-Century America* (Princeton, NJ: Princeton University Press, 2005).
56. Zaragosa Vargas, "Tejana Radical: Emma Tenayuca and the San Antonio Labor Movement during the Great Depression," *Pacific Historical Review* 66, no. 4 (1997): 553–80; Vargas, *Labor Rights Are Civil Rights*; Emma Tenayuca and Homer Brooks, "The Mexican Question in the Southwest," *Communist* 18, no. 3 (1939): 157–68.
57. Justin Akers Chacon, *Radicals in the Barrio: Magonistas, Socialists, Wobblies, and Communists in the Mexican-American Working Class* (Chicago: Haymarket Books, 2017).
58. Pulido, "Race, Class, and Political Activism."
59. See, e.g., Churchill, *Marxism and Native Americans*.
60. Sandy Grande, *Red Pedagogy: Native American Social and Political Thought*, 10th anniv. ed. (Lanham, MD: Rowman & Littlefield, 2015).
61. Coulthard, *Red Skin, White Masks*; Curry S. Malott, "In Defense of Communism: Against Critical Pedagogy, Capitalism, and Trump," *Critical Education* 8, no. 1 (2017): 1–24.
62. V. I. Lenin, "The Socialist Revolution and the Right of Nations to Self-Determination: Theses," Marxists Internet Archive, [1916] 2005, https://www.marxists.org/archive/lenin/works/1916/jan/x01.htm.
63. Ibid.
64. Ibid.
65. Malott, "In Defense of Communism."
66. De Lissovoy, *Education and Emancipation in the Neoliberal Era*, 106–107.
67. Coulthard, *Red Skin, White Masks*, 115.
68. Curry S. Malott and Derek R. Ford, *Marx, Capital, and Education: Towards a Critical Pedagogy of Becoming* (New York: Peter Lang, 2015), 45.
69. Coulthard, *Red Skin, White Masks*, 15.
70. For a discussion and debunking of these critiques, see Au, *Reclaiming Communist Philosophy*; John Bellamy Foster, "Marxism and Ecology: Common Fonts of a Great Transition," *Monthly Review* 67, no. 7 (2015), http://monthlyreview.org/2015/12/01/marxism-and-ecology/; John Bellamy Foster, "The Return of Engels: On the Occasion of His Birthday, Let's Celebrate the Incredible Contributions of Marx Col-

laborator Friedrich Engels," *Jacobin* 68, no. 10 (March, 2017), https://www.jacobinmag.com/2016/11/engels-marx-ecology-climate-crisis-materialism/.

71. Harvey, "Neoliberalism as Creative Destruction"; David Harvey, "The 'New' Imperialism: Accumulation by Dispossession," *Socialist Register* 40 (2004): 63–87.
72. As quoted in, Mick Brooks, "An Introduction to Marx's Labour Theory of Value—Part Two," *In Defence of Marxism*, October 15, 2002, n.p., https://www.marxist.com/marx-marxist-labour-theory-value2.htm.
73. Karl Marx, *Capital: The Process of Circulation of Capital*, vol. 2 (New York: International Publishers, 1967), 158–59.
74. Michael J. Dumas, "'Waiting for Superman' to Save Black People: Racial Representation and the Official Antiracism of Neoliberal School Reform," *Discourse: Studies in the Cultural Politics of Education* 34, no. 4 (2013): 531–47, doi:http://dx.doi.org/10.1080/01596306.2013.822621; Michael J. Dumas, "My Brother as 'Problem': Neoliberal Governmentality and Interventions for Black Young Men and Boys," *Educational Policy* 30, no. 1 (2015): 94–113; Leigh Patel, *Decolonizing Educational Research: From Ownership to Answerability* (New York: Routledge, 2016); Eve Tuck and K. Wayne Yang, "Decolonization Is Not a Metaphor," *Decolonization: Indigeneity, Education, and Society* 1, no. 1 (2012): 1–40.
75. Taylor, *From #Blacklivesmatter to Black Liberation*, 216.
76. For a recent meta-discussion of the shifting "critical" politics of education, see Isaac Gottesman, *The Critical Turn in Education: From Marxist Critique to Poststructuralist Feminism to Critical Theories of Race* (New York: Routledge, 2016); see also Michael W. Apple and Wayne Au, eds., *Critical Education*, 4 vols. (New York: Routledge, 2014) for a discussion of the tensions of race and class in the critical educational tradition.
77. Zeus Leonardo, "The Unhappy Marriage between Marxism and Race Critique: Political Economy and the Production of Racialized Knowledge," *Policy Futures in Education* 2, nos. 3 and 4 (2004): 483–93; Zeus Leonardo, "The Race for Class: Reflections on a Critical Raceclass Theory of Education," *Educational Studies* 58, no. 5 (2012): 427–49.
78. Anthony L. Brown and Noah De Lissovoy, "Economies of Racism: Grounding Education Policy Research in the Complex Dialectic of Race, Class, and Capital," *Journal of Education Policy* 26, no. 5 (2011): 612.
79. Ibid., 596.
80. Taylor, *From #Blacklivesmatter to Black Liberation*, 206.

81. Jodi Melamed, *Represent and Destroy: Rationalizing Violence in the New Racial Capitalism* (Minneapolis: University of Minnesota Press, 2011).
82. Wayne Au, "Meritocracy 2.0: High-Stakes, Standardized Testing as a Racial Project of Neoliberal Multiculturalism," *Educational Policy* 30, no. 1 (2016): 39–62, doi:10.1177/0895904815614916.
83. Gilbert, "Is Marxism Relevant?"
84. Taylor, *From #Blacklivesmatter to Black Liberation*, 216.

Chapter 3

1. Engels, "Engels to C. Schmidt in Berlin," 699.
2. Wayne Au, "Hiding behind High-Stakes Testing: Meritocracy, Objectivity, and Inequality in U.S. Education," *International Education Journal: Comparative Perspectives* 12, no. 2 (2013): 7–19; Au, "Meritocracy 2.0."
3. David C. Berliner, "Effects of Inequality and Poverty vs. Teachers and Schooling on America's Youth," *Teachers College Record* 115, no. 12 (2013), http://www.tcrecord.org.
4. For a great critique and analysis of these trends, see Paul C. Gorski, *Reaching and Teaching Students in Poverty: Strategies for Erasing the Opportunity Gap* (New York: Teachers College Press, 2013).
5. Anna K. Chmielewski and Sean F. Reardon, "State of the Union—The Poverty and Inequality Report 2016," Stanford Center on Poverty and Inequality (2016), https://cepa.stanford.edu/content/state-union-poverty-and-inequality-report-2016-education; Gloria Ladson-Billings, "From the Achievement Gap to the Education Debt: Understanding Achievement in U.S. Schools," *Educational Researcher* 35, no. 7 (October 2006): 3–12; Selcuk R. Sirin, "Socioeconomic Status and Student Achievement: A Meta-Analytic Review of Research," *Review of Educational Research* 75, no. 3 (2005): 417–53.
6. J. S. Coleman et al., *Equality of Educational Opportunity* (Washington, DC: US Government Printing Office, 1966); Jeannie Oakes, *Keeping Track: How Schools Structure Inequality*, 2nd ed. (New Haven, CT: Yale University Press, 2005).
7. Marx, "Preface to a Contribution to the Critique of Political Economy," 183.
8. Stuart Hall, "Gramsci's Relevance for the Study of Race and Ethnicity," *Journal of Communication Inquiry* 10, no. 2 (1986): 10.
9. Antonio Gramsci, *Selections from the Prison Notebooks*, Q. Hoare, ed. (New York: International Publishers, 1971).; Althusser, *Lenin and Philosophy and Other Essays*.

10. Jean Anyon, *Marx and Education*, Routledge Key Ideas in Education (New York: Routledge, 2011); Au and Apple, "Rethinking Reproduction"; Gottesman, *The Critical Turn in Education.*
11. Bowles and Gintis, *Schooling in Capitalist America*, 130.
12. Ibid., 131.
13. See, e.g., Michael W. Apple, "The Other Side of the Hidden Curriculum: Correspondence Theories and the Labor Process," *Interchange* 11, no. 3 (1980): 5–22; Michael W. Apple, "Reproduction, Contestation, and Curriculum: An Essay in Self-Criticism," *Interchange* 12, nos. 2–3 (1981): 27–47; Dennis L. Carlson, "Beyond the Reproductive Theory of Teaching," in Mike Cole, ed., *Bowles and Gintis Revisited: Correspondence and Contradiction in Educational Theory* (New York: The Falmer Press, 1988), 158–73; Henry A. Giroux, "Beyond the Correspondence Theory: Notes on the Dynamics of Educational Reproduction and Transformation," *Curriculum Inquiry* 10, no. 3 (1980): 225–47; Henry A. Giroux, "Ideology and Agency in the Process of Schooling," *Journal of Education* 165, no. 1 (1983): 12–34; M. Sarup, *Marxism and Education* (Boston: Routledge & Kegan Paul, 1978); Rachel Sharp, *Knowledge, Ideology, and the Politics of Schooling: Towards a Marxist Analysis of Education* (London and Boston: Routledge & Kegan Paul, 1980).
14. Michael W. Apple, *Education and Power*, 2nd ed. (New York: Routledge, 1995); Michael W. Apple, "Reproduction and Contradiction in Education: An Introduction," in Michael W. Apple, ed., *Cultural and Economic Reproduction in Education: Essays on Class, Ideology, and the State*, 1st ed. (Boston: Routledge & Kegan Paul, 1982), 1–31.
15. See, e.g., Wayne Au, "Against Economic Determinism: Revisiting the Roots of Neo-Marxism in Critical Educational Theory," *Journal for Critical Education Policy Studies* 4, no. 2 (2006), http://www.jceps.com/archives/520; Wayne Au, "Defending Dialectics: Rethinking the Neo-Marxist Turn in Critical Education Theory," in Sheila Macrine, Peter McLaren, and Dave Hill, eds., *Organizing Pedagogy: Educating for Social Justice and Socialism* (New York: Routledge, 2008); Au and Apple, "Rethinking Reproduction."
16. Bowles and Gintis, *Schooling in Capitalist America*, 12.
17. Ibid., 129.
18. Ibid., 246.
19. Au, "High-Stakes Testing."
20. Jean Anyon, "Social Class and the Hidden Curriculum of Work," *Journal of Education* 162, no. 1 (1980): 67–92; Jean Anyon, "Social Class

and School Knowledge," *Curriculum Inquiry* 11, no. 1 (1981): 3–42.

21. Andy Hargreaves, "Resistance and Relative Autonomy Theories: Problems of Distortion and Incoherence in Recent Marxist Analyses of Education," *British Journal of Sociology of Education* 3, no. 2 (1982): 109.
22. McLaren and Jaramillo, "Not Neo-Marxist, Not Post-Marxist, Not Marxian, Not Autonomist Marxism."
23. Paula Allman, *Revolutionary Social Transformation: Democratic Hopes, Political Possibilities, and Critical Education*, 1st ed. (Westport, CT: Bergin & Garvey, 1999); D. Coben, "Revisiting Gramsci," *Studies in the Education of Adults* 27, no. 1 (1995): 36–52.
24. Gramsci, *Prison Notebooks*, 12.
25. Ibid., 182.
26. Ibid., 12.
27. Martin Carnoy, "Education, Economy, and the State," in Michael W. Apple, ed., *Cultural and Economic Reproduction in Education: Essays on Class, Ideology, and the State* (Boston: Routledge & Kegan Paul, 1982), 79–126.
28. Gramsci, *Prison Notebooks*, 366, original emphasis.
29. Allman, *Revolutionary Social Transformation*; Paula Allman, *Critical Education against Global Capitalism: Karl Marx and Revolutionary Critical Education*, 1st ed. (Westport, CT: Bergin & Garvey, 2001).
30. Michael W. Apple and Kristen L. Buras, "Introduction," in Michael W. Apple and Kristen L. Buras, eds., *The Subaltern Speak: Curriculum, Power, and Educational Struggles* (New York: Routledge, 2006), 1–39; Michael W. Apple and Thomas C. Pedroni, "Conservative Alliance Building and African American Support of Vouchers: The End of Brown's Promise or a New Beginning?," *Teachers College Record* 107, no. 9 (2005): 2068–105; Michael W. Apple, *Official Knowledge: Democratic Education in a Conservative Age*, 2nd ed. (New York: Routledge, 2000), 64.
31. Kristen L. Buras, "Questioning Core Assumptions: A Critical Reading of and Response to E. D. Hirsch's *The Schools We Need and Why We Don't Have Them*," *Harvard Educational Review* 69, no. 1 (1999): 67–93; Henry A. Giroux, "Rethinking Cultural Politics and Radical Pedagogy in the Work of Antonio Gramsci," *Educational Theory* 49, no. 1 (1999): 1–19; John D. Holst, "The Affinities of Lenin and Gramsci: Implications for Radical Adult Education Theory and Practice," *International Journal of Lifelong Education* 18, no. 5 (1999): 407–21; B. Jessop, "Bringing the State Back In (Yet Again): Reviews, Revisions, Rejections, and Redirections," *International Review of*

Sociology 11, no. 2 (2001): 149–73.

32. Jessop, "Bringing the State Back In (Yet Again)," 151.
33. Allman, *Revolutionary Social Transformation*; Henry A. Giroux, "Theories of Reproduction and Resistance in the New Sociology of Education: A Critical Analysis," *Harvard Educational Review* 53, no. 3 (1983): 257–93.
34. See Hoare and Smith in the preface to Gramsci, *Prison Notebooks*, xii–xiv.
35. Althusser, *Lenin and Philosophy and Other Essays*, 135.
36. Ibid., 136.
37. Ibid., 153, original emphasis.
38. Ibid., 157.
39. Apple, *Education and Power*, 26.
40. Pierre Bourdieu and J. Passeron, *Reproduction in Education, Society, and Culture* (Beverly Hills, CA: Sage, 1977); Basil B. Bernstein, *The Structuring of Pedagogic Discourse*, 1st ed., Class, Codes, and Control, vol. 4. (New York: Routledge, 1990).
41. Giroux, "Theories of Reproduction and Resistance in the New Sociology of Education," 260.
42. Paul Willis, *Learning to Labor: How Working-Class Kids Get Working-Class Jobs* (New York: Columbia University Press, 1977); Paul Willis, "Foot Soldiers of Modernity: The Dialectics of Cultural Consumption and the 21st-Century School," *Harvard Educational Review* 73, no. 3 (2003): 392–93.
43. J. L. Dance, *Tough Fronts: The Impact of Street Culture on Schooling*, 1st ed. (New York: RoutledgeFalmer, 2002); Henry A. Giroux, "Hegemony, Resistance, and the Paradox of Educational Reform," *Interchange* 12, nos. 2–3 (1981): 3–26.
44. Steven B. Smith, "Althusser's Marxism without a Knowing Subject," *American Political Science Review* 79, no. 3 (1985): 649.
45. Louis Althusser, *For Marx* (New York: Pantheon Books, 1969); Mark Poster, "Althusser on History without Man," *Political Theory* 2, no. 4 (1974): 393–409.
46. Giroux, "Beyond the Correspondence Theory"; Giroux, "Theories of Reproduction and Resistance in the New Sociology of Education: A Critical Analysis"; Henry A. Giroux, "Public Pedagogy and the Politics of Resistance: Notes on a Critical Theory of Educational Struggle," *Educational Philosophy and Theory* 35, no. 1 (2003): 5–16.
47. Glenn Rikowski, "Scorched Earth: Rebuilding Marxist Educational Theory," *British Journal of Sociology of Education* 18, no. 4 (1997):

551–74.

48. Kenneth J. Saltman and David A. Gabbard, eds., *Education as Enforcement: The Militarization and Corporatization of Schools* (New York: RoutledgeFalmer, 2003).
49. See Au, Brown, and Calderon, *Reclaiming the Multicultural Roots of U.S. Curriculum.*
50. "Test, Punish, and Push out: How 'Zero Tolerance' and High-Stakes Testing Funnel Youth into the School-to-Prison Pipeline," The Advancement Project, Washington, DC, 2010, https://b.3cdn.net/advancement/d05cb2181a4545db07_r2im6caqe.pdf; Erica R. Meiners and Maisha T. Winn, eds., *Education and Incarceration* (New York: Routledge, 2012).
51. See, e.g., Leonardo, "The Unhappy Marriage between Marxism and Race Critique"; Steven B. Smith, "Althusser and the Overdetermined Self," *Review of Politics* 46, no. 4 (1984): 516–38.
52. Karl Marx and Frederick Engels, "The German Ideology: Part I," in R. C. Tucker, ed., *The Marx-Engels Reader* (New York: W. W. Norton & Company, 1978), 146–200.
53. Ibid., 172–73, original emphasis.
54. Ibid., 174.
55. Karl Marx, "The Class Struggles in France, 1848–1850," in Tucker, *The Marx-Engels Reader*, 586–93.
56. Carnoy, "Education, Economy, and the State."
57. Engels, "Engels to J. Bloch in Konigsberg," 692, original emphasis.
58. Ibid.; see also Engels, "Ludwig Feuerbach and the End of Classical German Philosophy."
59. Frederick Engels, "Engels to H. Borgius in Breslau," in *Marx and Engels: Selected Works*, 704–5, original emphasis.
60. Gramsci, *Prison Notebooks*, 162; Althusser, *Lenin and Philosophy and Other Essays*, 135.
61. Marx, "The Eighteenth Brumaire of Louis Bonaparte,"171.
62. Engels, "Engels to H. Borgius in Breslau," 705.
63. Frederick Engels, "Engels to F. Mehring in Berlin," in Marx and Engles, *Selected Works*, 700, original emphasis.
64. Engels, "Engels to J. Bloch in Konigsberg," 693.
65. See Engels, "Engels to F. Mehring in Berlin," 701.
66. Allman, *Revolutionary Social Transformation*; Au, *Reclaiming Communist Philosophy*; Frederick Engels, *Dialectics of Nature*, C. Dutt, trans., 1st ed. (New York: International Publishers, 1940); Sean Sayers, "Marxism and the Dialectical Method: A Critique of G. A. Cohen,"

in Sean Sayers and Peter Osborne, eds., *Socialism, Feminism, and Philosophy: A Radical Philosophy Reader* (New York: Routledge, 1990), 140–68; Woods and Grant, *Reason in Revolt.*

67. See, e.g., Rikowski, "Scorched Earth."
68. Sayers, "Marxism and the Dialectical Method," 143.
69. Ibid., 164.
70. Au, *Unequal by Design*; Michael Bochenek and A. Widney Brown, "Hatred in the Hallways: Violence and Discrimination against Lesbian, Gay, Bisexual, and Transgender Students in U.S. Schools," Human Rights Watch, 2001, http://www.hrw.org/reports/2001/uslgbt/toc.htm; N. Lopez, *Hopeful Girls, Troubled Boys: Race and Gender Disparity in Urban Education* (New York: Routledge, 2003); Bree Picower and Edwin Mayorga, eds., *What's Race Got to Do with It?: How Current School Reform Policy Maintains Racial and Economic Inequality* (New York: Peter Lang, 2015).
71. Au, "Devising Inequality"; Bernstein, *The Structuring of Pedagogic Discourse.*
72. Au, "Hiding behind High-Stakes Testing"; Bowles and Gintis, *Schooling in Capitalist America.*
73. Au, "Hiding behind High-Stakes Testing."
74. Apple, *Education and Power*, 53, original emphasis.
75. Wayne Au and Jesse Hagopian, "How One Elementary School Sparked a Citywide Movement to Make Black Students' Lives Matter," *Rethinking Schools* 32, no. 1 (2017): 11–18; Wayne Au, "Social Justice and Resisting Neoliberal Education Reform in the USA," *Forum* 58, no. 3 (2016): 315–24, doi:http://dx.doi.org/10.15730/forum.2016.58.3.315; Taylor, *From #Blacklivesmatter to Black Liberation*; Hagopian, *More Than a Score.*
76. Coulthard, *Red Skin, White Masks.*
77. Au, Brown, and Calderon, *Reclaiming the Multicultural Roots of U.S. Curriculum*; Grande, *Red Pedagogy.*
78. See, e.g., Augustine Romero, Sean Arce, and Julio Cammarota, "A Barrio Pedagogy: Identity, Intellectualism, Activism, and Academic Achievement through the Evolution of Critically Compassionate Intellectualism," *Race Ethnicity and Education* 12, no. 2 (2009): 217–33; Allyson Tintiangco-Cubales et al., "Toward an Ethnic Studies Pedagogy: Implications for K–12 Schools from the Research," *Urban Review* 47, no. 1 (2015): 104–25, doi:10.1007/s11256-014-0280-y.
79. S. A. Ginwright, *Black in School: Afrocentric Reform, Urban Youth, and the Promise of Hip-Hop Culture*, 1st ed. (New York: Teachers College

Press, 2004); Gloria Ladson-Billings, *The Dreamkeepers: Successful Teachers of African American Children* (San Francisco: Jossey-Bass Publishers, 1994).

80. Au, "High-Stakes Testing: A Tool for White Supremacy for 100 Years"; Dumas, "'Waiting for Superman' to Save Black People."
81. Au, *Reclaiming Communist Philosophy*; Malott and Ford, *Marx, Capital, and Education*.
82. Marx, "The Eighteenth Brumaire of Louis Bonaparte," 97.
83. Engels, "Ludwig Feuerbach and the End of Classical German Philosophy," 622.
84. V. I. Lenin, *What Is to Be Done?: Burning Questions of Our Movement* (Peking: Foreign Language Press, 1975); Vygotsky, *Mind in Society*; Vygotsky, "Thinking and Speech"; Freire, *Pedagogy of the Oppressed*, 1974 ed.
85. Perry Anderson, *Arguments within English Marxism* (London: New Left Books, 1980), ch. 2.
86. Bowles and Gintis, *Schooling in Capitalist America*; Michael W. Apple, *Ideology and Curriculum*, 3rd ed. (New York: RoutledgeFalmer, 2004); Apple, *Education and Power*; Martin Carnoy and Henry M. Levin, *Schooling and Work in the Democratic State* (Stanford, CA: Stanford University Press, 1985).
87. Dance, *Tough Fronts*; Hagopian, *More Than a Score*; Ira Shor, *Empowering Education: Critical Teaching for Social Change*, 1st ed. (Chicago: The University of Chicago Press, 1992); Willis, "Foot Soldiers of Modernity."
88. Allman, *Revolutionary Social Transformation*; Paula Allman, Peter McLaren, and Glenn Rikowski, "After the Box People: The Labour-Capital Relation as Class Constitution—and Its Consequences for Marxist Educational Theory and Human Resistance," 2000, http://www.ieps.org.uk.cwc.net/afterthebox.pdf; Michael W. Apple, *Teachers and Texts: A Political Economy of Class and Gender Relations in Education* (New York: Routledge & Kegan Paul, 1986); Mary Compton and Lois Weiner, eds., *The Global Assault on Teaching, Teachers, and Their Unions: Stories for Resistance* (New York: Palgrave Macmillan, 2008).
89. Michael W. Apple, *Can Education Change Society?* (New York: Routledge, 2012); George S. Counts, *Dare the Schools Build a New Social Order?* (New York: John Day, 1932).

Chapter 4

1. Michael Fabricant and Michelle Fine, *The Changing Politics of Education: Privatization and the Dispossessed Lives Left Behind* (Boulder,

CO: Paradigm Publishers, 2013).

2. Harvey, "Neoliberalism as Creative Destruction," 22.
3. Pauline Lipman, *The New Political Economy of Urban Education: Neoliberalism, Race, and the Right to the City* (New York: Routledge, 2011), 6.
4. Au, *Unequal by Design*, chs. 2 and 3.
5. On teachers' unions, see Compton and Weiner, *The Global Assault on Teaching, Teachers, and Their Unions*; and Brian Jones, "Keys to the Schoolhouse: Black Teachers, Privatization, and the Future of Teacher Unions," in Bree Picower and Edwin Mayorga, eds., *What's Race Got to Do with It?: How Current School Reform Policy Maintains Racial and Economic Inequality*, Critical Multicultural Perspectives on Whiteness, vol. 2 (New York: Peter Lang, 2015), 81–102. On the improper use of high-stakes test scores to evaluate teachers, see Audrey Amrein-Beardsley, *Rethinking Value-Added Models in Education: Critical Perspectives on Tests and Assessment-Based Accountability* (New York: Routledge, 2014); and American Statistical Association, "ASA Statement on Using Value-Added Models for Educational Assessment," American Statistical Association, 2014, https://www.amstat.org/policy/pdfs/ASA_VAM_Statement.pdf. On the role of testing to control teaching and curriculum, see Wayne Au, "Teaching under the New Taylorism: High-Stakes Testing and the Standardization of the 21st Century Curriculum," *Journal of Curriculum Studies* 43, no. 1 (2011): 25–45, doi:10.1080/00220272.2010.521261. On the use of high-stakes tests to improperly evaluate teacher education programs, see Kerry Kretchmar, Beth Sondel, and Joseph J. Ferrare, "Mapping the Terrain: Teach For America, Charter School Reform, and Corporate Sponsorship," *Journal of Education Policy* 29, no. 6 (2014): 742-759, doi:10.1080/02680939.2014.880812; and Kenneth M. Zeichner and Cesar Pena-Sandoval, "Venture Philanthropy and Teacher Education Policy in the U.S.: The Role of the New Schools Venture Fund," *Teachers College Record* 117, no. 6 (2015), http://www.tcrecord.org. On the neoliberal revisioning of public education, see Fabricant and Fine, *The Changing Politics of Education*; and Michael W. Apple, "Comparing Neo-Liberal Projects and Inequality in Education," *Comparative Education* 37, no. 4 (2001): 409–23.
6. Apple, "Comparing Neo-Liberal Projects and Inequality in Education"; Lipman, *The New Political Economy of Urban Education*.
7. Lipman, *The New Political Economy of Urban Education*.
8. Ibid., 13, original emphasis.
9. David Stovall, "Mayoral Control: Reform, Whiteness, and Critical

Race Analysis of Neoliberal Educational Policy," in Picower and Mayorga, *What's Race Got to Do with It?*, 45–58; Kenneth K. Wong and Francis X. Shen, "When Mayors Lead Urban Schools: Assessing the Effects of Mayoral Takeovers," in William G. Howell, ed., *Besieged: School Boards and the Future of Education Politics* (Washington, DC: Brookings Institutions Press, 2005), 81–101; Michael W. Kirst, "Mayoral Influence, New Regimes, and Public School Governance," Consortium for Policy Research in Education, University of Pennsylvania, May 2002, http://www.cpre.org/Publications/rr49.pdf.

10. Wayne Au and Christopher A. Lubienski, "The Role of the Gates Foundation and the Philanthropic Sector in Shaping the Emerging Education Market: Lessons from the US on Privatization of Schools and Educational Governance," in Antoni Verger, Christopher A. Lubienski, and Gita Steiner-Khamsi, eds., *World Yearbook of Education 2016: The Global Education Industry* (New York: Taylor & Francis, 2016), 27–43; Michael J. Barker, "Bill Gates as Social Engineer: Introducing the World's Largest Liberal Philanthropist," *ZNet*, July 16, 2008, https://zcomm.org/znetarticle/bill-gates-philanthropy-and-social-engineering-part-1-of-3-by-michael-barker/; Michael Klonsky, "Power Philanthropy: Taking the Public out of Public Education," in Phillip E. Kovacs, ed., *The Gates Foundation and the Future of U.S. "Public" Schools* (New York: Routledge, 2011), 21–38; Kenneth J. Saltman, "From Carnegie to Gates: The Bill and Melinda Gates Foundation and the Venture Philanthropy Agenda for Public Education," in Kovacs, *The Gates Foundation and the Future of U.S. "Public" Schools*, 1–20; Wayne Au and Joseph J. Ferrare, "Sponsors of Policy: A Network Analysis of Wealthy Elites, Their Affiliated Philanthropies, and Charter School Reform in Washington State," *Teachers College Record* 116, no. 8 (2014), 1–24; Joanne Barkan, "Got Dough?: How Billionaires Rule Our Schools," *Dissent* 58, no. 1 (2011): 49–57, doi:10.1353/dss.2011.0023; Joanne Barkan, "Hired Guns on Astroturf: How to Buy and Sell School Reform," *Dissent* 59, no. 2 (2012): 49–57; Anthony Cody, "Gates Money Attempts to Shift the Education Conversation to Successes," *Living in Dialogue*, December 12, 2014, http://www.livingindialogue.com/money-attempts-shift-education-conversation-successes/; Zeichner and Pena-Sandoval, "Venture Philanthropy and Teacher Education Policy in the U.S."

11. Lyndsey Layton, "How Bill Gates Pulled off the Swift Common Core Revolution," *Washington Post*, June 7, 2014, https://www.washingtonpost.com/politics/how-bill-gates-pulled-off-the-swift

-common-core-revolution/2014/06/07/a830e32e-ec34-11e3-9f5c-9075d5508f0a_story.html?utm_term=.82889327c859.

12. Au and Ferrare, "Sponsors of Policy."
13. Diane Ravitch, *Reign of Error: The Hoax of the Privatization Movement and the Danger to America's Public Schools* (New York: Vintage Books, 2014).
14. Valerie Strauss, "Bill Gates: 'It Would Be Great If Our Education Stuff Worked But . . . '," The Answer Sheet, *Washington Post*, 2013, http://www.washingtonpost.com/blogs/answer-sheet/wp/2013/09/27/bill-gates-it-would-be-great-if-our-education-stuff-worked-but/.
15. Klonsky, "Power Philanthropy."
16. KrazyTA, "KrazyTA Explains What Bill Gates Wants for His Own Children," *Diane Ravitch's Blog*, March 19, 2014, https://dianeravitch.net/2014/03/19/krazyta-explains-what-bill-gates-wants-for-his-own-children/; HiPointDem, "Bill Gates Tells Us Why 'His' High School Was a Great Learning Environment," *Seattle Education*, June 18, 2012, https://seattleducation2010.wordpress.com/2012/06/18/bill-gates-tells-us-why-his-high-school-was-a-great-learning-environment/.
17. Bill Gates Jr., "Speech Delivered to the National Conference of State Legislatures," 2009, http://www.gatesfoundation.org/media-center/speeches/2009/07/bill-gates-national-conference-of-state-legislatures-ncsl.
18. Fabricant and Fine, *Changing Politics of Education*, 25.
19. Patricia Burch, "The New Educational Privatization: Educational Contracting and High Stakes Accountability," *Teachers College Record* 108, no. 12 (2006): 2582–2610; Patricia Burch, *Hidden Markets: The New Education Privatization* (New York: Routledge, 2009).
20. W. James Popham, *The Truth about Testing: An Educator's Call to Action* (Alexandria, VA: Association for Supervision and Curriculum Development (ASCD), 2001); Au, *Unequal by Design*.
21. G. W. Bush, "The Future of Educational Reform" (speech, Manhattan Institute, New York, October 5, 1999, retrieved from http://www.manhattan-institute.org/html/bush_speech.htm).
22. George Joseph, "What Betsy DeVos Didn't Say about School Choice," *CityLab*, January 19, 2017, http://www.citylab.com/politics/2017/01/what-betsy-devos-didnt-say-about-school-choice/513269/.
23. Leigh Dingerson et al., eds., *Keeping the Promise?: The Debate over Charter Schools* (Milwaukee, WI: Rethinking Schools, 2008); Stan Karp, "Charter Schools and the Future of Public Education: It's Time to Refocus Public Policy on Providing Excellent Public Schools for

All," *New Jersey Education Association Review*, March 2013, http://www.njea.org/news-and-publications/njea-review/march-2013/charter-schools-and-the-future-of-public-education.

24. Wayne Au, "Learning to Read: Charter Schools, Public Education, and the Politics of Educational Research" (presentation at the Washington State PTA Public Charter School Forum, Seattle, WA, February 29, 2012).
25. The Center for Popular Democracy and Integrity in Education, *Charter School Vulnerabilities to Waste, Fraud, and Abuse*, report, May 2014, https://www.scribd.com/doc/221993993/Charter-School-Vulnerabilities-to-Waste-Fraud-Abuse; Sharon Higgins, "Charter School Scandals," 2013, *Charter School Scandals*, http://charterschoolscandals.blogspot.com; Preston C. Green III, Bruce D. Baker, and Joseph O. Oluwole, "Having It Both Ways: How Charter Schools Try to Obtain Funding of Public Schools and the Autonomy of Private Schools," *Emory Law Journal* 63 (2013): 303–37.
26. Robin J. Lake, "In the Eye of the Beholder: Charter Schools and Innovation," *Journal of School Choice* 2, no. 2 (2008): 115–27, doi:http://dx.doi.org/10.1080/15582150802136090; C. Preston et al., "School Innovation in District Context: Comparing Traditional Public Schools and Charter Schools," *Economics of Education Review* 31, no. 2 (2012): 318–30, doi:https://doi.org/10.1016/j.econedurev.2011.07.016.
27. Gary Miron and Jessica Urschel, "The Impact of School Choice Reforms on Student Achievement," in Kevin G. Welner, Patricia H. Hinchey, and William J. Mathis, eds., *Exploring the School Choice Universe: Evidence and Recommendations* (Charlotte, NC: Information Age Publishing, 2012), 211–36.
28. Center for Research on Education Outcomes (CREDO), *Multiple Choice: Charter School Performance in 16 States*, report, June 2009, http://credo.stanford.edu/reports/MULTIPLE_CHOICE_CREDO.pdf.
29. CREDO, *National Charter School Study 2013*, report, June 2013, http://credo.stanford.edu.
30. Myron Orfield and Thomas Luce, "An Analysis of Student Performance in Chicago's Charter Schools," *Education Policy Analysis Archives* 24, no. 111 (2016): 3, doi:http://dx.doi.org/10.14507/epaa.24.2203.
31. Stephanie Simon, "Special Report: Class Struggle—How Charter Schools Get the Students They Want," *Reuters*, February 17, 2013, http://www.reuters.com/article/2013/02/15/us-usa-charters-admissions-idUSBRE91E0HF20130215; see also Kevin G. Welner,

"The Dirty Dozen: How Charter Schools Influence Student Enrollment," *Teachers College Record*, May 5, 2013, http://www.tcrecord.org/Content.asp?ContentID=17104.

32. Erica Frankenberg, Genevieve Siegel-Hawley, and Jia Wang, "Choice without Equity: Charter School Segregation," *Educational Policy Analysis Archives* 19, no. 1 (2013), http://epaa.asu.edu/ojs/article/view/779; Simon, "Special Report: Class Struggle—How Charter Schools Get the Students They Want"; Gary Miron et al., *Schools without Diversity: Education Management Organizations, Charter Schools, and the Demographic Stratification of the American School System*, policy brief, Education and the Public Interest Center and Education Policy Research Unit, 2010, http://nepc.colorado.edu/files/EMO-Seg.pdf; Julian Vasquez Heilig et al., "The Problematic Segregation of Special Populations in Charter Schools Relative to Traditional Public Schools," *Stanford Law and Policy Review* 27 (2016): 251–94.
33. Mark Weber, "Steve Perry: The Final Debunk," *Jersey Jazzman*, May 27, 2013, http://jerseyjazzman.blogspot.com/2013/05/dr-steve-perry-final-debunk.html.
34. Ibid.
35. Ibid.
36. Wayne Au, and Jesslyn Hollar, "Opting out of the Education Reform Industry," *Monthly Review* 67, no. 10 (2016), 29–37.
37. Amrein-Beardsley, *Rethinking Value-Added Models in Education.*
38. Peter Z. Schochet and Hanley S. Chiang, "Error Rates in Measuring Teacher and School Performance Based on Test Score Gains," Institute of Educational Sciences, US Department of Education, August 23, 2010, http://ies.ed.gov/ncee/pubs/20104004/pdf/20104004.pdf.
39. Tim R. Sass, "The Stability of Value-Added Measures of Teacher Quality and Implication for Teacher Compensation," policy brief, National Center for Analysis of Longitudinal Data in Educational Research, November 2008, https://eric.ed.gov/?id=ED508273.
40. Eva L. Baker et al., "Problems with the Use of Student Test Scores to Evaluate Teachers," Economic Policy Institute, August 29, 2010, http://www.epi.org/publication/bp278/; Amrein-Beardsley, *Rethinking Value-Added Models in Education*.
41. Dan DiMaggio, "The Loneliness of the Long-Distance Test Scorer," *Monthly Review* 62, no. 7 (2012), http://monthlyreview.org/2010/12/01/the-loneliness-of-the-long-distance-test-scorer.
42. Ibid.
43. Todd Farley, *Making the Grades: My Misadventures in the Standardized*

Testing Industry (San Francisco: Berrett-Koehler Publishers, 2009); see also Farley, "My Misadventures in the Standardized Testing Industry," The Answer Sheet, *Washington Post*, December, 18, 2009, http://voices.washingtonpost.com/answer-sheet/standardized-tests/-gerald-martineaupost-today-my.html; Farley, "A Test Scorer's Lament," *Rethinking Schools* 23, no. 2 (2010), http://www.rethinkingschools.org/archive/23_02/test232.shtml.

44. Berliner, "Effects of Inequality and Poverty vs. Teachers and Schooling on America's Youth."
45. Board of Governors of the Federal Reserve, "Changes in U.S. family Finances from 2013 to 2016: Evidence from the Survey of Consumer Finances," *Federal Reserve Bulletin* 103, no 3 (2017), 1–42, https://www.federalreserve.gov/publications/files/scf17.pdf; Matt Bruenig, "Wealth Inequality Is Higher Than Ever," *Jacobin* (October 1, 2017), https://www.jacobinmag.com/2017/10/wealth-inequality-united-states-federal-reserve.
46. Yang Jiang, Maribel R. Granja, and Heather Koball, "Basic Facts about Low-Income Children: Children under 18 Years, 2015," fact sheet, National Center for Children in Poverty, Columbia University, 2017, http://www.nccp.org/publications/pdf/text_1170.pdf.
47. Wayne Au, "Neither Fair nor Accurate: Research Based Reasons Why High-Stakes Tests Should Not Be Used to Evaluate Teachers," *Rethinking Schools* 25, no. 2 (2010): 34–38.
48. Gerald W. Bracey, *Setting the Record Straight* (Portsmouth, NH: Heinemann, 2004); Philip Harris, Bruce M. Smith, and Joan Harris, *The Myths of Standardized Tests: Why They Don't Tell You What You Think They Do* (New York: Rowman & Littlefield Publishers, Inc., 2011).
49. Ravitch, *Reign of Error*; M. Hout and S. W. Elliott, eds., *Incentives and Test-Based Accountability in Education*, National Research Council, Committee on Incentives and Test-Based Accountability in Public Education, Washington, DC, 2011.
50. Sharon L. Nichols and David C. Berliner, *Collateral Damage: How High-Stakes Testing Corrupts America's Schools* (Cambridge, MA: Harvard Education Press, 2007); Angela Valenzuela, ed., *Leaving Children behind: How "Texas Style" Accountability Fails Latino Youth*, Social Context of Education (New York: State University of New York Press, 2005).
51. Ray Hart et al., *Student Testing in America's Great City Schools: An Inventory and Preliminary Analysis* (Washington, DC: Council of the Great City Schools, 2015), https://www.cgcs.org/cms/lib/DC00001581/Centricity/Domain/87/Testing%20Report.pdf.

52. Melissa Lazarin, *Testing Overload in America's Schools*, report, Center for American Progress, Washington, DC, 2014, 3, https://cdn.americanprogress.org/wp-content/uploads/2014/10/LazarinOvertestingReport.pdf.
53. Mark Weber, "Standardized Tests: Symptoms, Not Causes," *Jersey Jazzman*, May 24, 2015, http://jerseyjazzman.blogspot.com/2015/05/standardized-tests-symptoms-not-causes.html; see also Popham, *The Truth about Testing*.
54. Xuan Tan and Rochelle Michel, "Why Do Standardized Testing Programs Report Scaled Scores?: Why Not Just Report the Raw or Percent-Correct Scores?," *ETS R&D Connections*, 2011, https://www.ets.org/Media/Research/pdf/RD_Connections16.pdf; Mark Weber, "Common Core Testing: Who's the Real 'Liar'?," *Jersey Jazzman*, September 25, 2015, http://jerseyjazzman.blogspot.com/2015/09/common-core-testing-whos-real-liar.html.
55. Wayne Au, "Can We Test for Liberation?: Moving from Retributive to Restorative and Transformative Assessment in Schools," *Critical Education* 8, no. 13 (2017).
56. National Poverty Center, "Poverty in the United States: Frequently Asked Questions," National Poverty Center, official website, 2017, http://www.npc.umich.edu/poverty/; Huizhong Wu, "The 'Model Minority' Myth: Why Asian-American Poverty Goes Unseen," *Mashable*, December 14, 2015, http://mashable.com/2015/12/14/asian-american-poverty/#_7xAoYLYigqs; Christian E. Weller and Jeffrey Thompson, *Wealth Inequality among Asian Americans Greater than among Whites*, report, Center for American Progress, Washington, DC, December 20, 2016, https://www.americanprogress.org/issues/race/reports/2016/12/20/295359/wealth-inequality-among-asian-americans-greater-than-among-whites/.
57. Wayne Au, "High-Stakes Testing and Discursive Control: The Triple Bind for Non-Standard Student Identities," *Multicultural Perspectives* 11, no. 2 (2009): 65–71; Nichols and Berliner, *Collateral Damage*.
58. Kevin D. Vinson and E. Wayne Ross, "Controlling Images: The Power of High-Stakes Testing," in Saltman and Gabbard, *Education as Enforcement*, 241–58.
59. Olesya Baker and Kevin Lang, "The Effect of High School Exit Exams on Graduation, Employment, Wages, and Incarceration" (working paper, National Bureau of Economic Research, Cambridge, MA, 2013, http://www.nber.org/papers/w19182.pdf); see also Michelle Fine and Jessica Ruglis, "Circuits and Consequences of Dispossession: The Ra-

cialized Realignment of the Public Sphere for U.S. Youth," *Transforming Anthropology* 17, no. 1 (2009): 20–33, doi:10.1111/j.1548-7466.2009.01037.x.

60. Linda Darling-Hammond, "Race, Inequality, and Educational Accountability: The Irony of 'No Child Left Behind,'" *Race, Ethnicity, and Education* 10, no. 3 (2007): 245–60.
61. Daniel J. Losen et al., "Charter Schools, Civil Rights and Schools Discipline: A Comprehensive Review," Center for Civil Rights Remedies, The Civil Rights Project, Los Angeles, 2016, https://civilrightsproject.ucla.edu/resources/projects/center-for-civil-rights-remedies/school-to-prison-folder/federal-reports/charter-schools-civil-rights-and-school-discipline-a-comprehensive-review/losen-et-al-charter-school-discipline-review-2016.pdf.
62. George Joseph, "Where Charter-School Suspensions Are Concentrated," *Atlantic*, September 16, 2016, https://www.theatlantic.com/education/archive/2016/09/the-racism-of-charter-school-discipline/500240/.
63. Ibid.
64. R. Balfanz, V. Byrnes, and J. Fox, "Sent Home and Put off Track: The Antecedents, Disproportionalities, and Consequences of Being Suspended in the 9th Grade," in Daniel J. Losen ed., *Closing the School Discipline Gap: Equitable Remedies for Excessive Exclusion*, (New York, NY: Teachers College Press, 2015), 17–30; A. L. Noltemeyer, R. M. Ward, and C. Mcloughlin, "Relationship between School Suspension and Student Outcomes: A Meta-Analysis," *School Psychology Review* 44, no. 2 (2015): 224–40, doi:10.17105/spr-14-0008.1; T. L. Shollenberger, "Racial Disparities in School Suspension and Subsequent Outcomes: Evidence from the National Longitudinal Survey of Youth," in Losen, *Closing the School Discipline Gap*, 31–43.
65. Stephanie Ewert, Bryan L. Sykes, and Becky Pettit, "The Degree of Disadvantage: Incarceration and Inequality in Education," *Annals of the American Academy of Political and Social Science* 651 (2014): 24–43, doi:10.1177/0002716213503100.
66. Frankenberg, Siegel-Hawley, and Wang, "Choice without Equity"; Miron et al., "Schools without Diversity."
67. Linda A. Renzulli and Lorraine Evans, "School Choice, Charter Schools, and White Flight," *Social Problems* 52, no. 3 (2005): 398–418; Christopher Bonastia, "The Racist History of the Charter School Movement: Touted as the Cure for What Ails Public Education, Charter Schools Have Historical Roots That Are Rarely Discussed,"

AlterNet, January 6, 2015, http://www.alternet.org/education/racist-history-charter-school-movement.

68. Renzulli and Evans, "School Choice, Charter Schools, and White Flight," 412.

69. Helen F. Ladd, Charles T. Clotfelter, and John B. Holbein, "The Growing Segmentation of the Charter School Sector in North Carolina," *Education Finance and Policy* 19, no. 55 (2017): 1–28, doi:10.1162/edfp_a_00226; see also Joseph, "What Betsy DeVos Didn't Say about School Choice."

70. Josh Eidelson, "Christie's Charter School Nightmare: 'White Flight, and They're Bankrupting Us,'" *Salon*, May 13, 2014, http://www.salon.com/2014/03/13/christies_charter_school_nightmare_white_flight_and_they're_bankrupting_us/.

71. Joy Resmovits, "Murdoch Education Affiliate's $2.7 Million Consulting Contract Approved by New York City," *Huffington Post*, July 15, 2011, http://www.huffingtonpost.com/2011/07/15/murdoch-education-affiliate-contract-approved_n_900379.html.

72. Lee Fang, "Venture Capitalists Are Poised to 'Disrupt' Everything about the Education Market," *Nation*, September 25, 2014, https://www.thenation.com/article/venture-capitalists-are-poised-disrupt-everything-about-education-market/.

73. P. Murphy, E. Regenstein, and K. McNamara, "Putting a price tag on the Common Core: How much will smart implementation cost?,"Thomas B. Fordham Institute, Washington, DC, http://www.edexcellence.net/publications/putting-a-price-tag-on-the-common-core.html.

74. Accountability Works, "National Cost of Aligning States and Localities to the Common Core Standards," Pioneer Institute American Principles Project Pacific Research Institute, Boston, retrieved from http://www.accountabilityworks.org/photos/Cmmn_Cr_Cst_Stdy.Fin.2.22.12.pdf.

75. M. Rich, "New Schools Fund Attracts More Capital," *New York Times*, May 1, 2013, http://www.nytimes.com/2013/05/01/education/newschools-venture-fund-links-with-rethink-education.html?ref=education&_r=1&.

76. A. J. Vicens, "Bill Gates Spent More than $200 Million to Promote Common Core. Here's Where It Went: The Gates Foundation Has Bankrolled a Sprawling Network of Groups to Advance the Standards," *Mother Jones*, September 4, 2014, http://www.motherjones.com/politics/2014/09/bill-melinda-gates-foundation-common-core/.

77. Layton, "How Bill Gates Pulled off the Swift Common Core Revolution."
78. Kristin Rawls, "Who Is Profiting from Charters?: The Big Bucks behind Charter School Secrecy, Financial Scandal and Corruption," *AlterNet*, May 13, 2013, http://www.alternet.org/education/who-profiting-charters-big-bucks-behind-charter-school-secrecy-financial-scandal-and?paging=off.
79. Ibid.
80. Ibid.
81. Ibid.; see also Daniel Wolff, "Speculating on Education," *Counterpunch*, September 25, 2009, http://www.counterpunch.org/2009/09/25/speculating-on-education/.
82. Carol Burris, "School Choice a Sham, Profits on the Taxpayers' Dime," *Capitol Times*, April 6, 2017, http://azcapitoltimes.com/news/2017/04/06/school-choice-profits-on-the-taxpayers-dime/.
83. Jeremy Pelzer, "Charter School Operator Owns Property Bought with Public Money, Ohio Supreme Court Rules," *Cleveland.com*, September 12, 2015, http://www.cleveland.com/open/index.ssf/2015/09/charter_school_operator_owns_p.html.
84. Bruce D. Baker, "Exploring the Consequences of Charter School Expansion in U.S. Cities," Economic Policy Institute, Washington, DC, November 30, 2016, http://epi.org/109218; David Lapp et al., *The Fiscal Impact of Charter School Expansion: Calculation in Six Pennsylvania School Districts*, report, Research for Action, Philadelphia, 2017, https://www.researchforaction.org/publications/fiscal-impact-charter-school-expansion-calculations-six-pennsylvania-school-districts/.
85. Fabricant and Fine, *The Changing Politics of Education*, 25.
86. Harvey, "The 'New' Imperialism," 74.
87. KrazyTA, "KrazyTA Explains What Bill Gates Wants for His Own Children"; Mark Weber, "How Every Kid Could Go to Bill Gate's Private School," *Jersey Jazzman*, April 24, 2013, http://jerseyjazzman.blogspot.com/2013/04/how-every-kid-could-go-to-bill-gatess.html; HiPointDem, "Bill Gates Tells Us Why 'His' High School Was a Great Learning Environment."
88. Wayne Au and Joseph J. Ferrare, "Other People's Policy: Wealthy Elites and Charter School Reform in Washington State," in Au and Ferrare, *Mapping Corporate Education Reform*, 147–64.
89. Au, "Meritocracy 2.0"; Wayne Au, "Just Whose Rights Do These Civil Rights Groups Think They Are Protecting?," The Answer Sheet, *Washington Post*, May 9, 2015, http://www.washingtonpost.com/blogs/answer-sheet/wp/2015/05/09/just-whose-rights-do-these-civil-rights

-groups-think-they-are-protecting/; Au and Ferrare, "Other People's Policy"; Picower and Mayorga, *What's Race Got to Do with It?*.

90. Bowles and Gintis, *Schooling in Capitalist America*; see also my discussion of Bowles and Gintis in chapter 3 of this book.
91. Jesse Hagopian, "Our Destination Is Not on the MAP," in Hagopian, *More Than a Score*, 31–47.
92. Ibid.
93. Rethinking Schools, "Leading Educators Support Teacher Test Boycott," *Rethinking Schools Blog*, January 21, 2013, https://rethinkingschoolsblog.wordpress.com/2013/01/21/leading-educators-support-teacher-test-boycott/; see also: Au, "Proud to Be a Garfield Bulldog."
94. Hagopian, "Our Destination Is Not on the MAP."
95. Aaron Dixon, *My People Are Rising: Memoir of a Black Panther Party Captain* (Chicago: Haymarket Books, 2012).
96. John Bellamy Foster, "The Opt Out Revolt: Democracy and Education," *Monthly Review* 67, no. 10 (2016), http://monthlyreview.org/2016/03/01/the-opt-out-revolt/; Jesse Hagopian, "Obama Regrets 'Taking the Joy out of Teaching and Learning' with Too Much Testing," *Common Dreams*, October 30, 2015, http://www.commondreams.org/views/2015/10/30/obama-regrets-taking-joy-out-teaching-and-learning-too-much-testing.
97. Robert Pondiscio, "Opting Out, Race, and Reform," Common Core Watch, Thomas B. Fordham Institute, March 25, 2015, https://edexcellence.net/articles/opting-out-race-and-reform.
98. Jesse Hagopian and Network for Public Education, "Resistance to High Stakes Tests Serves the Cause of Equity in Education: A Reply to 'We Oppose Anti-Testing Efforts,'" Network for Public Education, May 5, 2015, http://www.networkforpubliceducation.org/2015/05/resistance-to-high-stakes-tests-serves-the-cause-of-equity-in-education/; Rethinking Schools, "The Gathering Resistance to Standardized Tests," *Rethinking Schools*, 2014, http://www.rethinkingschools.org/archive/28_03/edit2283.shtml.
99. Hagopian, *More Than a Score*.
100. Jesse Hagopian, "Salt of the Earth School: 'They Can't Break Us.' Interview with Jia Lee," in ibid., 107–12.
101. Sarah Chambers, "Ice the ISAT: Boycotting the Test under Mayor Rahm Emanuel's Regime," in ibid., 113–22.
102. Dao X. Tran, "Forget Teaching to the Test–Castle Bridge Boycotts It!," in ibid., 211–18.
103. "The Journey for Justice Alliance Education Platform: An Equitable

and Just School System Now!," Journey for Justice Alliance, 2016, https://www.j4jalliance.com/wp-content/uploads/2016/09/J4J_Final_Education_Platform.pdf.

104. Ibid.

105. Ibid.

106. Jonathan Stith, Hiram Rivera, and Chinyere Tutashinda, "A Vision for Black Lives: Policy Demands for Black Power, Freedom, and Justice: An End to the Privatization of Education and Real Community Control by Parents, Students, and Community Members of Schools Including Democratic School Boards and Community Control of Curriculum, Hiring, Firing, and Discipline Policies," Movement for Black Lives, 2016, https://policy.m4bl.org/wp-content/uploads/2016/07/Community-Control-of-Schools-Policy-Brief.pdf.

107. Au, "Just Whose Rights Do These Civil Rights Groups Think They Are Protecting?"

108. NAACP, "Statement Regarding the NAACP's Resolution on a Moritorium on Charter Schools," NAACP, official website, October 15, 2016, http://www.naacp.org/latest/statement-regarding-naacps-resolution-moratorium-charter-schools/.

109. Michelle Fine and Michael Fabricant, "What It Takes to Unite Teachers Unions and Communities of Color: Overcoming Years of Tensions and Divisions, Parents and Teachers Are Linking Arms to Save Public Schools," *Nation*, October 13, 2014, https://www.thenation.com/article/what-it-takes-unite-teachers-unions-and-communities-color/.

110. Luke Whelan, "Seattle Teacher Strike Is the Latest Front Line in America's Public School Wars: It's about Much More than a Wage Dispute," *Mother Jones*, September 15, 2015, http://www.motherjones.com/politics/2015/09/heres-why-seattle-teacheres-are-strike/.

111. Wayne Au, "When Multicultural Education Is Not Enough," *Multicultural Perspectives* 19, no. 3 (2017): 1–4, doi:10.1080/15210960.2017.1331741.

112. Fine and Fabricant, "What It Takes to Unite Teachers Unions and Communities of Color."

113. Hagopian, "Obama Regrets 'Taking the Joy out of Teaching and Learning' with Too Much Testing"; Au and Hollar, "Opting out of the Education Reform Industry."

114. Arianna Prothero, "Public Support for Charter School Plummets, Poll Finds," *Education Week*, August 16, 2017, http://www.edweek.org/ew/articles/2017/08/15/public-support-for-charter-schools

-plummets-poll.html.
115. Michael W. Apple, *Educating the "Right" Way: Markets, Standards, God, and Inequality*, 2nd ed. (New York: RoutledgeFalmer, 2006).

Chapter 5

1. Marx and Engels, "The German Ideology: Part I," 158.
2. Au, "Teaching about the WTO."
3. Stephen Toulmin, "The Mozart of Psychology," *New York Review of Books*, September 28, 1978; Jerome S. Bruner, "Prologue to the English Edition," in Robert W. Rieber and Aaron Carton, eds., *The Collected Works of L. S. Vygotsky: Problems of General Psychology Including the Volume Thinking and Speech*, Norris Minick, trans., Cognition and Language, vol. 1 (New York: Plenum Press, 1987), 1–16.
4. See, e.g., Yuriy V. Karpov, "Vygotsky's Doctrine of Scientific Concepts: Its Role for Contemporary Education," in Alex Kozulin et al., eds., *Vygotsky's Educational Theory in Cultural Context*, Learning in Doing: Social, Cognitive, and Computational Perspectives (New York: Cambridge University Press, 2003), 65–82; S. J. Meacham, "Vygotsky and the Blues: Re-Reading Cultural Connections and Conceptual Development," *Theory into Practice* 40, no. 3 (2001): 190; Seth Chaiklin, "The Zone of Proximal Development in Vygotsky's Analysis of Learning and Instruction," in Kozulin et al., *Vygotsky's Educational Theory in Cultural Context*, 39–64.
5. See, e.g., Guillermo Blanck, "Vygotsky: The Man and His Cause," in Luis C. Moll, ed., *Vygotsky and Education: Instructional Implications and Applications of Sociohistorical Psychology* (Cambridge; New York: Cambridge University Press, 1990), 31–58; Fred Newman and Lois Holzman, *Lev Vygotsky: Revolutionary Scientist*, Critical Psychology (London and New York: Routledge, 1993); Michael Cole and Sylvia Scribner, "Introduction," in Vygotsky, *Mind in Society*, 1–14; Loren R. Graham, *Science and Philosophy in the Soviet Union* (New York: Alfred A. Knopf, 1972); James V. Wertsch, *Vygotsky and the Social Formation of Mind* (Cambridge, MA: Harvard University Press, 1985); Jerome S. Bruner, "Vygotsky's Zone of Proximal Development: The Hidden Agenda," in Barbara Rogoff and James V. Wertsch, eds., *Children's Learning in the "Zone of Proximal Development,"* New Directions for Child Development, vol. 23 (San Francisco: Jossey-Bass, 1984), 93–97; Alberto Rosa and Ignacio Montero, "The Historical Context of Vygotsky's Work: A Sociohistorical Approach," in Moll, *Vygotsky and Education*, 59–88.

6. See also Jeremy Sawyer, "Vygotsky's Revolutionary Theory of Psychological Development," *International Socialist Review* 93 (2014), http://isreview.org/issue/93/vygotskys-revolutionary-theory-psychological-development, for a good discussion of Vygotsky.
7. Lev S. Vygotsky, *Thought and Language*, E. Hanfmann, trans. (Cambridge, MA: The MIT Press, 1962).
8. Graham, *Science and Philosophy in the Soviet Union.*
9. Vygotsky, *Thought and Language.*
10. Vygotsky, "Thinking and Speech."
11. Wertsch, *Vygotsky and the Social Formation of Mind*; Vassily V. Davydov, "The Basic Concepts of Contemporary Psychology," *Soviet Education* 30, no. 8 (1988): 15–43.
12. As quoted in Cole and Scribner, "Introduction," 8.
13. Lenin, *What Is to Be Done?*, 34.
14. Ibid., 35.
15. Ibid., 36.
16. Ibid.
17. Ibid.
18. Ibid.
19. Ibid., 125.
20. Ibid., 86.
21. Ibid., 200.
22. Ibid., 35, 36, 86, 125, 200.
23. Kenneth Burke, *A Rhetoric of Motives* (Berkeley, CA: University of California Press, 1950).
24. Marx and Engels, "The German Ideology: Part I," 154–55.
25. V. V. Davydov, "From the History of General and Child Psychology," *Soviet Education* 30, no. 10 (1988): 42–77.
26. Vygotsky, "Thinking and Speech," 190.
27. Ibid., 192.
28. Ibid., 190–91.
29. Ibid., 192–93.
30. Although there is not enough space to fully address the issue here, it should be noted that Vygotsky's uses of the terms "science" and "scientific" are most likely quite different than what these terms are regularly accepted to connote. In current usage, the term "science" commonly serves as a marker for what we know as the positivistic sciences. The positivistic conception of science is quite problematic for a wide range of reasons. Suffice to say, if we accept the proposition that Vygotsky worked within the Marxist tradition, then we have to also accept the

proposition that he was working within a dialectical materialist conception of science—one that is in many ways antithetical to the positivistic conception. See chapter 5 of this book for further discussion.

31. It should be noted that throughout the text of "Thinking and Speech" Vygotsky uses "nonspontaneous" and "scientific" somewhat interchangeably in reference to concepts; "spontaneous" and "everyday" are used interchangeably as well. However, the text does seem to assert that "scientific" concepts are more specific types of "nonspontaneous" concepts.
32. Vygotsky, "Thinking and Speech," 172.
33. Ibid., 191.
34. Ibid., 190.
35. Ibid., 234.
36. Lenin, *What Is to Be Done?*, 36.
37. Vygotsky, "Thinking and Speech," 180.
38. Ibid., 190.
39. Ibid., 177.
40. Ibid., 180.
41. Ibid., 220.
42. Lenin, *What Is to Be Done?*, 36.
43. It should be noted that Lenin's use of the term "Social Democracy" was different from the way it is popularly used now. For Lenin, Social Democrats were interested in a socialist revolution that included the overthrow of the ruling class and the complete restructuring of the state. More contemporary usages of the term refer to the idea of using existing liberal democracies to support socialist ideals and policies.
44. Lenin, *What Is to Be Done?*, 97.
45. Vygotsky, "Thinking and Speech," 194.
46. Ibid., 201, 211.
47. Lev S. Vygotsky, "Interaction between Learning and Development," in Vygotsky, *Mind in Society*, 86; see also Vygotsky, "Thinking and Speech," 201.
48. Vygotsky, "Interaction between Learning and Development," 90.
49. Ibid.; Vygotsky, "Thinking and Speech," 211.
50. Vygotsky, "Thinking and Speech," 209.
51. Lenin, *What Is to Be Done?*, 97.
52. Ibid., 36–37.
53. Ibid., 36–37.
54. Alan Shandro, "'Consciousness from Without': Marxism, Lenin, and the Proletariat," *Science and Society* 59, no. 3 (1995): 285.

55. Paul D'Amato, "The Myth of Lenin's Elitism," *International Socialist Review* 60 (2008), http://www.isreview.org/issues/60/feat-leninmyth.shtml.
56. Lenin, *What Is to Be Done?*, 37.
57. Ibid., 136.
58. Ibid., 138.
59. Ibid., 136, emphasis added.
60. Ibid., 199, emphasis added.
61. Ibid., 138, 150.
62. D'Amato, "The Myth of Lenin's Elitism."
63. Vygotsky, "Thinking and Speech," 216.
64. Vygotsky's conception of learning reflects the uneven distribution of knowledge in this basic sense. See Wertsch, *Vygotsky and the Social Formation of Mind*; William Frawley, *Vygotsky and Cognitive Science: Language and the Unification of the Social and Computational Mind* (Cambridge, MA: Harvard University Press, 1997); Michael Cole and Yrjö Engeström, "A Cultural-Historical Approach to Distributed Cognition," in Gavriel Salomon, ed., *Distributed Cognitions: Psychological and Educational Considerations* (Cambridge, UK: Cambridge University Press, 1997), 1–46; Bonnie A. Nardi, "Studying Context: A Composition of Activity Theory, Situated Action Models, and Distributed Cognition," in Bonnie A. Nardi, ed., *Context and Consciousness: Activity Theory and Human-Computer Interaction* (Cambridge, MA: The MIT Press, 1996), 69–102.
65. Luis S. Villacana de Castro, "A Critique of Vygotsky's Misapprehension of Marx's 'Phenomenal Forms,'" *Science and Society* 79, no. 1 (2015): 90–113.
66. Vygotsky, "Thinking and Speech," 176.
67. V. John-Steiner and Holbrook Mahn, "Sociocultural Approaches to Learning and Development: A Vygotskian Framework," *Educational Psychologist* 31 (1996): 191–206.
68. Au, *Reclaiming Communist Philosophy*.
69. Freire, *Pedagogy of the Oppressed*, 1974 ed.; Freire, *Education for Critical Consciousness* (New York: Continuum, 1982).
70. Lenin, *What Is to Be Done?*, 48.
71. As quoted in, Frederic Lilge, "Lenin and the Politics of Education," *Slavic Review* 27, no. 2 (1968): 235–36.
72. Lilge, "Lenin and the Politics of Education."
73. Lev S. Vygotsky, "The Genesis of Higher Mental Functions," in James V. Wertsch, ed. and trans., *The Concept of Activity in Soviet Psychology* (Armonk, NY: M. E. Sharpe, 1981), 164.

74. Vygotsky, "The Genesis of Higher Mental Functions."
75. Ibid., 154.
76. Engels, *Dialectics of Nature.*
77. Cole and Scribner, "Introduction"; Villacana de Castro, "A Critique of Vygotsky's Misapprehension of Marx's 'Phenomenal Forms.'"
78. Vygotsky, "The Genesis of Higher Mental Functions," 162.
79. Ibid., 163.
80. Lev S. Vygotsky, "The Problem of the Cultural Development of the Child," *Journal of Genetic Psychology: Child Behavior, Animal Behavior, and Comparative Psychology* 36, no. 1 (1929): 427.
81. Vygotsky, "The Genesis of Higher Mental Functions," 158.
82. Ibid., 162.
83. Ibid., 164.
84. See, e.g., Pierre Bourdieu, *Distinction: A Social Critique of the Judgment of Taste,* R. Nice, trans. (Cambridge, MA: Routledge & Kegan Paul Ltd., 1984); Basil B. Bernstein, *Pedagogy, Symbolic Control, and Identity: Theory, Research, Critique: Critical Perspectives on Literacy and Education* (London: Taylor & Francis, 1996); Roy Nash, "The Cognitive Habitus: Its Place in a Realist Account of Inequality/Difference," *British Journal of Sociology of Education* 26, no. 5 (2005): 599–612.
85. Vygotsky, "The Genesis of Higher Mental Functions," 161.

Chapter 6

1. Apple, *Can Education Change Society?*
2. Apple, *Educating the Right Way.*
3. John D. Holst, "Paulo Freire in Chile, 1964–1969: Pedagogy of the Oppressed in Its Sociopolitical Economic Context," *Harvard Educational Review* 76, no. 2 (2006): 243–70.
4. Ana Maria Araujo Freire and Donaldo Macedo, "Introduction," in Ana Maria Araujo Freire and Donaldo Macedo, eds., *The Paulo Freire Reader* (New York: Continuum, 1998), 1–44.
5. Marx, *Capital,* vol. 1; Frantz Fanon, *The Wretched of the Earth,* 1st evergreen ed. (New York: Grove Press, 1966); Amílcar Cabral, *Revolution in Guinea: Selected Texts* (New York: Monthly Review, 1969); A. Memmi, *The Colonizer and the Colonized* (Boston: Beacon Press, 1967).
6. Jeremi Suri, *The Global Revolutions of 1968* (New York: W. W. Norton & Company, 2007).
7. Allan Luke, "Critical Literacy: Foundational Notes," *Theory into Practice* 51, no. 4 (2012): 4–11; Michael W. Apple and Wayne Au, "Introduction," and "General Introduction," in Michael W. Apple

and Wayne Au, eds., *Critical Education*, vol. 1 (New York: Routledge, 2015), 1–32; Makalani, "An Apparatus for Negro Women: Black Women's Organizing, Communism, and the Instutional Spaces for Radical Pan-African Thought"; Naison, *Communists in Harlem during the Depression*; Don-chean Chu, *Chairman Mao: Education of the Proletariat* (New York: Philosophical Library, 1980); Peter McLaren and Juha Suoranta, "Socialist Pedagogy," in Dave Hill, ed., *Contesting Neoliberal Education* (London: Routledge, 2009), 242–64.

8. Isaac Gottesman, "Sitting in the Waiting Room: Paulo Freire and the Critical Turn in the Field of Education," *Educational Studies* 46, no. 4 (2010): 376–99, doi:10.1080/00131941003782429.
9. Moacir Gadotti and Carlos Alberto Torres, "Paulo Freire: Education for Development," *Development and Change* 46, no. 2 (2009): 1255–67.
10. Paulo Freire, *Pedagogy of the Oppressed*, 30th anniv. ed. (New York: Bloomsbury Press, 2000).
11. Michael W. Apple, *Power, Meaning, and Identity: Essays in Critical Educational Studies*, Studies in the Postmodern Theories of Education (New York: Peter Lang, 1999); Daniel Schugurensky, "The Legacy of Paulo Freire: A Critical Review of His Contributions," *Convergence* 31, nos. 1–2 (1998): 17–29.
12. Au and Apple, "Freire, Critical Education, and the Environmental Crisis"; Rich Gibson, "Paulo Freire and Revolutionary Pedagogy for Social Justice," in E. W. Ross and Rich Gibson, eds., *Neoliberalism and Education Reform* (Cresskill, NJ: Hampton Press, 2006), 177–236; Ira Shor and Paulo Freire, *A Pedagogy for Liberation: Dialogues on Transforming Education* (South Hadley, MA: Bergin & Garvey Publishers, 1987); Ira Shor, ed., *Freire for the Classroom: A Sourcebook for Liberatory Teaching* (Portsmouth, NH: Boynton/Cook Publishers, Heinemann, 1987).
13. Peter McLaren, *Che Guevara, Paulo Freire, and the Pedagogy of Revolution*, Culture and Education Series (Lanham, MD: Rowman & Littlefield Publishers, 2000); Allman, *Revolutionary Social Transformation*; Antonia Darder, *Reinventing Paulo Freire* (Boulder, CO: Westview Press, 2002).
14. Here, I'm distinguishing between Freire's critical/liberatory pedagogy and Freire the person. As Gibson notes in "Paulo Freire and Revolutionary Pedagogy for Social Justice," Freire was Marxian in many areas, but he was also deeply religious in others. I would argue that Freire's pedagogy is perhaps more Marxist dialectical materialist than

is Freire the person.

15. M. Gadotti, *Pedagogy of Praxis: A Dialectical Philosophy of Education*, J. Milton, trans., 1st ed. (Albany, NY: State University of New York Press, 1996); see also Ollman, *Dance of the Dialectic*; Sayers, "Marxism and the Dialectical Method"; Allman, *Revolutionary Social Transformation*; Au, *Reclaiming Communist Philosophy*.
16. Benton and Craib, *Philosophy of Social Science*.
17. Cole and Scribner, "Introduction"; Engels, *Dialectics of Nature*; Au, *Reclaiming Communist Philosophy*; Lenin, *Materialism and Empirio-Criticism*.
18. Freire, *Pedagogy of the Oppressed*, 1974 ed.; Freire, *Education for Critical Consciousness*; Freire, *Pedagogy of Hope: Reliving Pedagogy of the Oppressed*, Robert R. Barr, trans., 2004 ed. (New York: Continuum Publishing Company, 1992); Freire, *Pedagogy of Indignation*, Series in Critical Narrative (Boulder, CO: Paradigm Publishers, 2004); Freire and Donaldo Macedo, *Literacy: Reading the Word and the World*, Donaldo Macedo, trans., Critical Studies in Education Series (Westport, CT: Bergin & Garvey, 1987); Shor and Freire, *A Pedagogy for Liberation*.
19. Freire, *Education for Critical Consciousness*, 146–47.
20. Paulo Freire, *Politics and Education*, Pia Lindquist Wong, trans. (Los Angeles: UCLA Latin American Center Publications, 1998), 19.
21. Raymond Allen Morrow and Carlos Alberto Torres, *Reading Freire and Habermas: Critical Pedagogy and Transformative Social Change* (New York: Teachers College Press, 2002), 34.
22. Lenin, *Materialism and Empirio-Criticism*; see also Roy Bhaskar, *Reclaiming Reality: A Critical Introduction to Contemporary Philosophy*, 2nd ed. (New York: Verso, 1989).
23. Freire, *Education for Critical Consciousness*, 3, 101, 149, 152, 161; see also Shor and Freire, *A Pedagogy for Liberation*, 100.
24. Peter Roberts, "Knowledge, Dialogue, and Humanization: Exploring Freire's Philosophy," in Michael Peters et al., eds., *Critical Theory and the Human Condition: Founders and Praxis*, Studies in the Post Modern Theory in Education, vol. 168 (New York: Peter Lang, 2003), 169–83.
25. Ibid.
26. Freire, *Education for Critical Consciousness*, 3, 4.
27. See Freire, *Pedagogy of the Oppressed*, 1974 ed.; Freire, *Education for Critical Consciousness*; Freire, *Pedagogy of Indignation*.
28. Grant Gilbert, "Marx, Wittgenstein, and the Problem of Consciousness," in Peters et al., *Critical Theory and the Human Condition*, 101–13; Marx and Engels, "The German Ideology: Part I."

29. Freire, in Rex Davis and Paulo Freire, "Education for Awareness: A Talk with Paulo Freire," in Robert Mackie, ed., *Literacy and Revolution: The Pedagogy of Paulo Freire* (New York: Continuum, 1981), 62.
30. Vygotsky, "Thinking and Speech"; Lenin, *What Is to Be Done?*.
31. Freire, *Pedagogy of the Oppressed*, 1974 ed., 107, original emphasis; Davis and Freire, "Education for Awareness: A Talk with Paulo Freire," 58, original emphasis.
32. Lev S. Vygotsky, "Development of Higher Mental Functions," in A. Leontyev, A. Luryia, and A. Smirnov, eds., *Psychological Research in the U.S.S.R.* (Moscow: Progress Publishers, 1966), 11–45.
33. Freire and Macedo, *Literacy: Reading the Word and the World*; Paulo Freire and Donaldo Macedo, "A Dialogue: Culture, Language, and Race," *Harvard Educational Review* 65, no. 3 (1995): 377–402; Roberts, "Knowledge, Dialogue, and Humanization."
34. Freire, *Education for Critical Consciousness*, 137.
35. Freire, *Politics and Education*, 20.
36. Freire, *Education for Critical Consciousness*, 102.
37. Davis and Freire, "Education for Awareness: A Talk with Paulo Freire"; Freire, *Pedagogy of the Oppressed*, 1974 ed.; Freire, *Education for Critical Consciousness*.
38. Roberts, "Knowledge, Dialogue, and Humanization."
39. Freire, in Shor and Freire, *A Pedagogy for Liberation*, 161.
40. Freire, *Pedagogy of the Oppressed*, 1974 ed.; Freire and Macedo, "A Dialogue: Culture, Language, and Race"; Shor and Freire, *A Pedagogy for Liberation: Dialogues on Transforming Education*.
41. Ronald D. Glass, "On Paulo Freire's Philosophy of Praxis and the Foundations of Liberation Education," *Educational Researcher* 30, no. 2 (2001): 15–25; Roberts, "Knowledge, Dialogue, and Humanization."
42. Davis and Freire, "Education for Awareness: A Talk with Paulo Freire," 59.
43. Freire, in ibid.
44. Rethinking Schools, official website; Zinn Education Project, "Zinn Education Project: Teaching a People's History," Zinn Education Project, 2017, https://zinnedproject.org.
45. Rowan Shafer, "The (young) People's Climate Conference: Teaching Global Warming to 3rd Graders," *Rethinking Schools* 31, no. 4 (2017), https://www.rethinkingschools.org/articles/the-young-people-s-climate-conference.
46. Freire, *Education for Critical Consciousness*, 56.
47. Shor and Freire, *A Pedagogy for Liberation*, 33.

48. Shafer, "The (Young) People's Climate Conference."
49. Freire, *Education for Critical Consciousness*, 107.
50. Shafer, "The (Young) People's Climate Conference."
51. Freire, *Pedagogy of the Oppressed*, 1974 ed., 70–71, original emphasis.
52. Freire, *Education for Critical Consciousness*, 154, original emphasis.
53. Ibid., 161.
54. Stephen Jay Gould, "The Geometer of Race," *Discover*, November 1, 1994, 65–69.
55. Haney Lopez, *White by Law: The Legal Construction of Race* (New York: New York University Press, 1996); Michael Omi and Howard Winant, *Racial Formations in the United States* (New York: Routledge, 2015).
56. Lopez, *White by Law*; Omi and Winant, *Racial Formations in the United States*.
57. Shor and Freire, *A Pedagogy for Liberation*, 98.
58. Freire, *Pedagogy of the Oppressed*, 1974 ed., 80–81.
59. Shor and Freire, *A Pedagogy for Liberation: Dialogues on Transforming Education*, 13.
60. Freire, *Pedagogy of the Oppressed*, 1974 ed., 77.
61. Ibid., 100, original emphasis.
62. Paulo Freire, *Pedagogy of Freedom: Ethics, Democracy, and Civic Courage*, Patrick Clarke, trans., 2001 ed., Critical Perspectives Series (New York: Rowman and Littlefield Publishers, 1998); Freire, *Education for Critical Consciousness*, 125.
63. Freire, *Pedagogy of the Oppressed*, 1974 ed., 67.
64. Freire, *Pedagogy of Hope*, 101, original emphasis.
65. Shor and Freire, *A Pedagogy for Liberation*, 46, original emphasis.
66. Ibid., 103.
67. Freire, *Pedagogy of Hope*, 66.
68. Shor and Freire, *A Pedagogy for Liberation*, 91.
69. Freire and Macedo, "A Dialogue: Culture, Language, and Race."
70. Wayne Au, "Addressing Redress: Japanese Americans' Reparations for Their Internment during World War II," in Edith Chen and Glenn Omatsu, eds., *Teaching about Asian Pacific Americans* (New York: Rowman & Littlefield, 2006), 163–80.
71. Jesse Hagopian, "My Greatest Teaching Moment," *Yes! Magazine*, March 14, 2012, http://www.yesmagazine.org/for-teachers/teacher-stories/my-greatest-teaching-moment.
72. Allman, *Revolutionary Social Transformation*.
73. C. A. Bowers and Frederique Apffel-Marglin, eds., *Rethinking Freire: Globalization and the Environmental Crisis* (Mahwah, NJ:

Lawrence Erlbaum Associates, 2005).

74. See, in *Rethinking Freire*, C. A. Bowers, "How the Ideas of Paulo Freire Contribute to the Cultural Roots of the Ecological Crisis"; Derek Rasmussen, "Cease to Do Evil, Then Learn to Do Good . . . (a Pedagogy for the Oppressor)"; Phyllis Robinson, "Whose Oppression Is This?: The Cultivation of Action in Dissolving the Dualistic Barrier"; Grimaldo Rengifo Vasquez, "Nurturance in the Andes"; Barbara Loyda Sanchez Bejarano, "Who Are the Oppressed?"; Gustavo Esteva, Dana L. Stuchul, and Madhu Suri Prakash, "From a Pedagogy of Liberation to Liberation from Pedagogy."

75. Au and Apple, "Freire, Critical Education, and the Environmental Crisis."

76. Bowers, "How the Ideas of Paulo Freire Contribute to the Cultural Roots of the Ecological Crisis"; Rasmussen, "Cease to Do Evil, Then Learn to Do Good"; Robinson, "Whose Oppression Is This?: The Cultivation of Action in Dissolving the Dualistic Barrier"; Vasquez, "Nurturance in the Andes."

77. See, e.g., Elizabeth Ellsworth, "Why Doesn't This Feel Empowering?: Working through the Repressive Myths of Critical Pedagogy," *Harvard Educational Review* 59, no. 3 (1989): 297–324; Kathleen Weiler, "Freire and a Feminist Pedagogy of Difference," *Harvard Educational Review* 61, no. 4 (1991): 449–74.

78. Curtis Acosta, "The Impact of Humanizing Pedagogies and Curriculum upon the Identities, Civic Engagement, and Political Activism of Chican@ Youth" (PhD diss., University of Arizona, 2015, http://hdl.handle.net/10150/556592).

79. Freire, *Pedagogy of the Oppressed*, 1974 ed.; Freire, *Education for Critical Consciousness*; Freire and Macedo, "A Dialogue."

80. Freire, *Education for Critical Consciousness*, 137.

81. Engels, *Dialectics of Nature*; Cole and Scribner, "Introduction"; David A. Gruenewald, "The Best of Both Worlds: A Critical Pedagogy of Place," *Educational Researcher* 32, no. 4 (2003): 3–12.

82. Bowers and Apffel-Marglin, eds., *Rethinking Freire*.

83. Bejarano, "Who Are the Oppressed?"; Esteva, Stuchul, and Prakash, "From a Pedagogy of Liberation to Liberation from Pedagogy"; Rasmussen, "Cease to Do Evil, Then Learn to Do Good"; Siddhartha, "From Conscientization to Interbeing: A Personal Journey," in *Rethinking Freire: Globalization and the Environmental Crisis*, C. A. Bowers and Frederique Apffel-Marglin, eds., 83–100 (Mahwah, NJ: Lawrence Erlbaum Associates, 2005).

84. McLaren, *Che Guevara, Paulo Freire, and the Pedagogy of Revolution.*
85. Freire, *Pedagogy of Hope*, 72.
86. Au and Apple, "Freire, Critical Education, and the Environmental Crisis."
87. Paulo Freire, "A Response," in Paulo Freire et al., eds., *Mentoring the Mentor: A Critical Dialogue with Paulo Freire*, Studies in the Postmodern Theories of Education (New York: Peter Lang, 1997), 328.
88. Au and Apple, "Freire, Critical Education, and the Environmental Crisis."
89. Freire, "A Response," 328; "Letters," *Harvard Educational Review* 60, no. 3 (1990): 388–405.
90. Ellsworth, "Why Doesn't This Feel Empowering?"
91. Rachel Sharp and Anthony Green, *Education and Social Control: A Study in Progressive Primary Education* (London: Routledge & Kegan Paul, 1975); Shor and Freire, *A Pedagogy for Liberation.*
92. Freire, "A Response," 328.
93. Weiler, "Freire and a Feminist Pedagogy of Difference."
94. Stephen Nathan Haymes, "Race, Pedagogy, and Paulo Freire," *Philosophy of Education Yearbook*, 2002, 151–59; Gloria Ladson-Billings, "I Know Why This Doesn't Feel Empowering: A Critical Race Analysis of Critical Pedagogy," in Freire et al., *Mentoring the Mentor*, 127–41; Zeus Leonardo, ed., *Critical Pedagogy and Race* (Malden, MA: Blackwell Publishing, 2005).
95. Weiler, "Freire and a Feminist Pedagogy of Difference."
96. Glass, "On Paulo Freire's Philosophy of Praxis and the Foundations of Liberation Education"; Ron Scapp, "The Subject of Education: Paulo Freire, Postmodernism, and Multiculturalism," in Freire et al., *Mentoring the Mentor*, 283–91; Weiler, "Freire and a Feminist Pedagogy of Difference."
97. Michelle Fine, "A Letter to Paulo," in Freire et al., *Mentoring the* Mentor, 89–97.
98. bell hooks, *Teaching to Transgress: Education as the Practice of Freedom* (New York: Routledge, 1994); Asgedet Stefanos, "African Women and Revolutionary Change: A Freirian and Feminist Perspective," in Freire et al., *Mentoring the Mentor*, 243–71; Weiler, "Freire and a Feminist Pedagogy of Difference."
99. See, e.g., Ricky Lee Allen, "Whiteness and Critical Pedagogy," in Leonardo, *Critical Pedagogy and Race*, 53–68; Daniel Solorzano and Tara Yosso, "Maintaining Social Justice Hopes within Academic Realities: A Freirean Approach to Critical Race/LatCrit Pedagogy," *Denver*

University Law Review, 78 (2001): 69–92.

100. Freire, "A Response," 309.
101. Freire and Macedo, "A Dialogue"; Freire and Macedo, *Literacy: Reading the Word and the World.*
102. Freire, "A Response," 309.
103. Freire, in Shor and Freire, *A Pedagogy for Liberation*, 11.
104. McLaren, *Che Guevara, Paulo Freire, and the Pedagogy of Revolution.*
105. See, e.g., Sol Stern, "Pedagogy of the Oppressor: Another Reason Why U.S. Ed Schools Are so Awful: The Ongoing Influence of Brazilian Marxist Paulo Freire," *City Journal*, 2009, https://www.city-journal.org/html/pedagogy-oppressor-13168.html.

Chapter 7

1. Herbert M. Kliebard, *The Struggle for the American Curriculum, 1893–1958*, 3rd ed. (New York: RoutledgeFalmer, 2004).
2. Au, *Unequal by Design*; Brown and Au, "Race, Memory, and Master Narratives: A Critical Essay on U.S. Curriculum History"; Au, Brown, and Calderon, *Reclaiming the Multicultural Roots of U.S. Curriculum.*
3. Christine Sleeter, "Ethnic Studies and the Struggle in Tucson," *Education Week* 31, no. 21 (2012), http://www.edweek.org/ew/articles/2012/02/15/21sleeter.h31.html?tkn=VRMFRGuUcYPvsaR7iQ0tSO0BuBkBdu8hRyIN&cmp=clp-edweek; J. Gabriel Ware, "Ethnic Studies Courses Break Down Barriers and Benefit Everyone—so Why the Resistance?," *Yes! Magazine*, March 23, 2017, http://www.yesmagazine.org/peace-justice/ethnic-studies-courses-break-down-barriers-and-benefit-everyone-so-why-the-resistance-20170323.
4. American Civil Liberties Union, "Campaigns to Undermine Sexuality Education in Public Schools," ACLU, official website, 2017, https://www.aclu.org/other/campaigns-undermine-sexuality-education-public-schools.
5. Eric Foner, "Twisting History in Texas," *Nation*, April 5, 2010, https://www.thenation.com/article/twisting-history-texas/; Bill Bigelow, "Those Awful Texas Social Studies Standards: And What about Yours?," *Rethinking Schools* 24, no. 4 (2010): 46–48.
6. Melinda D. Anderson, "Rethinking History Class on Columbus Day: The Importance of Exposing Students to the Many Truths about the Controversial Explorer," *Atlantic*, October 12, 2015, https://www.theatlantic.com/education/archive/2015/10/columbus-day-school

-holiday/409984/; Bigelow and Peterson, *Rethinking Columbus.*

7. Diana Hess, "Should Intelligent Design Be Taught in Social Studies?," *Social Education* 79, no. 3 (2006): 8–13; Eugenie C. Scott and Glenn Branch, eds., *Not in Our Classrooms: Why Intelligent Design Is Wrong for Our Schools* (Boston: Beacon Press, 2006).
8. Apple, *Official Knowledge.*
9. Wayne Au and Michael W. Apple, "The Curriculum and the Politics of Inclusion and Exclusion," in E. Tressou et al., eds., *Beyond Pedagogies of Exclusion in Diverse Childhood Contexts: Transnational Challenges* (New York: Palgrave Macmillan, 2009), 101–16.
10. Michael W. Apple, "Social Crisis and Curriculum Accords," *Educational Theory* 38, no. 2 (1988): 193.
11. Au and Apple, "The Curriculum and the Politics of Inclusion and Exclusion."
12. Hartsock, *The Feminist Standpoint Revisited and Other Essays*; Harding, "How Standpoint Methodology Informs Philosophy of Science."
13. Lukács, *History and Class Consciousness.*
14. Noah De Lissovoy, "Conceptualizing Oppression in Educational Theory: Toward a Compound Standpoint," *Cultural Studies–Critical Methodologies* 8, no. 1 (2008): 82–105, doi:10.1177/1532708607310794; Au, *Critical Curriculum Studies.*
15. Lukács, *History and Class Consciousness*, 164.
16. Harding, "How Standpoint Methodology Informs Philosophy of Science"; Benton and Craib, *Philosophy of Social Science.*
17. Chela Sandoval, *Methodology of the Oppressed* (Minneapolis: University of Minnesota Press, 2000); Hartsock, *The Feminist Standpoint Revisited and Other Essays*; Douglas A. Foley, Bradley A. Levinson, and Janise Hurtig, "Chapter 2: Anthropology Goes Inside: The New Educational Ethnography of Ethnicity and Gender," *Review of Research in Education* 25 (2000): 37–98, doi:10.3102/0091732X025001037.
18. Chela Sandoval, "U.S. Third World Feminism: The Theory and Method of Differential Oppositional Consciousness," in Harding, *The Feminist Standpoint Reader*, 195–210; Patricia Hill Collins, *Black Feminist Thought: Knowledge, Consciousness, and the Politics of Empowerment* (New York: Routledge, 2000).
19. Harding, "How Standpoint Methodology Informs Philosophy of Science," 67.
20. Collins, *Black Feminist Thought.*
21. Nick Wing, "When the Media Treats White Suspects and Killers Better than Black Victims," Black Voices, *Huffington Post*, August 14,

2014, http://www.huffingtonpost.com/2014/08/14/media-black-victims_n_5673291.html.

22. Sarah Ruiz-Grossman, "The Double Standard in How the Media Is Portraying the Las Vegas Shooter," Black Voices, *Huffington Post*, October 3, 2017, https://www.huffingtonpost.com/entry/double-standard-white-privilege-media-las-vegas-shooting_us_59d3da15e4b04b9f92058316.
23. Hartsock, *The Feminist Standpoint Revisited and Other Essays*, 107.
24. Hartsock, "The Feminist Standpoint: Developing the Ground for a Specifically Feminist Historical Materialism"; Hartsock, *The Feminist Standpoint Revisited and Other Essays*; Harding, "How Standpoint Methodology Informs Philosophy of Science"; Harding, "Rethinking Standpoint Empistemology."
25. Hartsock, *The Feminist Standpoint Revisited and Other Essays*; Harding, "How Standpoint Methodology Informs Philosophy of Science."
26. Hartsock, *The Feminist Standpoint Revisited and Other Essays*, 229.
27. Harding, "How Standpoint Methodology Informs Philosophy of Science," 68.
28. Hartsock, *The Feminist Standpoint Revisited and Other Essays*, 107.
29. Harding, "How Standpoint Methodology Informs Philosophy of Science," 68.
30. Hartsock, *The Feminist Standpoint Revisited and Other Essays*, 229.
31. Ibid.
32. Harding, "How Standpoint Methodology Informs Philosophy of Science," 68–69.
33. Sandoval, *Methodology of the Oppressed*.
34. Patricia Hill Collins, "The Social Construction of Black Feminist Thought," *Signs* 14, no. 4 (1989): 745–73.
35. Harding, "Rethinking Standpoint Epistemology," 128.
36. Hartsock, *The Feminist Standpoint Revisited and Other Essays*, 80.
37. Harding, "Rethinking Standpoint Epistemology," 134; Taylor, *From #Blacklivesmatter to Black Liberation*.
38. Harding, "Rethinking Standpoint Epistemology," 131.
39. Hartsock, *The Feminist Standpoint Revisited and Other Essays*, 236.
40. Harding, "What Is 'Strong Objectivity'?,"; Donna Haraway, *Simians, Cyborgs, and Women* (New York: Routledge, 1991).
41. Harding, "What Is 'Strong Objectivity'?," 136.
42. Ibid., 137.
43. See Wayne Au, "The Long March towards Revitalization: Developing Standpoint in Curriculum Studies," *Teachers College Record* 114, no.

5 (2012), http://www.tcrecord.org.

44. Bill Bigelow, "Scholastic Inc. Pushing Coal: A 4th-Grade Curriculum Lies through Omission," *Rethinking Schools* 25, no. 4 (2011), http://www.rethinkingschools.org/archive/25_04/25_04_bigelow.shtml.
45. Josh Golin et al., "Scholastic Severs Ties with the Coal Industry: Controversial Elementary School Materials Withdrawn after Protests," press release, Campaign for a Commercial-Free Childhood, Rethinking Schools, May 14, 2011, http://www.commercialfreechildhood.org/pressreleases/coalandscholasticwin.html.
46. Linda Christensen, "Putting out the Linguistic Welcome Mat," in Au, *Rethinking Multicultural Education*, 137–44.
47. Ibid., 138–39.
48. Eric Gutstein, "Math, SATs, and Racial Profiling," in Au, *Rethinking Multicultural Education*, 341–47.
49. Ibid., 342.
50. Au, "When Multicultural Education Is Not Enough."
51. Wayne Au, "What Curriculum Could Be: Utopian Dreams amidst a Dystopian Reality," *Kappa Delta Pi Record* 48, no. 2 (2012): 55–58.

Chapter 8

1. Au, *Unequal by Design*; Au, "Devising Inequality"; Au, "Teaching under the New Taylorism"; Au, "High-Stakes Testing and Curricular Control: A Qualitative Metasynthesis," *Educational Researcher* 36, no. 5 (2007): 258–67.
2. Au and Ferrare, "Sponsors of Policy."
3. See also Wayne Au, "Chartering Charade in Washington State: The Anti-Democratic Politics of the Charter School Movement and the Removal of the Public from Public Education," in Jamel K. Donner and Tara L. Affolter, eds., *The Charter School Solution: Distinguishing Fact from Rhetoric* (New York: Routledge, 2016), 1–19.
4. Au, "High-Stakes Testing and Curricular Control."
5. Au, "Devising Inequality."
6. Au, "Vygotsky and Lenin on Learning"; see also chapter 5 of this book.
7. Minerva Chavez, "Autoethnography, a Chicana's Methodological Research Tool: The Role of Storytelling for Those Who Have No Choice but to Do Critical Race Theory," *Equity and Excellence in Education* 45, no. 2 (2012): 334–48, doi:10.1080/10665684.2012.669196; H. Chang, *Autoethnography as Method* (Walnut Creek, CA: Left Coast Press, 2008).

8. Gabriella Gutiérrez y Muhs et al., eds., *Presumed Incompetent: The Intersections of Race and Class for Women in Academia* (Boulder, CO: University Press of Colorado, 2012).
9. For an example—where I am told by a local charter school advocate that I don't know how to read the research—see Robin Lake, "State Law and Implementation Matter," *Seattle Times*, October 23, 2012, http://seattletimes.com/html/northwestvoices/2017418193_arecharterschoolsthebestsolution.html?syndication=rss; see also Au, "Learning to Read," for my public response.
10. Au and Hagopian, "How One Elementary School Sparked a Citywide Movement to Make Black Students' Lives Matter"; Au, "Proud to Be a Garfield Bulldog"; Au, "The Idiocy of Policy: The Anti-Democratic Curriculum of High-Stakes Testing," *Critical Education* 1, no. 1 (2010): 1–16; Au, "Policy Memo on Washington State Initiative 1240," *Seattle Education*, October 22, 2012, http://seattleducation2010.wordpress.com/2012/10/22/policy-memo-on-washington-state-initiative-1240/.
11. Ellen Brantlinger, "An Application of Gramsci's 'Who Benefits?' to High-Stakes Testing," *Workplace* 6, no. 1 (2006), http://www.louisville.edu/journal/workplace/issue6p1/brantlinger.html.
12. Levine and Au, "Rethinking Schools: Enacting a Vision for Social Justice within US Education."
13. Hagopian, "Seattle Test Boycott."
14. Au, "Proud to Be a Garfield Bulldog."
15. Rethinking Schools, "Leading Educators Support Teacher Test Boycott."
16. Au, "Learning to Read."
17. Wayne Au, "The False Promise of Charter Schools," *Seattle Times*, October 23, 2012, http://seattletimes.com/html/opinion/2017379325_guest31au.html; Au, "Pro-Con: Charter Schools—Con: Statistics Show No Significant Advantage over Regular Public Education," *Spokesman-Review*, January 29, 2012, http://www.spokesman.com/stories/2012/jan/29/con-statistics-show-no-significant-advantage-over/.
18. Au, "Policy Memo on Washington State Initiative 1240."
19. Wayne Au, "Letter to the Editor: 'Half-Truths, Spin, and Obfuscation about Summit Sierra Charter,'" *International Examiner*, May 6, 2016, http://www.iexaminer.org/2016/05/letter-to-the-editor-half-truths-spin-and-obfuscation-about-summit-sierra-charter/.
20. Au, "A Perfect Education Storm in Washington State."
21. Ibid.
22. Ann Pelo, ed., *Rethinking Early Childhood Education* (Milwaukee,

WI: Rethinking Schools, 2008); Linda Christensen et al., eds., *Rethinking Elementary Education* (Milwaukee, WI: Rethinking Schools, 2012); Au, *Rethinking Multicultural Education.*

23. Bigelow and Peterson, *Rethinking Columbus.*
24. Vygotsky, "The Genesis of Higher Mental Functions," 161.
25. Otto Bell, dir., *The Eagle Huntress* (UK, USA: Kisaki Films, 2016), 1hr. 27min.
26. Credit to Brian Jones who, in his feedback on an earlier draft of this final chapter, came up with the phraseology about being the lone Marxist without having to be the lonely Marxist.
27. Albert L. Terry III, "A Few Words on Marxism and Identity Politics," *Left Voice*, January 8, 2017, http://www.leftvoice.org/A-Few-Words-on-Marxism-and-Identity-Politics; Kelton Sears, "A Marxist Critiques Identity Politics: A Q & A with Asad Haider, Founding Editor of Viewpoint Magazine, on an Ideology Fracturing the Left," *Seattle Weekly*, April 25, 2017, http://www.seattleweekly.com/news/a-marxist-critiques-identity-politics/; Rick Ayers, "Identity Politics—Considering a Few More Points," *Huffington Post*, June 16, 2017, http://www.huffingtonpost.com/entry/identity-politics-considering-a-few-more-points_us_5940537ee4b03e17eee0878f.
28. Keeanga-Yamahtta Taylor, ed., *How We Get Free: Black Feminism and the Combahee River Collective* (Chicago: Haymarket Books, 2017); Cherrie Moraga and Gloria Anzaldua, eds., *This Bridge Called My Back: Writings by Radical Women of Color*, 4th ed. (Albany, NY: State University of New York Press, 2015).
29. Taylor, *From #Blacklivesmatter to Black Liberation*, 216; see also, Gilbert, "Is Marxism Relevant?: Some Uses and Misuses."

Bibliography

Acosta, Curtis. "The Impact of Humanizing Pedagogies and Curriculum upon the Identities, Civic Engagement, and Political Activism of Chican@ Youth." PhD diss., University of Arizona, 2015. http://hdl.handle.net/10150/556592.

Accountability Works. "National cost of aligning states and localities to the Common Core Standards." Pioneer Institute American Principles Project Pacific Research Institute, Boston. Retrieved from http://www.accountabilityworks.org/photos/Cmmn_Cr_Cst_Stdy.Fin.2.22.12.pdf.

The Advancement Project. "Test, Punish, and Push Out: How 'Zero Tolerance' and High-Stakes Testing Funnel Youth into the School-to-Prison Pipeline." The Advancement Project, Washington, DC, 2010, https://b.3cdn.net/advancement/d05cb2181a4545db07_r2im6caqe.pdf.

Allen, Ricky Lee. "Whiteness and Critical Pedagogy." In *Critical Pedagogy and Race*, edited by Zeus Leonardo, 53–68. Malden, MA: Blackwell Publishing, 2005.

Allman, Paula. *Critical Education against Global Capitalism: Karl Marx and Revolutionary Critical Education*. 1st ed. Critical Studies in Education and Culture. Westport, CT: Bergin & Garvey, 2001.

———. *Revolutionary Social Transformation: Democratic Hopes, Political Possibilities, and Critical Education*. 1st ed. Critical Studies in Education and Culture Series. Westport, CT: Bergin & Garvey, 1999.

Allman, Paula, Peter McLaren, and Glenn Rikowski. "After the Box People: The Labour-Capital Relation as Class Constitution—and Its Consequences for Marxist Educational Theory and Human Resistance," 2000. http://www.ieps.org.uk.cwc.net/afterthebox.pdf.

Althusser, Louis. *For Marx*. New York: Pantheon Books, 1969.

———. *Lenin and Philosophy and Other Essays*. Translated by B. Brewster. New York: Monthly Review Books, 1971.

American Civil Liberties Union. "Campaigns to Undermine Sexuality Education in Public Schools." ACLU, 2017. https://www.aclu.org/other/campaigns-undermine-sexuality-education-public-schools.

American Statistical Association. "ASA Statement on Using Value-Added Models for Educational Assessment." American Statistical Association, 2014. https://www.amstat.org/policy/pdfs/ASA_VAM_Statement.pdf.

Amrein-Beardsley, Audrey. *Rethinking Value-Added Models in Education: Critical Perspectives on Tests and Assessment-Based Accountability*. New York: Routledge, 2014.

Anderson, Kevin B. *Marx at the Margins: On Nationalism, Ethnicity, and Non-Western Societies*. 2nd ed., expanded. Chicago: University of Chicago Press, 2016.

Anderson, Melinda D. "Rethinking History Class on Columbus Day: The Importance of Exposing Students to the Many Truths about the Controversial Explorer." *Atlantic*, October 12, 2015. https://www.theatlantic.com/education/archive/2015/10/columbus-day-school-holiday/409984/.

Anderson, Perry. *Arguments within English Marxism*. London: New Left Books, 1980.

Anyon, Jean. *Marx and Education*. Routledge Key Ideas in Education. New York: Routledge, 2011.

———. "Social Class and School Knowledge." *Curriculum Inquiry* 11, no. 1 (1981): 3–42.

———. "Social Class and the Hidden Curriculum of Work." *Journal of Education* 162, no. 1 (1980): 67–92.

Apple, Michael W. *Can Education Change Society?* New York: Routledge, 2012.

———. "Comparing Neo-Liberal Projects and Inequality in Education." *Comparative Education* 37, no. 4 (2001): 409–23.

———. *Educating the "Right" Way: Markets, Standards, God, and Inequality*. 2nd ed. New York: RoutledgeFalmer, 2006.

———. *Education and Power*. 2nd ed. New York: Routledge, 1995.

———. *Ideology and Curriculum*. 3rd ed. New York: RoutledgeFalmer, 2004.

———. *Official Knowledge: Democratic Education in a Conservative Age*. 2nd ed. New York: Routledge, 2000.

———. "The Other Side of the Hidden Curriculum: Correspondence Theories and the Labor Process." *Interchange* 11, no. 3 (1980): 5–22.

———. *Power, Meaning, and Identity: Essays in Critical Educational Studies*. Studies in the Postmodern Theories of Education. New York: Peter Lang, 1999.

———. "Reproduction and Contradiction in Education: An Introduction." In *Cultural and Economic Reproduction in Education: Essays on Class, Ideology, and the State*, edited by Michael W. Apple, 1st ed., 1–31. Boston: Routledge & Kegan Paul, 1982.

———. "Reproduction, Contestation, and Curriculum: An Essay in Self-Criticism." *Interchange* 12, nos. 2–3 (1981): 27–47.

———. "Social Crisis and Curriculum Accords." *Educational Theory* 38, no. 2 (1988): 191–201.

———. *Teachers and Texts: A Political Economy of Class and Gender Relations in Education*. New York: Routledge & Kegan Paul, 1986.

Apple, Michael W., and Wayne Au, eds. *Critical Education*. 4 vols. Major Themes in Education. New York: Routledge, 2014.

Apple, Michael W., and Kristen L. Buras. "Introduction." In *The Subaltern Speak: Curriculum, Power, and Educational Struggles*, edited by Michael W. Apple and Kristen L. Buras, 1–39. New York: Routledge, 2006.

Apple, Michael W., and Thomas C. Pedroni. "Conservative Alliance Building and African American Support of Vouchers: The End of Brown's Promise or a New Beginning?" *Teachers College Record* 107, no. 9 (2005): 2068–2105.

Au, Wayne. "Addressing Redress: Japanese Americans' Reparations for Their Internment during World War II." In *Teaching about Asian Pacific Americans*, edited by Edith Chen and Glenn Omastu, 163–80. New York: Rowman & Littlefield 2006.

———. "Against Economic Determinism: Revisiting the Roots of Neo-Marxism in Critical Educational Theory." *Journal for Critical Education Policy Studies* 4, no. 2 (2006). http://www.jceps.com/archives/520.

———. "And Ya Don't Stop." *Rethinking Schools* 12, no. 2 (1998): 16–17, 19.

———. "Between Education and the Economy: High-Stakes Testing and the Contradictory Location of the New Middle Class." *Journal of Education Policy* 23, no. 5 (2008): 501–13.

———. "Can We Test for Liberation?: Moving from Retributive to Restorative and Transformative Assessment in Schools." *Critical Education* 18, no. 13 (2017). http://ices.library.ubc.ca/index.php/criticaled/article/view/186313.

———. "Chartering Charade in Washington State: The Anti-Democratic Politics of the Charter School Movement and the Removal of the Public from Public Education." In *The Charter School Solution: Distinguishing Fact from Rhetoric*, edited by Jamel K. Donner and Tara L. Affolter, 1–19. New York: Routledge, 2016.

———. *Critical Curriculum Studies: Education, Consciousness, and the Politics of Knowing*. Critical Social Thought. New York: Routledge, 2011.

———. "Decolonizing the Classroom: Lessons in Multicultural Education." *Rethinking Schools* 23, no. 2 (2009): 27–30.

———. "Defending Dialectics: Rethinking the Neo-Marxist Turn in Critical Education Theory." In *Organizing Pedagogy: Educating for Social Justice and Socialism*, edited by Sheila Macrine, Peter McLaren, and Dave Hill. New York: Routledge, 2008.

———. "Devising Inequality: A Bernsteinian Analysis of High-Stakes Testing and Social Reproduction in Education." *British Journal of Sociology of Education* 29, no. 6 (2008): 639–51.

———. "Epistemology of the Oppressed: The Dialectics of Paulo Freire's Theory of Knowledge." *Journal for Critical Education Policy Studies* 5, no. 2 (2007). http://www.jceps.com/archives/551.

———. "The False Promise of Charter Schools." *Seattle Times*, October 23, 2012. http://seattletimes.com/html/opinion/2017379325_guest31au.html.

———. "Fighting with the Text: Critical Issues in the Development of Freirian Pedagogy." In *The Routledge Handbook of Critical Education*, edited by Michael W. Apple, Wayne Au, and Luis Armando Gandin, 83–95. New York: Routledge, 2009.

———. "Hiding behind High-Stakes Testing: Meritocracy, Objectivity, and Inequality in U.S. Education." *International Education Journal: Comparative Perspectives* 12, no. 2 (2013): 7–19.

———. "High-Stakes Testing and Curricular Control: A Qualitative Metasynthesis." *Educational Researcher* 36, no. 5 (2007): 258–67.

———. "High-Stakes Testing and Discursive Control: The Triple Bind for Non-Standard Student Identities." *Multicultural Perspectives* 11, no. 2 (2009): 65–71.

———. "High-Stakes Testing: A Tool for White Supremacy for 100 Years." In *What's Race Got to Do with It?: How Current School Reform Policy Maintains Racial and Economic Inequality*, edited by Bree Picower and Edwin Mayorga, 21–44. New York: Peter Lang, 2015.

———. "The Idiocy of Policy: The Anti-Democratic Curriculum of High-Stakes Testing." *Critical Education* 1, no. 1 (2010): 1–16.

———. "Just Whose Rights Do These Civil Rights Groups Think They Are Protecting?" The Answer Sheet, *Washington Post*, May 9, 2015. http://www.washingtonpost.com/blogs/answer-sheet/wp/2015/05/09/just-whose-rights-do-these-civil-rights-groups-think-they-are-protecting/.

———. "Learning to Read: Charter Schools, Public Education, and the Politics of Educational Research." Presentation at the Washington State

PTA Public Charter School Forum, Seattle, WA, February 29, 2012.

———. "Letter to the Editor: 'Half-Truths, Spin, and Obfuscation about Summit Sierra Charter.'" *International Examiner*, May 6, 2016. http://www.iexaminer.org/2016/05/letter-to-the-editor-half-truths-spin-and-obfuscation-about-summit-sierra-charter/.

———. "The Long March towards Revitalization: Developing Standpoint in Curriculum Studies." *Teachers College Record* 114, no. 5 (2012). http://www.tcrecord.org.

———. "Meritocracy 2.0: High-Stakes, Standardized Testing as a Racial Project of Neoliberal Multiculturalism." *Educational Policy* 30, no. 1 (2016): 39–62. doi:10.1177/0895904815614916.

———. "Neither Fair nor Accurate: Research Based Reasons Why High-Stakes Tests Should Not Be Used to Evaluate Teachers." *Rethinking Schools* 25, no. 2 (2010): 34–38.

———. "A Perfect Education Storm in Washington State." The Answer Sheet, *Washington Post*, September 10, 2015. https://www.washingtonpost.com/blogs/answer-sheet/wp/2015/09/10/a-perfect-education-storm-in-washington-state/.

———. "Policy Memo on Washington State Initiative 1240." *Seattle Education*, October 22, 2012. http://seattleducation2010.wordpress.com/2012/10/22/policy-memo-on-washington-state-initiative-1240/.

———. "Pro-Con: Charter Schools—Con: Statistics Show No Significant Advantage over Regular Public Education." *Spokesman-Review*, January 29, 2012. http://www.spokesman.com/stories/2012/jan/29/con-statistics-show-no-significant-advantage-over/.

———. "Proud to Be a Garfield Bulldog." *Rethinking Schools Blog*, January 12, 2013. http://rethinkingschoolsblog.wordpress.com/2013/01/12/proud-to-be-a-garfield-bulldog/.

———, ed. *Rethinking Multicultural Education: Teaching for Racial and Cultural Justice*. 2nd ed. Milwaukee, WI: Rethinking Schools, 2014.

———. "Social Justice and Resisting Neoliberal Education Reform in the USA." *Forum* 58, no. 3 (2016): 315–24. doi:http://dx.doi.org/10.15730/forum.2016.58.3.315.

———. "Teaching about the WTO." *Rethinking Schools* 14, no. 3 (2000): 4–5.

———. "Teaching in Dystopia: High-Stakes Testing's Stranglehold on Education." *Rethinking Schools* 22, no. 3 (2008): 22–24.

———. "Teaching under the New Taylorism: High-Stakes Testing and the Standardization of the 21st Century Curriculum." *Journal of Curriculum Studies* 43, no. 1 (2011): 25–45. doi:10.1080/00220272.2010.521261.

———. "Techies, the Tea Party, and the Common Core: The Rise of the New Upper Middle Class and Tensions in the Rightist Politics of Federal Education Reform." *Educational Forum* 80, no. 2 (2016). doi: 10.1080/00131725.2016.1135378.

———. *Unequal by Design: High-Stakes Testing and the Standardization of Inequality*. Critical Social Thought. New York: Routledge, 2009.

———. "Vygotsky and Lenin on Learning: The Parallel Structures of Individual and Social Development." *Science and Society* 71, no. 3 (2007): 273–98.

———. "What Curriculum Could Be: Utopian Dreams amidst a Dystopian Reality." *Kappa Delta Pi Record* 48, no. 2 (2012): 55–58.

———. "What's a Nice Test like You Doing in a Place like This?: The edTPA and Corporate Education Reform." *Rethinking Schools* 27, no. 4 (2013). http://www.rethinkingschools.org/archive/27_04/27_04_au.shtml.

———. "What the Tour Guide Didn't Tell Me: Paradise and the Politics of Tourist Hawai'i." In *Rethinking Our Classroom: Teaching for Equity and Justice*, edited by Bill Bigelow, Brenda Harvey, Stan Karp, and Larry Miller, 2:76–80. Milwaukee, WI: Rethinking Schools, 2001.

———. "When Multicultural Education Is Not Enough." *Multicultural Perspectives* 19, no. 3 (2017): 1–4. doi:10.1080/15210960.2017.1331741.

Au, Wayne, and Michael W. Apple. "The Curriculum and the Politics of Inclusion and Exclusion." In *Beyond Pedagogies of Exclusion in Diverse Childhood Contexts: Transnational Challenges.*, edited by E. Tressou, S. Mitakidou, Beth Swadener, Carl Grant, and W. Secada, 101–16. New York: Palgrave Macmillan, 2009.

———. "Freire, Critical Education, and the Environmental Crisis." *Educational Policy* 21, no. 3 (2007): 457–70.

———. "Rethinking Reproduction: Neo-Marxism in Critical Educational Theory." In *The Routledge Handbook of Critical Education*, edited by Michael W. Apple, Wayne Au, and Luis Armando Gandin, 83–95. New York: Routledge, 2009.

Au, Wayne, Anthony L. Brown, and Dolores Calderon. *Reclaiming the Multicultural Roots of U.S. Curriculum: Communities of Color and Official Knowledge in Education*. New York: Teachers College Press, 2016.

Au, Wayne, and Joseph J. Ferrare, eds. *Mapping Corporate Education Reform: Power and Policy Networks in the Neoliberal State*. New York: Routledge, 2015.

———. "Other People's Policy: Wealthy Elites and Charter School Reform in Washington State." In *Mapping Corporate Education Reform: Power and Policy Networks in the Neoliberal State*, edited by Wayne Au and Joseph J. Ferrare, 147–64. New York: Routledge, 2015.

———. "Sponsors of Policy: A Network Analysis of Wealthy Elites, Their Affiliated Philanthropies, and Charter School Reform in Washington State." *Teachers College Record* 116, no. 8 (2014): 1–24.

Au, Wayne, and Jesse Hagopian. "How One Elementary School Sparked a Citywide Movement to Make Black Students' Lives Matter." *Rethinking Schools* 32, no. 1 (2017): 11–18.

Au, Wayne, and Jesslyn Hollar. "Opting out of the Education Reform Industry." *Monthly Review* 67, no. 10 (2016): 29–37.

Au, Wayne, and Christopher A. Lubienski. "The Role of the Gates Foundation and the Philanthropic Sector in Shaping the Emerging Education Market: Lessons from the US on Privatization of Schools and Educational Governance." In *World Yearbook of Education 2016: The Global Education Industry*, edited by Antoni Verger, Christopher A. Lubienski, and Gita Steiner-Khamsi, 27–43. New York: Taylor & Francis, 2016.

Au, Wilson W. S. *Reclaiming Communist Philosophy: Marx, Lenin, Mao, and the Dialectics of Nature*. Marxist, Socialist, and Communist Studies in Education. Charlotte, NC: Information Age Publishing, 2017.

Ayers, Rick. "Identity Politics—Considering a Few More Points." *Huffington Post*, June 16, 2017. http://www.huffingtonpost.com/entry/identity-politics-considering-a-few-more-points_us_5940537ee4b03e17eee0878f.

Baker, Bruce D. "Exploring the Consequences of Charter School Expansion in U.S. Cities." Economic Policy Institute, November 30, 2016. http://epi.org/109218.

Baker, Eva L., Paul E. Barton, Linda Darling-Hammond, Edward Haertel, Helen F. Ladd, Robert L. Linn, Diane Ravitch, Richard Rothstein, Richard J. Shavelson, and Lorrie A. Shepard. "Problems with the Use of Student Test Scores to Evaluate Teachers." Economic Policy Institute, August 29, 2010. http://www.epi.org/publication/bp278/.

Baker, Olesya, and Kevin Lang. "The Effect of High School Exit Exams on Graduation, Employment, Wages, and Incarceration." Working paper. National Bureau of Economic Research, Cambridge, MA, 2013. http://www.nber.org/papers/w19182.pdf.

Baldoz, Rick. "'Comrade Carlos Bulosan': U.S. State Surveillance and the Cold War Suppression of Filipino Radicals." *Asia-Pacific Journal* 11, no. 33 (2014): 1–18.

Balfanz, R., V. Byrnes, and J. Fox. "Sent Home and Put off Track: The Antecedents, Disproportionalities, and Consequences of Being Suspended in the 9th Grade." In *Closing the School Discipline Gap: Equitable Remedies for Excessive Exclusion*, edited by Daniel J. Losen, 17–30. New York: Teachers College Press, 2015.

Barkan, Joanne. "Got Dough?: How Billionaires Rule Our Schools." *Dissent* 58, no. 1 (2011): 49–57. doi:10.1353/dss.2011.0023.

———. "Hired Guns on Astroturf: How to Buy and Sell School Reform." *Dissent* 59, no. 2 (2012): 49–57.

Barker, Michael J. "Bill Gates as Social Engineer: Introducing the World's Largest Liberal Philanthropist." *ZNet*. July 16, 2008. https://zcomm.org/znetarticle/bill-gates-philanthropy-and-social-engineering-part-1-of-3-by-michael-barker/.

Bejarano, Barbara Loyda Sanchez. "Who Are the Oppressed?" In *Rethinking Freire: Globalization and the Environmental Crisis*, edited by C. A. Bowers and Frederique Apffel-Marglin, 49–67. Mahwah, NJ: Lawrence Erlbaum Associates, 2005.

Bell, Otto, dir. *The Eagle Huntress*. UK, USA: Kisaki Films, 2016. 1 hr. 27 min.

Benton, Ted, and Ian Craib. *Philosophy of Social Science: The Philosophical Foundations of Social Thought*. Traditions in Social Theory. New York: Palgrave, 2001.

Berliner, David C. "Effects of Inequality and Poverty vs. Teachers and Schooling on America's Youth." *Teachers College Record* 115, no. 12 (2013). http://www.tcrecord.org.

Bernal, Martin. *Black Athena: The Afroasiatic Roots of Classical Civilization*. 3 vols. New Brunswick, NJ: Rutgers University Press, 1987.

Bernstein, Basil B. *Class Codes and Control Volume 3: Towards a Theory of Educational Transmissions*. 2nd ed. Primary Socialization, Language and Education, vol. 3. London: Routledge & Kegan Paul, 1977.

———. *Pedagogy, Symbolic Control, and Identity: Theory, Research, Critique*. Critical Perspectives on Literacy and Education. London: Taylor & Francis, 1996.

———. *The Structuring of Pedagogic Discourse*. 1st ed. Class, Codes, and Control, vol. 4. New York: Routledge, 1990.

Bhaskar, Roy. *Reclaiming Reality: A Critical Introduction to Contemporary Philosophy*. 2nd ed. New York: Verso, 1989.

Bigelow, Bill. "Scholastic Inc. Pushing Coal: A 4th-Grade Curriculum Lies through Omission." *Rethinking Schools* 25, no. 4 (2011). http://www.rethinkingschools.org/archive/25_04/25_04_bigelow.shtml.

———. "Those Awful Texas Social Studies Standards: And What about Yours?" *Rethinking Schools* 24, no. 4 (2010): 46–48.

Bigelow, Bill, and Bob Peterson, eds. *Rethinking Columbus: The next 500 Years*. 2nd ed. Milwaukee, WI: Rethinking Schools, 1998.

Bigelow, Bill, and Tim Swinehart, eds. *A People's Curriculum for the Earth: Teaching Climate Change and the Environmental Crisis*. Milwaukee, WI: Rethinking Schools, 2014.

Blanck, Guillermo. "Vygotsky: The Man and His Cause." In *Vygotsky and Education: Instructional Implications and Applications of Sociohistorical Psychology*, edited by Luis C. Moll, 31–58. New York: Cambridge University Press, 1990.

Board of Governors of the Federal Reserve. "Changes in U.S. Family Finances from 2013 to 2016: Evidence from the Survey of Consumer Finances." *Federal Reserve Bulletin* 103, no. 3 (2017): 1–42. https://www.federalreserve.gov/publications/files/scf17.pdf.

Bochenek, Michael, and A. Widney Brown. *Hatred in the Hallways: Violence and Discrimination against Lesbian, Gay, Bisexual, and Transgender Students in U.S. Schools*. Report. Human Rights Watch, 2001. http://www.hrw.org/reports/2001/uslgbt/toc.htm.

Bonastia, Christopher. "The Racist History of the Charter School Movement: Touted as the Cure for What Ails Public Education, Charter Schools Have Historical Roots That Are Rarely Discussed." *AlterNet*, January 6, 2015. http://www.alternet.org/education/racist-history-charter-school-movement.

Bourdieu, Pierre. *Distinction: A Social Critique of the Judgment of Taste*. Translated by R. Nice. Cambridge, MA: Routledge & Kegan Paul Ltd., 1984.

Bourdieu, Pierre, and J. Passeron. *Reproduction in Education, Society, and Culture*. Beverly Hills, CA: Sage, 1977.

Bowers, C. A. "How the Ideas of Paulo Freire Contribute to the Cultural Roots of the Ecological Crisis." In *Rethinking Freire: Globalization and the Environmental Crisis*, edited by C. A. Bowers and Frederique Apffel-Marglin, 133–50. Mahwah, NJ: Lawrence Erlbaum Associates, 2005.

Bowers, C. A., and Frederique Apffel-Marglin, eds. *Rethinking Freire: Globalization and the Environmental Crisis*. Mahwah, NJ: Lawrence Erlbaum Associates, 2005.

Bowles, S., and H. Gintis. *Schooling in Capitalist America: Educational Reform and the Contradictions of Economic Life*. 1st ed. New York: Basic Books, 1976.

Bracey, Gerald W. *Setting the Record Straight*. Portsmouth, NH: Heinemann, 2004.

Brantlinger, Ellen. "An Application of Gramsci's 'Who Benefits?' to High-

Stakes Testing." *Workplace* 6, no. 1 (2006). http://www.louisville.edu/journal/workplace/issue6p1/brantlinger.html.

Brooks, Mick. "An Introduction to Marx's Labour Theory of Value—Part Two." *In Defence of Marxism*, October 15, 2002. https://www.marxist.com/marx-marxist-labour-theory-value2.htm.

Brown, Anthony L., and Wayne Au. "Race, Memory, and Master Narratives: A Critical Essay on U.S. Curriculum History." *Curriculum Inquiry* 44, no. 3 (2014): 358–89. doi:10.1111/curi.12049.

Brown, Anthony L., and Noah De Lissovoy. "Economies of Racism: Grounding Education Policy Research in the Complex Dialectic of Race, Class, and Capital." *Journal of Education Policy* 26, no. 5 (2011): 595–619.

Bruenig, Matt. "Wealth Inequality Is Higher than Ever." *Jacobin*, October 1, 2017. https://www.jacobinmag.com/2017/10/wealth-inequality-united-states-federal-reserve.

Bruner, Jerome S. "Prologue to the English Edition." In *The Collected Works of L. S. Vygotsky: Problems of General Psychology Including the Volume Thinking and Speech*, edited by Robert W. Rieber and Aaron Carton, translated by Norris Minick, 1–16. Cognition and Language, vol. 1. New York: Plenum Press, 1987.

———. "Vygotsky's Zone of Proximal Development: The Hidden Agenda." In *Children's Learning in the "Zone of Proximal Development,"* edited by Barbara Rogoff and James V. Wertsch, 93–97. New Directions for Child Development, vol. 23. San Francisco: Jossey-Bass Inc., 1984.

Buras, Kristen L. "Questioning Core Assumptions: A Critical Reading of and Response to E. D. Hirsch's *The Schools We Need and Why We Don't Have Them*." *Harvard Educational Review* 69, no. 1 (1999): 67–93.

Burch, Patricia. *Hidden Markets: The New Education Privatization*. New York: Routledge, 2009.

———. "The New Educational Privatization: Educational Contracting and High Stakes Accountability." *Teachers College Record* 108, no. 12 (2006): 2582–2610.

Burke, Kenneth. *A Rhetoric of Motives*. Berkeley: University of California Press, 1950.

Burris, Carol. "School Choice a Sham, Profits on the Taxpayers' Dime." *Capitol Times*, April 6, 2017. http://azcapitoltimes.com/news/2017/04/06/school-choice-profits-on-the-taxpayers-dime/.

Bush, G. W. "The future of educational reform." Speech at the Manhattan Institute, New York, October 5, 1999. Retrieved from http://www.manhattan-institute.org/html/bush_speech.htm.

Butler-Wall, Annika, Kim Cosier, Rachel Harper, Jeff Sapp, Jody Sokolower, and Melissa Bollow Tempel, eds. *Rethinking Sexism, Gender, and Sexuality*. Milwaukee, WI: Rethinking Schools, 2016.

Cabral, Amílcar. *Revolution in Guinea; Selected Texts*. New York: Monthly Review Press, 1969.

Carlson, Dennis L. "Beyond the Reproductive Theory of Teaching." In *Bowles and Gintis Revisited: Correspondence and Contradiction in Educational Theory*, edited by Mike Cole, 158–73. New York: The Falmer Press, 1988.

Carnoy, Martin. "Education, Economy, and the State." In *Cultural and Economic Reproduction in Education: Essays on Class, Ideology, and the State*, edited by Michael W. Apple, 79–126. Boston: Routledge & Kegan Paul, 1982.

Carnoy, Martin, and Henry M. Levin. *Schooling and Work in the Democratic State*. Stanford, CA: Stanford University Press, 1985.

The Center for Popular Democracy, and Integrity in Education. *Charter School Vulnerabilities to Waste, Fraud, and Abuse.* Report. May 2014, https://www.scribd.com/doc/221993993/Charter-School-Vulnerabilities-to-Waste-Fraud-Abuse.

Center for Research on Education Outcomes (CREDO). *Multiple Choice: Charter School Performance in 16 States*. Report. June 2009. http://credo.stanford.edu/reports/MULTIPLE_CHOICE_CREDO.pdf.

———. *National Charter School Study 2013.* Report. June 2013. http://credo.stanford.edu.

Chacon, Justin Akers. *Radicals in the Barrio: Magonistas, Socialists, Wobblies, and Communists in the Mexican-American Working Class.* Chicago: Haymarket Books, 2017.

Chaiklin, Seth. "The Zone of Proximal Development in Vygotsky's Analysis of Learning and Instruction." In *Vygotsky's Educational Theory in Cultural Context*, edited by Alex Kozulin, Boris Gindis, Vladimir S. Ageyev, and Suzanne M. Miller, 39–64. Learning in Doing: Social, Cognitive, and Computational Perspectives. New York: Cambridge University Press, 2003.

Chambers, Sarah. "Ice the ISAT: Boycotting the Test under Mayor Rahm Emanuel's Regime." In *More Than a Score: The New Uprising against High-Stakes Testing*, edited by Jesse Hagopian, 113–22. Chicago: Haymarket Books, 2014.

Chang, H. *Autoethnography as Method.* Walnut Creek, CA: Left Coast Press, 2008.

Chang, Jeff. *Can't Stop Won't Stop: A History of the Hip Hop Generation.*

New York: St. Martin's Press, 2005.

Chavez, Minerva. "Autoethnography, a Chicana's Methodological Research Tool: The Role of Storytelling for Those Who Have No Choice but to Do Critical Race Theory." *Equity and Excellence in Education* 45, no. 2 (2012): 334–48. doi:10.1080/10665684.2012.669196.

Chin, Frank, and J. P. Chan. "Racist Love." In *Seeing through Shuck*, edited by Richard Kostelanetz. New York: Ballantine Books, 1972.

Chmielewski, Anna K., and Sean F. Reardon. "State of the Union—The Poverty and Inequality Report 2016: Education." Stanford Center on Poverty and Inequality, 2016.

Choy, Christine, and Renee Tajima-Pena, dirs. *Who Killed Vincent Chin?* 35 mm, documentary. Public Broadcasting Service, 1987.

Christensen, Linda. "Putting out the Linguistic Welcome Mat." In *Rethinking Multicultural Education: Teaching for Racial and Cultural Justice*, edited by Wayne Au, 2nd ed. 137–44. Milwaukee, WI: Rethinking Schools, 2014.

Christensen, Linda, Mark Hansen, Bob Peterson, Elizabeth Schlessman, and Dyan Watson, eds. *Rethinking Elementary Education*. Milwaukee, WI: Rethinking Schools, 2012.

Chu, Don-chean. *Chairman Mao: Education of the Proletariat*. New York: Philosophical Library, 1980.

Churchill, Ward, ed. *Marxism and Native Americans*. Boston: South End Press, 1983.

Coben, D. "Revisiting Gramsci." *Studies in the Education of Adults* 27, no. 1 (1995): 36–52.

Cody, Anthony. "Gates Money Attempts to Shift the Education Conversation to Successes." *Living in Dialogue*, December 12, 2014. http://www.livingindialogue.com/money-attempts-shift-education-conversation-successes/.

Coleman, J. S., et al. *Equality of Educational Opportunity*. Washington, DC: US Government Printing Office, 1966.

Cole, Michael, and Yrjö Engeström. "A Cultural-Historical Approach to Distributed Cognition." In *Distributed Cognitions: Psychological and Educational Considerations*, edited by Gavriel Salomon, 1–46. Cambridge, UK: Cambridge University Press, 1997.

Cole, Michael, and Sylvia Scribner. "Introduction." In *Mind in Society*, by L. S. Vygotsky, 1–14. Cambridge, MA: Harvard University Press, 1978.

Cole, Mike, ed. *Bowles and Gintis Revisited: Correspondence and Contradiction in Educational Theory*. 1st ed. Philadelphia: The Falmer Press, 1988.

Collins, Patricia Hill. *Black Feminist Thought: Knowledge, Consciousness, and the Politics of Empowerment*. New York: Routledge, 2000.

———. "The Social Construction of Black Feminist Thought." *Signs* 14, no. 4 (1989): 745–73.

Compton, Mary, and Lois Weiner, eds. *The Global Assault on Teaching, Teachers, and Their Unions: Stories for Resistance*. New York: Palgrave Macmillan, 2008.

Coulthard, Glen Sean. *Red Skin, White Masks: Rejecting the Colonial Politics of Recognition*. Minneapolis: University of Minnesota Press, 2014.

Counts, George S. *Dare the Schools Build a New Social Order?* New York: John Day, 1932.

Crowley, Thomas. "The Many Faces of the Indian Left: In India, Even as Prominent Left Parties Falter, Radicalism Persists." *Jacobin*, May 12, 2014. https://www.jacobinmag.com/2014/05/the-many-faces-of-the-indian-left/.

D'Amato, Paul. "The Myth of Lenin's Elitism." *International Socialist Review* 60 (2008). http://www.isreview.org/issues/60/feat-leninmyth.shtml.

Dance, J. L. *Tough Fronts: The Impact of Street Culture on Schooling*. 1st ed. Critical Social Thought. New York: RoutledgeFalmer, 2002.

Darder, Antonia. *Reinventing Paulo Freire*. Boulder, CO: Westview Press, 2002.

Darling-Hammond, Linda. "Race, Inequality, and Educational Accountability: The Irony of 'No Child Left Behind.'" *Race, Ethnicity, and Education* 10, no. 3 (2007): 245–60.

Davis, Rex, and Paulo Freire. "Education for Awareness: A Talk with Paulo Freire." In *Literacy and Revolution: The Pedagogy of Paulo Freire*, edited by Robert Mackie, 57–69. New York: Continuum, 1981.

Davydov, Vassily V. "The Basic Concepts of Contemporary Psychology." *Soviet Education* 30, no. 8 (1988): 15–43.

———. "From the History of General and Child Psychology." *Soviet Education* 30, no. 10 (1988): 42–77.

De Lissovoy, Noah. "Conceptualizing Oppression in Educational Theory: Toward a Compound Standpoint." *Cultural Studies–Critical Methodologies* 8, no. 1 (2008): 82–105. doi:10.1177/1532708607310794.

———. *Education and Emancipation in the Neoliberal Era: Being, Teaching, and Power*. New York: Palgrave Macmillan, 2015.

DiMaggio, Dan. "The Loneliness of the Long-Distance Test Scorer." *Monthly Review* 62, no. 7 (2012). http://monthlyreview.org/2010/12/01/the-loneliness-of-the-long-distance-test-scorer.

Dingerson, Leigh, Barbara Miner, Bob Peterson, and Stephanie Walters, eds. *Keeping the Promise?: The Debate over Charter Schools*. Milwaukee, WI: Rethinking Schools, 2008.

Diop, Cheikh Anta. *The African Origin of Civilization: Myth or Reality*. Chicago: Lawrence Hill, 1974.

———. *Civilization or Barbarism: An Authentic Anthropology*. Chicago: Chicago Review Press, 1991.

Dirlik, Arif. "Mao Zedong and 'Chinese Marxism.'" In *Marxism beyond Marxism*, edited by Saree Makdisi, Cesare Casarino, and Rebecca E. Karl, 119–48. New York: Routledge, 1996.

Dixon, Aaron. *My People Are Rising: Memoir of a Black Panther Party Captain*. Chicago: Haymarket Books, 2012.

Dumas, Michael J. "My Brother as 'Problem': Neoliberal Governmentality and Interventions for Black Young Men and Boys." *Educational Policy* 30, no. 1 (2015): 94–113.

———. "'Waiting for Superman' to Save Black People: Racial Representation and the Official Antiracism of Neoliberal School Reform." *Discourse: Studies in the Cultural Politics of Education* 34, no. 4 (2013): 531–47. doi:http://dx.doi.org/10.1080/01596306.2013.822621.

Eidelson, Josh. "Christie's Charter School Nightmare: 'White Flight, and They're Bankrupting Us.'" *Salon*, May 13, 2014. http://www.salon.com/2014/03/13/christies_charter_school_nightmare_white_flight_and_they're_bankrupting_us/.

Ellsworth, Elizabeth. "Why Doesn't This Feel Empowering?: Working through the Repressive Myths of Critical Pedagogy." *Harvard Educational Review* 59, no. 3 (1989): 297–324.

Engels, Frederick. *Dialectics of Nature*. Translated by C. Dutt. 1st ed. New York: International Publishers, 1940.

———. "Engels to C. Schmidt in Berlin." In Karl Marx and Frederick Engels, *Selected Works*, 694–99. New York: International Publishers, 1968.

———. "Engels to F. Mehring in Berlin." In Marx and Engels, *Selected Works*, 699–703.

———. "Engels to H. Borgius in Breslau." In Marx and Engels, *Selected Works*, 704–6.

———. "Engels to J. Bloch in Konigsberg." In Marx and Engels, *Selected Works*, 692–93.

———. "Ludwig Feuerbach and the End of Classical German Philosophy." In Marx and Engels, *Selected Works*, 596–618.

Esteva, Gustavo, Dana L. Stuchul, and Madhu Suri Prakash. "From a Pedagogy of Liberation to Liberation from Pedagogy." In *Rethinking Freire: Globalization and the Environmental Crisis*, edited by C. A. Bowers and Frederique Apffel-Marglin, 13–30. Mahwah, NJ: Lawrence Erlbaum Associates, 2005.

Ewert, Stephanie, Bryan L. Sykes, and Becky Pettit. "The Degree of Disadvantage: Incarceration and Inequality in Education." *Annals of the American Academy of Political and Social Science* 651 (2014): 24–43. doi:10.1177/0002716213503100.

Fabricant, Michael, and Michelle Fine. *The Changing Politics of Education: Privatization and the Dispossessed Lives Left Behind.* Boulder, CO: Paradigm Publishers, 2013.

Fang, Lee. "Venture Capitalists Are Poised to 'Disrupt' Everything about the Education Market." *Nation*, September 25, 2014. https://www.thenation.com/article/venture-capitalists-are-poised-disrupt-everything-about-education-market/.

Fanon, Frantz. *The Wretched of the Earth.* 1st evergreen ed. New York: Grove Press, 1966.

Farley, Todd. *Making the Grades: My Misadventures in the Standardized Testing Industry.* San Francisco: Berrett-Koehler, 2009.

———. "My Misadventures in the Standardized Testing Industry." The Answer Sheet, *Washington Post*, December 18, 2009. http://voices.washingtonpost.com/answer-sheet/standardized-tests/-gerald-martineaupost-today-my.html.

———. "A Test Scorer's Lament." *Rethinking Schools* 23, no. 2 (2010). http://www.rethinkingschools.org/archive/23_02/test232.shtml.

Fine, Michelle. "A Letter to Paulo." In *Mentoring the Mentor: A Critical Dialogue with Paulo Freire*, edited by Paulo Freire, with James W. Fraser, Donaldo Macedo, Tanya McKinnon, William T. Stokes, and Shirley Steinberg, 89–97. Studies in the Postmodern Theories of Education. New York: Peter Lang, 1997.

Fine, Michelle, and Michael Fabricant. "What It Takes to Unite Teachers Unions and Communities of Color: Overcoming Years of Tensions and Divisions, Parents and Teachers Are Linking Arms to Save Public Schools." *Nation*, October 13, 2014. https://www.thenation.com/article/what-it-takes-unite-teachers-unions-and-communities-color/.

Fine, Michelle, and Jessica Ruglis. "Circuits and Consequences of Dispossession: The Racialized Realignment of the Public Sphere for U.S. Youth." *Transforming Anthropology* 17, no. 1 (2009): 20–33. doi:10.1111/j.1548-7466.2009.01037.x.

Foley, Douglas A., Bradley A. Levinson, and Janise Hurtig. "Chapter 2: Anthropology Goes Inside: The New Educational Ethnography of Ethnicity and Gender." *Review of Research in Education* 25 (2000): 37–98. doi:10.3102/0091732X025001037.

Foner, Eric. "Twisting History in Texas." *Nation*, April 5, 2010. 48638510.

Foster, John Bellamy. "Marxism and Ecology: Common Fonts of a Great Transition." *Monthly Review* 67, no. 7 (2015). http://monthlyreview.org/2015/12/01/marxism-and-ecology/.

———. "The Opt Out Revolt: Democracy and Education." *Monthly Review* 67, no. 10 (2016). http://monthlyreview.org/2016/03/01/the-opt-out-revolt/.

———. "The Return of Engels: On the Occasion of His Birthday, Let's Celebrate the Incredible Contributions of Marx Collaborator Friedrich Engels." *Jacobin* 68, no. 10 (March, 2017). https://www.jacobinmag.com/2016/11/engels-marx-ecology-climate-crisis-materialism/.

Frankenberg, Erica, Genevieve Siegel-Hawley, and Jia Wang. "Choice without Equity: Charter School Segregation." *Educational Policy Analysis Archives* 19, no. 1 (2013). http://epaa.asu.edu/ojs/article/view/779.

Fraser, Nancy. "From Redistribution to Recognition? Dilemmas of Justice in a 'Post-Socialist' Age." *New Left Review* 212 (1995): 68–93.

Frawley, William. *Vygotsky and Cognitive Science: Language and the Unification of the Social and Computational Mind.* Cambridge, MA: Harvard University Press, 1997.

Freire, Ana Maria Araujo, and Donaldo Macedo. "Introduction." In *The Paulo Freire Reader*, edited by Ana Maria Araujo Freire and Donaldo Macedo, 1–44. New York: Continuum, 1998.

Freire, Paulo. *Education for Critical Consciousness.* New York: Continuum, 1982.

———. *Pedagogy of Freedom: Ethics, Democracy, and Civic Courage.* Translated by Patrick Clarke. 2001 ed. Critical Perspectives Series. New York: Rowman and Littlefield, 1998.

———. *Pedagogy of Hope: Reliving Pedagogy of the Oppressed.* Translated by Robert R. Barr. 2004 ed. New York: Continuum, 1992.

———. *Pedagogy of Indignation.* Series in Critical Narrative. Boulder, CO: Paradigm Publishers, 2004.

———. *Pedagogy of the Oppressed.* Translated by Myra Bergman Ramos. New York: Seabury Press, 1974.

———. *Pedagogy of the Oppressed.* 30th anniversary edition. New York: Bloomsbury Press, 2000.

———. *Politics and Education.* Translated by Pia Lindquist Wong. Los Angeles: UCLA Latin American Center Publications, 1998.

———. "A Response." In *Mentoring the Mentor: A Critical Dialogue with Paulo Freire*, edited by Paulo Freire, with James W. Fraser, Donaldo Macedo, Tanya McKinnon, William T. Stokes, and Shirley Steinberg, 303–29. Studies in the Postmodern Theories of Education. New York:

Peter Lang, 1997.

Freire, Paulo, and Donaldo Macedo. "A Dialogue: Culture, Language, and Race." *Harvard Educational Review* 65, no. 3 (1995): 377–402.

———. *Literacy: Reading the Word and the World.* Translated by Donaldo Macedo. Critical Studies in Education Series. Westport, CT: Bergin & Garvey, 1987.

Gadotti, M. *Pedagogy of Praxis: A Dialectical Philosophy of Education.* Translated by J. Milton. 1st ed. Albany, NY: State University of New York Press, 1996.

Gadotti, Moacir, and Carlos Alberto Torres. "Paulo Freire: Education for Development." *Development and Change* 46, no. 2 (2009): 1255–67.

Galeano, Eduardo. *Open Veins of Latin America: Five Centuries of the Pillage of a Continent.* New York: New York University Press, 1998.

Garza, Alicia. "Our Cynicism Will Not Build a Movement. Collaboration Will." *Mic*, January 26, 2017. https://mic.com/articles/166720/blm-co-founder-protesting-isnt-about-who-can-be-the-most-radical-its-about-winning#.JzNEW3kZQ.

Gates, Bill, Jr. "Speech Delivered to the National Conference of State Legislatures," 2009. http://www.gatesfoundation.org/media-center/speeches/2009/07/bill-gates-national-conference-of-state-legislatures-ncsl.

Gibson, Rich. "Paulo Freire and Revolutionary Pedagogy for Social Justice." In *Neoliberalism and Education Reform*, edited by E. W. Ross and Rich Gibson, 177–236. Cresskill, NJ: Hampton Press, 2006.

Gilbert, David. "Is Marxism Relevant?: Some Uses and Misuses." *Abolition*, January 16, 2017. https://abolitionjournal.org/is-marxism-relevant-some-uses-and-misuses-by-david-gilbert-political-prisoner/.

Gilbert, Grant. "Marx, Wittgenstein, and the Problem of Consciousness." In *Critical Theory and the Human Condition: Founders and Praxis*, edited by Michael Peters, Colin Lankshear, Mark Olssen, and Shirley R. Steinberg, 101–13. Studies in the Post Modern Theory in Education, vol. 168. New York: Peter Lang, 2003.

Ginwright, S. A. *Black in School: Afrocentric Reform, Urban Youth, and the Promise of Hip-Hop Culture.* 1st ed. New York: Teachers College Press, 2004.

Giroux, Henry A. "Beyond the Correspondence Theory: Notes on the Dynamics of Educational Reproduction and Transformation." *Curriculum Inquiry* 10, no. 3 (1980): 225–47.

———. "Hegemony, Resistance, and the Paradox of Educational Reform." *Interchange* 12, nos. 2–3 (1981): 3–26.

———. "Ideology and Agency in the Process of Schooling." *Journal of*

Education 165, no. 1 (1983): 12–34.

———. "Public Pedagogy and the Politics of Resistance: Notes on a Critical Theory of Educational Struggle." *Educational Philosophy and Theory* 35, no. 1 (2003): 5–16.

———. "Rethinking Cultural Politics and Radical Pedagogy in the Work of Antonio Gramsci." *Educational Theory* 49, no. 1 (1999): 1–19.

———. "Theories of Reproduction and Resistance in the New Sociology of Education: A Critical Analysis." *Harvard Educational Review* 53, no. 3 (1983): 257–93.

Glass, Ronald D. "On Paulo Freire's Philosophy of Praxis and the Foundations of Liberation Education." *Educational Researcher* 30, no. 2 (2001): 15–25.

Golin, Josh, Bill Bigelow, Nick Berning, and Kyle Ash. "Scholastic Severs Ties with the Coal Industry: Controversial Elementary School Materials Withdrawn after Protests." Press release. Campaign for a Commercial-Free Childhood, May 14, 2011. http://www.commercialfreechildhood .org/pressreleases/coalandscholasticwin.html.

Gorski, Paul C. *Reaching and Teaching Students in Poverty: Strategies for Erasing the Opportunity Gap*. Multicultural Education Series. New York: Teachers College Press, 2013.

Gottesman, Isaac. "Sitting in the Waiting Room: Paulo Freire and the Critical Turn in the Field of Education." *Educational Studies* 46, no. 4 (2010): 376–99. doi:10.1080/00131941003782429.

———. *The Critical Turn in Education: From Marxist Critique to Poststructuralist Feminism to Critical Theories of Race*. New York: Routledge, 2016.

Gould, Stephen Jay. "The Geometer of Race." *Discover*, November 1, 1994, 65–69.

———. *The Mismeasure of Man*. Rev ed. New York: Norton, 1996.

Graham, Loren R. *Science and Philosophy in the Soviet Union*. New York: Alfred A. Knopf, 1972.

Gramsci, A. *Selections from the Prison Notebooks*. Translated by Q. Hoare. New York: International Publishers, 1971.

Grande, Sandy. *Red Pedagogy: Native American Social and Political Thought*. 10th anniversary ed.. Lanham, Maryland: Rowman & Littlefield, 2015.

Green III, Preston C., Bruce D. Baker, and Joseph O. Oluwole. "Having It Both Ways: How Charter Schools Try to Obtain Funding of Public Schools and the Autonomy of Private Schools." *Emory Law Journal* 63 (2013): 303–37.

Gruenewald, David A. "The Best of Both Worlds: A Critical Pedagogy of Place." *Educational Researcher* 32, no. 4 (2003): 3–12.

Gutierrez y Muhs, Gabriella, Yolanda Flores Niemann, Carmen G. Gonzalez, and Angela P. Harris, eds. *Presumed Incompetent: The Intersections of Race and Class for Women in Academia*. Boulder, CO: University Press of Colorado, 2012.

Gutstein, Eric. "Math, SATs, and Racial Profiling." In *Rethinking Multicultural Education: Teaching for Racial and Cultural Justice*, edited by Wayne Au, 341–47. Milwaukee, WI: Rethinking Schools, Ltd., 2009.

Hagopian, Jesse, ed. *More Than a Score: The New Uprising against High-Stakes Testing*. Chicago: Haymarket Books, 2014.

———. "My Greatest Teaching Moment." *Yes! Magazine*, March 14, 2012. http://www.yesmagazine.org/for-teachers/teacher-stories/my-greatest-teaching-moment.

———. "Obama Regrets 'Taking the Joy out of Teaching and Learning' with Too Much Testing." *CommonDreams*, October 30, 2015. http://www.commondreams.org/views/2015/10/30/obama-regrets-taking-joy-out-teaching-and-learning-too-much-testing.

———. "Our Destination Is Not on the MAP." In *More Than a Score: The New Uprising against High-Stakes Testing*, edited by Jesse Hagopian, 31–47. Chicago: Haymarket Books, 2014.

———. "Salt of the Earth School: 'They Can't Break Us.' Interview with Jia Lee." In *More Than a Score: The New Uprising against High-Stakes Testing*, edited by Jesse Hagopian, 107–12. Chicago: Haymarket Books, 2014.

———. "Seattle Test Boycott: Our Destination Is Not on the MAP." *Rethinking Schools* 27, no. 3 (2014). http://www.rethinkingschools.org/archive/27_03/27_03_hagopian.shtml.

Hagopian, Jesse, and Network for Public Education. "Resistance to High Stakes Tests Serves the Cause of Equity in Education: A Reply to 'We Oppose Anti-Testing Efforts.'" The Network for Public Education, May 5, 2015. http://www.networkforpubliceducation.org/2015/05/resistance-to-high-stakes-tests-serves-the-cause-of-equity-in-education/.

Hall, Stuart. "Gramsci's Relevance for the Study of Race and Ethnicity." *Journal of Communication Inquiry* 10, no. 2 (1986): 5–27.

Haraway, Donna. *Simians, Cyborgs, and Women*. New York: Routledge, 1991.

Harding, Sandra. "How Standpoint Methodology Informs Philosophy of Science." In *Approaches to Qualitative Research*, edited by Sharlene Nagy Hesse-Biber and Patricia Leavy, 62–80. New York: Oxford University Press, 2004.

———, ed. *The "Racial Economy of Science": Toward a Democratic Future*. Indianapolis: Indiana University Press, 1993.

———. "Rethinking Standpoint Epistemology: What Is 'Strong Objectivity'?" In *The Feminist Standpoint Reaader*, edited by Sandra Harding, 127–40. New York: Routledge, 2004.

Hargreaves, Andy. "Resistance and Relative Autonomy Theories: Problems of Distortion and Incoherence in Recent Marxist Analyses of Education." *British Journal of Sociology of Education* 3, no. 2 (1982): 107–26.

Harris, Philip, Bruce M. Smith, and Joan Harris. *The Myths of Standardized Tests: Why They Don't Tell You What You Think They Do*. New York: Rowman & Littlefield, 2011.

Hart, Ray, Michael Casserly, Renata Uzzell, Moses Palacios, Amanda Corcoran, and Liz Spurgeon. *Student Testing in America's Great City Schools: An Inventory and Preliminary Analysis.* Report. Council of the Great City Schools, Washington, DC, 2015. https://www.cgcs.org/cms/lib/DC00001581/Centricity/Domain/87/Testing%20Report.pdf.

Hartsock, Nancy C. M. "The Feminist Standpoint: Developing the Ground for a Specifically Feminist Historical Materialism." In *Discovering Reality: Feminist Perspectives on Epistemology, Metaphysics, Methodology, and Philosophy of Science*, edited by Sandra Harding and M. B. Hintikka, 283–310. Dordrecht, Holland: D. Reidel, 1983.

———. *The Feminist Standpoint Revisited and Other Essays*. Boulder, CO: Westview Press, 1998.

Harvey, David. "Neoliberalism as Creative Destruction." *Annals of the American Academy of Political and Social Science* 610 (2007): 22–44.

———. "The 'New' Imperialism: Accumulation by Dispossession." *Socialist Register* 40 (2004): 63–87.

Haymes, Stephen Nathan. "Race, Pedagogy, and Paulo Freire." *Philosophy of Education Yearbook*, 2002, 151–59.

Haywood, Harry. *A Black Communist in the Freedom Struggle: The Life of Harry Haywood.* Edited by Gwendolyn Midlo Hall. Minneapolis: University of Minnesota Press, 2012.

Hess, Diana. "Should Intelligent Design Be Taught in Social Studies?" *Social Education* 79, no. 3 (2006): 8–13.

Higgins, Sharon. "Charter School Scandals," 2013. *Charter School Scandals.* http://charterschoolscandals.blogspot.com/.

HiPointDem. "Bill Gates Tells Us Why 'His' High School Was a Great Learning Environment." *Seattle Education*, June 18, 2012. https://seattleducation2010.wordpress.com/2012/06/18/bill-gates-tells-us-why-his-high-school-was-a-great-learning-environment/.

Ho, Fred. "Fists for Revolution: The Revolutionary History of I Wor

Kuen/League of Revolutionary Struggle." In *Legacy to Liberation: Politics and Culture of Revolutionary Asian Pacific America*, edited by Fred Ho, 3–14. San Francisco: Big Red Media and AK Press, 2000.

Holst, John D. "The Affinities of Lenin and Gramsci: Implications for Radical Adult Education Theory and Practice." *International Journal of Lifelong Education* 18, no. 5 (1999): 407–21.

———. "Paulo Freire in Chile, 1964–1969: Pedagogy of the Oppressed in Its Sociopolitical Economic Context." *Harvard Educational Review* 76, no. 2 (2006): 243–70.

hooks, bell. *Teaching to Transgress: Education as the Practice of Freedom*. New York: Routledge, 1994.

Hook, Sydney. "The Enlightenment and Marxism." *Journal of the History of Ideas* 29, no. 1 (1968): 93–108.

Hout, M. and S. W. Elliott, eds. *Incentives and Test-Based Accountability in Education*. National Research Council, Committee on Incentives and Test-Based Accountability in Public Education, Washington, DC, 2011.

Hughes, Arnold. "The Appeal of Marxism to Africans." *Journal of Communist Studies* 8, no. 2 (1992): 4–20.

Ichioka, Yuji. "A Buried Past: Early Issei Socialists and the Japanese Community." *Amerasia Journal* 1, no. 2 (1971): 1–25.

Jameson, Fredric. *Postmodernism, or, The Cultural Logic of Late Capitalism*. Durham, NC: Duke University Press, 1999.

Jessop, B. "Bringing the State Back In (Yet Again): Reviews, Revisions, Rejections, and Redirections." *International Review of Sociology* 11, no. 2 (2001): 149–73.

Jiang, Yang, Maribel R. Granja, and Heather Koball. "Basic Facts about Low-Income Children: Children under 18 Years, 2015." Fact sheet. National Center for Children in Poverty, Columbia University, 2017. http://www.nccp.org/publications/pdf/text_1170.pdf.

John-Steiner, V., and Holbrook Mahn. "Sociocultural Approaches to Learning and Development: A Vygotskian Framework." *Educational Psychologist* 31 (1996): 191–206.

Jones, Brian. "Keys to the Schoolhouse: Black Teachers, Privatization, and the Future of Teacher Unions." In *What's Race Got to Do with It?: How Current School Reform Policy Maintains Racial and Economic Inequality*, edited by Bree Picower and Edwin Mayorga, 81–102. Critical Multicultural Perspectives on Whiteness, vol. 2. New York: Peter Lang, 2015.

Jong, Alex de. "The War Is Over: In the Philippines, One of the World's Longest Running Communist Insurgencies Is Being Worn down by the

Passage of History." *Jacobin*, August 12, 2015. https://www.jacobinmag.com/2015/08/phillipines-maoists-communists-marcos-aquino/.

Joseph, George. "What Betsy DeVos Didn't Say about School Choice." *CityLab*, January 19, 2017. http://www.citylab.com/politics/2017/01/what-betsy-devos-didnt-say-about-school-choice/513269/.

———. "Where Charter-School Suspensions Are Concentrated." *Atlantic*, September 16, 2016. https://www.theatlantic.com/education/archive/2016/09/the-racism-of-charter-school-discipline/500240/.

Journey for Justice Alliance. "The Journey for Justice Alliance Education Platform: An Equitable and Just School System Now!" Journey for Justice Alliance, Chicago, 2016. https://www.j4jalliance.com/wp-content/uploads/2016/09/J4J_Final_Education_Platform.pdf.

Karpov, Yuriy V. "Vygotsky's Doctrine of Scientific Concepts: Its Role for Contemporary Education." In *Vygotsky's Educational Theory in Cultural Context*, edited by Alex Kozulin, Boris Gindis, Vladimir S. Ageyev, and Suzanne M. Miller, 65–82. Learning in Doing: Social, Cognitive, and Computational Perspectives. New York: Cambridge University Press, 2003.

Karp, Stan. "Charter Schools and the Future of Public Education: It's Time to Refocus Public Policy on Providing Excellent Public Schools for All." *New Jersey Education Association Review*, March 2013. http://www.njea.org/news-and-publications/njea-review/march-2013/charter-schools-and-the-future-of-public-education.

Kelley, Robin D. G. *Race Rebels: Culture, Politics, and the Black Working Class*. 1st ed. New York: The Free Press, 1996.

Kelsh, Deborah, and Dave Hill. "The Culturalization of Class and the Occluding of Class Consciousness: The Knowledge Industry In/of Education." *Journal for Critical Education Policy Studies* 4, no. 1 (2006). http://www.jceps.com/?pageID=article&articleID=59.

Kirst, Michael W. "Mayoral Influence, New Regimes, and Public School Governance." Consortium for Policy Research in Education, University of Pennsylvania, May 2002. http://www.cpre.org/Publications/rr49.pdf.

Kliebard, Herbert M. *The Struggle for the American Curriculum, 1893–1958*. 3rd ed. New York, NY: RoutledgeFalmer, 2004.

Klonsky, Michael. "Power Philanthropy: Taking the Public out of Public Education." In *The Gates Foundation and the Future of U.S. "Public" Schools*, edited by Phillip E. Kovacs, 21–38. Routledge, 2011.

Knoester, Matthew, and Wayne Au. "Standardized Testing and School Segregation: Like Tinder to Fire?" *Race Ethnicity and Education* 20, no. 1 (2015): 1–14. doi:10.1080/13613324.2015.1121474.

KrazyTA. "KrazyTA Explains What Bill Gates Wants for His Own Children." *Diane Ravitch's Blog*, March 19, 2014. https://dianeravitch.net/2014/03/19/krazyta-explains-what-bill-gates-wants-for-his-own-children/.

Kretchmar, Kerry, Beth Sondel, and Joseph J. Ferrare. "Mapping the Terrain: Teach For America, Charter School Reform, and Corporate Sponsorship." *Journal of Education Policy* 29, no. 6 (2014): 742–59. doi:10.1080/02680939.2014.880812.

Ladd, Helen F., Charles T. Clotfelter, and John B. Holbein. "The Growing Segmentation of the Charter School Sector in North Carolina." *Education Finance and Policy* 19, no. 55 (2017): 1–28. doi:10.1162/edfp_a_00226.

Ladson-Billings, Gloria. "From the Achievement Gap to the Education Debt: Understanding Achievement in U.S. Schools." *Educational Researcher* 35, no. 7 (2006): 3–12.

———. *The Dreamkeepers: Successful Teachers of African American Children.* San Francisco: Jossey-Bass, 1994.

———. "I Know Why This Doesn't Feel Empowering: A Critical Race Analysis of Critical Pedagogy." In *Mentoring the Mentor: A Critical Dialogue with Paulo Freire*, edited by Paulo Freire, with James W. Fraser, Donaldo Macedo, Tanya McKinnon, William T. Stokes, and Shirley Steinberg, 127–41. Studies in the Postmodern Theories of Education. New York: Peter Lang, 1997.

Lai, Him Mark. "A Historical Survey of Organization of the Left among Chinese in America." *Bulletin of Concerned Asian Scholars* 4, no. 3 (1972): 10–20.

Lake, Robin. "State Law and Implementation Matter." *Seattle Times*, October 23, 2012. http://seattletimes.com/html/northwestvoices/2017418193_arecharterschoolsthebestsolution.html?syndication=rss.

Lake, Robin J. "In the Eye of the Beholder: Charter Schools and Innovation." *Journal of School Choice* 2, no. 2 (2008): 115–27. doi:http://dx.doi.org/10.1080/15582150802136090.

Lapp, David, Joshua Lin, Erik Dolson, and Della Moran. *The Fiscal Impact of Charter School Expansion: Calculation in Six Pennsylvania School Districts*. Report. Research for Action, Philadelphia, 2017. https://www.researchforaction.org/publications/fiscal-impact-charter-school-expansion-calculations-six-pennsylvania-school-districts/.

Layton, Lyndsey. "How Bill Gates Pulled off the Swift Common Core Revolution." *Washington Post*. June 7, 2014. http://www.washingtonpost.com/politics/how-bill-gates-pulled-off-the-swift-common-core-revolution/2014/06/07/a830e32e-ec34-11e3-9f5c-9075d5508f0a_story.html.

Lazarin, Melissa. *Testing Overload in America's Schools*. Report. Center for American Progress, 2014. https://cdn.americanprogress.org/wp-content/uploads/2014/10/LazarinOvertestingReport.pdf.

Lenin, V. I. *Materialism and Empirio-Criticism*. 1st English ed. Peking: Foreign Language Press, 1972.

———. "The Socialist Revolution and the Right of Nations to Self-Determination: Theses." Marxists Internet Archive, [1916] 2005. https://www.marxists.org/archive/lenin/works/1916/jan/x01.htm.

———. *What Is to Be Done?: Burning Questions of Our Movement*. Peking: Foreign Language Press, 1975.

Leonardo, Zeus, ed. *Critical Pedagogy and Race*. Malden, MA: Blackwell Publishing, 2005.

———. "The Race for Class: Reflections on a Critical Raceclass Theory of Education." *Educational Studies* 58, no. 5 (2012): 427–49.

———. "The Unhappy Marriage between Marxism and Race Critique: Political Economy and the Production of Racialized Knowledge." *Policy Futures in Education* 2, nos. 3–4 (2004): 483–93.

"Letters." *Harvard Educational Review* 60, no. 3 (1990): 388–405.

Levine, David, and Wayne Au. "Rethinking Schools: Enacting a Vision for Social Justice within US Education." *Critical Studies in Education* 54, no. 1 (2013): 72–84. doi:http://dx.doi.org/10.1080/17508487.2013.738693.

Lilge, Frederic. "Lenin and the Politics of Education." *Slavic Review* 27, no. 2 (1968): 230–57.

Lipman, Pauline. *The New Political Economy of Urban Education: Neoliberalism, Race, and the Right to the City*. New York: Routledge, 2011.

Lopez, Haney. *White by Law: The Legal Construction of Race*. New York: New York University Press, 1996.

Lopez, N. *Hopeful Girls, Troubled Boys: Race and Gender Disparity in Urban Education*. New York: Routledge, 2003.

Losen, Daniel J., Michael A. Keith II, Cheri L. Hodson, and Tia E. Martinez. "Charter Schools, Civil Rights and Schools Discipline: A Comprehensive Review." Center for Civil Rights Remedies, UCLA Civil Rights Project, 2016. https://civilrightsproject.ucla.edu/resources/projects/center-for-civil-rights-remedies/school-to-prison-folder/federal-reports/charter-schools-civil-rights-and-school-discipline-a-comprehensive-review/losen-et-al-charter-school-discipline-review-2016.pdf.

Lukács, Georg. *History and Class Consciousness*. Cambridge, MA: MIT Press, 1971.

Luke, Allan. "Critical Literacy: Foundational Notes." *Theory into Practice*

51, no. 4 (2012): 4–11.

Mackerras, Colin, and Nick Knight. *Marxism in Asia*. Sydney: Croom Helm, 1985.

Maffie, James. "Aztec Philosophy." *Internet Encyclopedia of Philosophy: A Peer-Reviewed Academic Resource*. Accessed February 6, 2017. http://www.iep.utm.edu/aztec/#SH2b.

———. *Aztec Philosophy: Understanding a World in Motion*. Boulder: University Press of Colorado, 2015.

Makalani, Minkah. "An Apparatus for Negro Women: Black Women's Organizing, Communism, and the Institutional Spaces for Radical Pan-African Thought." *Women, Gender, and Families of Color* 4, no. 2 (2016): 250–73.

———. "Internationalizing the Third International: The African Blood Brotherhood, Asian Radicals, and Race, 1919–1922." *Journal of African American History* 96, no. 2 (2011): 151–78.

Malott, Curry S. "In Defense of Communism: Against Critical Pedagogy, Capitalism, and Trump." *Critical Education* 8, no. 1 (2017): 1–24.

———. "Social Class and Rebellion: The Role of Knowledge Production in Capitalist Society." In *Education and the Reproduction of Capital: Neoliberal Knowledge and Counterstrategies*, edited by Ravi Kumar, 15–40. Marxism and Education. New York: Palgrave Macmillan, 2012.

Malott, Curry S., and Derek R. Ford. *Marx, Capital, and Education: Towards a Critical Pedagogy of Becoming*. Education and Struggle. New York: Peter Lang, 2015.

Marx, Karl. *Capital: A Critique of Political Economy*. Translated by S. Moore and E. Aveling. Vol. 1. New York: International Publishers, 1967.

———. *Capital: The Process of Circulation of Capital*. Vol. 2. New York: International Publishers, 1967.

———. "Preface to a Contribution to the Critique of Political Economy." In Marx and Engels, *Selected Works*, 181–85. New York: International Publishers, 1968.

———. "The Class Struggles in France, 1848–1850." In *The Marx-Engels Reader*, edited by R. C. Tucker, 586–93. 2nd ed. New York: W. W. Norton & Company, 1978.

———. "The Eighteenth Brumaire of Louis Bonaparte." In Marx and Engels, *Selected Works*, 95–180. New York: International Publishers, 1968.

Marx, Karl, and Frederick Engels. "The German Ideology: Part I." In *The Marx-Engels Reader*, edited by R. C. Tucker, 146–200. New York: W.W. Norton & Company, 1978.

———. *Manifesto of the Communist Party*. Peking: Foreign Language Press, 1848.

———. *Selected Works*. New York. International Publishers, 1968

McLaren, Peter. *Che Guevara, Paulo Freire, and the Pedagogy of Revolution*. Culture and Education Series. Lanham, MD.: Rowman & Littlefield, 2000.

McLaren, Peter, and Ramin Farahmandpur. "Reconsidering Marx in Post-Marxist Times: A Requiem for Postmodernism?" *Educational Researcher* 29, no. 3 (2000): 25–33.

McLaren, Peter, and Nathalia E. Jaramillo. "Not Neo-Marxist, Not Post-Marxist, Not Marxian, Not Autonomist Marxism: Reflections on a Revolutionary (Marxist) Critical Pedagogy." *Cultural Studies–Critical Methodologies* 10, no. 3 (2010): 251–62. doi:10.1177/1532708609354317.

McLaren, Peter, and Juha Suoranta. "Socialist Pedagogy." In *Contesting Neoliberal Education*, edited by Dave Hill, 242–64. London: Routledge, 2009.

Meacham, S. J. "Vygotsky and the Blues: Re-Reading Cultural Connections and Conceptual Development." *Theory into Practice* 40, no. 3 (2001): 190, 8 pgs.

Meiners, Erica R., and Maisha T. Winn, eds. *Education and Incarceration*. New York: Routledge, 2012.

Melamed, Jodi. *Represent and Destroy: Rationalizing Violence in the New Racial Capitalism*. Minneapolis: University of Minnesota Press, 2011.

Memmi, A. *The Colonizer and the Colonized*. Boston: Beacon Press, 1967.

Menkhart, D., A. D. Murray, and J. L. View, eds. *Putting the Movement Back into Civil Rights Teaching*. Washington, DC: Teaching for Change, 2004.

Meyer, Robinson. "American Trees Are Moving West, and No One Knows Why: Climate Change Explains Only 20 Percent of the Movement." *Atlantic*, May 17, 2017. https://www.theatlantic.com/science/archive/2017/05/go-west-my-sap/526899/.

Miron, Gary, and Jessica Urschel. "The Impact of School Choice Reforms on Student Achievement." In *Exploring the School Choice Universe: Evidence and Recommendations*, edited by Kevin G. Welner, Patricia H. Hinchey, and William J. Mathis, 211–36. Charlotte, NC: Information Age Publishing, 2012.

Miron, Gary, Jessica L. Urschel, William J. Mathis, and Elana Tornquist. *Schools without Diversity: Education Management Organizations, Charter Schools, and the Demographic Stratification of the American School System*. Policy brief. Education and the Public Interest Center and

Education Policy Research Unit, Boulder, CO, and Tempe, AZ, 2010. http://nepc.colorado.edu/files/EMO-Seg.pdf.

Moraga, Cherrie, and Gloria Anzaldua, eds. *This Bridge Called My Back: Writings by Radical Women of Color*. 4th ed. Albany, NY: State Univesity of New York Press, 2015.

Morrow, Raymond Allen, and Carlos Alberto Torres. *Reading Freire and Habermas: Critical Pedagogy and Transformative Social Change*. New York: Teachers College Press, 2002.

Murphy, P., E. Regenstein, and K. McNamara. "Putting a price tag on the Common Core: How much will smart implementation cost?." Thomas B. Fordham Institute, Washington, DC. http://www.edexcellence.net/publications/putting-a-price-tag-on-the-common-core.html.

NAACP. "Statement Regarding the NAACP's Resolution on a Moritorium on Charter Schools." NAACP, official website, October 15, 2016. http://www.naacp.org/latest/statement-regarding-naacps-resolution-moratorium-charter-schools/.

Naison, Mark. *Communists in Harlem during the Depression*. New York: Grove Press, 1985.

Nardi, Bonnie A. "Studying Context: A Composition of Activity Theory, Situated Action Models, and Distributed Cognition." In *Context and Consciousness: Activity Theory and Human-Computer Interaction*, edited by Bonnie A. Nardi, 69–102. Cambridge, MA: The MIT Press, 1996.

Nash, Roy. "The Cognitive Habitus: Its Place in a Realist Account of Inequality/Difference." *British Journal of Sociology of Education* 26, no. 5 (2005): 599–612.

National Poverty Center. "Poverty in the United States: Frequently Asked Questions." National Poverty Center, official website, 2017. http://www.npc.umich.edu/poverty/.

Newman, Fred, and Lois Holzman. *Lev Vygotsky: Revolutionary Scientist*. Critical Psychology. London and New York: Routledge, 1993.

Nichols, Sharon L., and David C. Berliner. *Collateral Damage: How High-Stakes Testing Corrupts America's Schools*. Cambridge, MA: Harvard Education Press, 2007.

Noltemeyer, A. L., R. M. Ward, and C. Mcloughlin. "Relationship between School Suspension and Student Outcomes: A Meta-Analysis." *School Psychology Review* 44, no. 2 (2015): 224–40. doi:10.17105/spr-14-0008.1.

Oakes, Jeannie. *Keeping Track: How Schools Structure Inequality*. 2nd ed. New Haven, CT: Yale University Press, 2005.

Ollman, Bertell. *Dance of the Dialectic: Steps in Marx's Method*. 1st ed.

Chicago: University of Illinois Press, 2003.

Omi, Michael, and Howard Winant. *Racial Formations in the United States*. New York: Routledge, 2015.

Orfield, Myron, and Thomas Luce. "An Analysis of Student Performance in Chicago's Charter Schools." *Education Policy Analysis Archives* 24, no. 111 (2016). doi:http://dx.doi.org/10.14507/epaa.24.2203.

Patel, Leigh. *Decolonizing Educational Research: From Ownership to Answerability*. New York: Routledge, 2016.

Pelo, Ann, ed. *Rethinking Early Childhood Education*. Milwaukee, WI: Rethinking Schools, 2008.

Pelzer, Jeremy. "Charter School Operator Owns Property Bought with Public Money, Ohio Supreme Court Rules." *Cleveland.com*, September 12, 2015. http://www.cleveland.com/open/index.ssf/2015/09/charter_school_operator_owns_p.html.

Picower, Bree, and Edwin Mayorga, eds. *What's Race Got to Do with It?: How Current School Reform Policy Maintains Racial and Economic Inequality*. New York: Peter Lang, 2015.

Pondiscio, Robert. "Opting Out, Race, and Reform." Common Core Watch, Thomas B. Fordham Institute, March 25, 2015. https://edexcellence.net/articles/opting-out-race-and-reform.

Popham, W. James. *The Truth about Testing: An Educator's Call to Action*. Alexandria, VA: Association for Supervision and Curriculum Development (ASCD), 2001.

Poster, Mark. "Althusser on History without Man." *Political Theory* 2, no. 4 (1974): 393–409.

Preston, C., Ellen Goldring, Mark Berends, and Marisa Cannata. "School Innovation in District Context: Comparing Traditional Public Schools and Charter Schools." *Economics of Education Review* 31, no. 2 (2012): 318–30. doi:https://doi.org/10.1016/j.econedurev.2011.07.016.

Prothero, Arianna. "Public Support for Charter School Plummets, Poll Finds." *Education Week*, August 16, 2017. http://www.edweek.org/ew/articles/2017/08/15/public-support-for-charter-schools-plummets-poll.html.

Pulido, Laura. "Race, Class, and Political Activism: Black, Chicano/a, and Japanese-American Leftists in Southern California, 1968–1978." *Antipode* 34, no. 4 (2002): 762–88.

Rasmussen, Derek. "Cease to Do Evil, Then Learn to Do Good . . . (a Pedagogy for the Oppressor)." In *Rethinking Freire: Globalization and the Environmental Crisis*, edited by C. A. Bowers and Frederique Apffel-Marglin, 115–31. Mahwah, NJ: Lawrence Erlbaum Associates, 2005.

Ravitch, Diane. *Reign of Error: The Hoax of the Privatization Movement and the Danger to America's Public Schools*. New York: Vintage Books, 2014.

Rawls, Kristin. "Who Is Profiting from Charters?: The Big Bucks behind Charter School Secrecy, Financial Scandal and Corruption." *AlterNet*, May 13, 2013. http://www.alternet.org/education/who-profiting-charters-big-bucks-behind-charter-school-secrecy-financial-scandal-and?paging=off.

Renzulli, Linda A., and Lorraine Evans. "School Choice, Charter Schools, and White Flight." *Social Problems* 52, no. 3 (2005): 398–418.

Resmovits, Joy. "Murdoch Education Affiliate's $2.7 Million Consulting Contract Approved by New York City." *Huffington Post*, July 15, 2011. http://www.huffingtonpost.com/2011/07/15/murdoch-education-affiliate-contract-approved_n_900379.html.

Rethinking Schools. Official website, 2017. http://www.rethinkingschools.org.

———. "The Gathering Resistance to Standardized Tests." *Rethinking Schools*, 2014. http://www.rethinkingschools.org/archive/28_03/edit2283.shtml.

———. "Leading Educators Support Teacher Test Boycott." *Rethinking Schools Blog*, January 21, 2013. https://rethinkingschoolsblog.wordpress.com/2013/01/21/leading-educators-support-teacher-test-boycott/.

Rich, M. "New Schools fund attracts more capital." *New York Times*, May 1, 2013. http://www.nytimes.com/2013/05/01/education/newschools-venture-fund-links-with-rethink-education.html?ref=education&_r=1&.

Rikowski, Glenn. "Scorched Earth: Rebuilding Marxist Educational Theory." *British Journal of Sociology of Education* 18, no. 4 (1997): 551–74.

Roberts, Peter. "Knowledge, Dialogue, and Humanization: Exploring Freire's Philosophy." In *Critical Theory and the Human Condition: Founders and Praxis*, edited by Michael Peters, Colin Lankshear, Mark Olssen, and Shirley R. Steinberg, 169–83. Studies in the Post Modern Theory in Education, vol. 168. New York: Peter Lang, 2003.

Robinson, Cedric J. *Black Marxism: The Making of the Black Radical Tradition*. London: Zed, 1983.

Robinson, Phyllis. "Whose Oppression Is This?: The Cultivation of Action in Dissolving the Dualistic Barrier." In *Rethinking Freire: Globalization and the Environmental Crisis*, edited by C. A. Bowers and Frederique Apffel-Marglin, 101–14. Mahwah, NJ: Lawrence Erlbaum Associates, 2005.

Romero, Augustine, Sean Arce, and Julio Cammarota. "A Barrio Pedagogy: Identity, Intellectualism, Activism, and Academic Achievement through the Evolution of Critically Compassionate Intellectualism." *Race Ethnicity and Education* 12, no. 2 (2009): 217–33.

Rosa, Alberto, and Ignacio Montero. "The Historical Context of Vygotsky's Work: A Sociohistorical Approach." In *Vygotsky and Education: Instructional Implications and Applications of Sociohistorical Psychology*, edited by Luis C. Moll, 59–88. New York: Cambridge University Press, 1990.

Ruiz-Grossman, Sarah. "The Double Standard in How the Media Is Portraying the Las Vegas Shooter." Black Voices, *Huffington Post*, October 3, 2017. https://www.huffingtonpost.com/entry/double-standard-white-privilege-media-las-vegas-shooting_us_59d3da15e4b04b9f92058316.

Sader, Emir. *The New Mole: Paths of the Latin American Left*. New York: Verso, 2011.

Said, Edward W. *Orientalism*. 1st ed. New York: Pantheon Books, 1978.

Saltman, Kenneth J. "From Carnegie to Gates: The Bill and Melinda Gates Foundation and the Venture Philanthropy Agenda for Public Education." In *The Gates Foundation and the Future of U.S. "Public" Schools*, edited by Phillip E. Kovacs, 1–20. New York: Routledge, 2011.

Saltman, Kenneth J., and David A. Gabbard, eds. *Education as Enforcement: The Militarization and Corporatization of Schools*. New York: RoutledgeFalmer, 2003.

Sandoval, Chela. *Methodology of the Oppressed*. Minneapolis: University of Minnesota Press, 2000.

———. "U.S. Third World Feminism: The Theory and Method of Differential Oppositional Consciousness." In *The Feminist Standpoint Reader*, edited by Sandra Harding, 195–210. New York: Routledge, 2004.

Sarup, M. *Marxism and Education*. Boston: Routledge & Kegan Paul, 1978.

Sass, Tim R. "The Stability of Value-Added Measures of Teacher Quality and Implication for Teacher Compensation." Policy brief. National Center for Analysis of Longitudinal Data in Educational Research, November 2008.

Sawyer, Jeremy. "Vygotsky's Revolutionary Theory of Psychological Development." *International Socialist Review* 93 (2014). http://isreview.org/issue/93/vygotskys-revolutionary-theory-psychological-development.

Sayers, Sean. "Marxism and the Dialectical Method: A Critique of G. A. Cohen." In *Socialism, Feminism, and Philosophy: A Radical Philosophy Reader*, edited by Sean Sayers and Peter Osborne, 140–68. New York: Routledge, 1990.

Scalapino, Robert A. *The Japanese Communist Movement, 1920–1966*. Los Angeles: University of California Press, 1967.

Scapp, Ron. "The Subject of Education: Paulo Freire, Postmodernism, and

Multiculturalism." In *Mentoring the Mentor: A Critical Dialogue with Paulo Freire*, edited by Paulo Freire, with James W. Fraser, Donaldo Macedo, Tanya McKinnon, William T. Stokes, and Shirley Steinberg, 283–91. Studies in the Postmodern Theories of Education. New York: Peter Lang, 1997.

Schochet, Peter Z., and Hanley S. Chiang. "Error Rates in Measuring Teacher and School Performance Based on Test Score Gains." National Center for Educational Evaluation and Regional Assistance, US Department of Education, August 23, 2010. http://ies.ed.gov/ncee/pubs/20104004/pdf/20104004.pdf.

Schugurensky, Daniel. "The Legacy of Paulo Freire: A Critical Review of His Contributions." *Convergence* 31, nos. 1–2 (1998): 17–29.

Scott, Eugenie C., and Glenn Branch, eds. *Not in Our Classrooms: Why Intelligent Design Is Wrong for Our Schools*. Boston: Beacon Press, 2006.

Sears, Kelton. "A Marxist Critiques Identity Politics: A Q & A with Asad Haider, Founding Editor of Viewpoint Magazine, on an Ideology Fracturing the Left." *Seattle Weekly*, April 25, 2017. http://www.seattleweekly.com/news/a-marxist-critiques-identity-politics/.

Shafer, Rowan. "The (young) People's Climate Conference: Teaching Global Warming to 3rd Graders." *Rethinking Schools* 31, no. 4 (2017). https://www.rethinkingschools.org/articles/the-young-people-s-climate-conference.

Shandro, Alan. "'Consciousness from Without': Marxism, Lenin, and the Proletariat." *Science and Society* 59, no. 3 (1995): 268–97.

Sharp, Rachel. *Knowledge, Ideology, and the Politics of Schooling: Towards a Marxist Analysis of Education*. London and Boston: Routledge & Kegan Paul, 1980.

Sharp, Rachel, and Anthony Green. *Education and Social Control: A Study in Progressive Primary Education*. London: Routledge & Kegan Paul, 1975.

Shollenberger, T. L. "Racial Disparities in School Suspension and Subsequent Outcomes: Evidence from the National Longitudinal Survey of Youth." In *Closing the School Discipline Gap: Equitable Remedies for Excessive Exclusion*, edited by Daniel J. Losen, 31–43. New York: Teachers College Press, 2015.

Shor, Ira. *Empowering Education: Critical Teaching for Social Change*. 1st ed. Chicago: The University of Chicago Press, 1992.

———, ed. *Freire for the Classroom: A Sourcebook for Liberatory Teaching*. Portsmouth, NH: Boynton/Cook Publishers, 1987.

Shor, Ira, and Paulo Freire. *A Pedagogy for Liberation: Dialogues on Transforming Education*. South Hadley, MA: Bergin & Garvey Publishers,

1987.

Siddhartha. "From Conscientization to Interbeing: A Personal Journey." In *Rethinking Freire: Globalization and the Environmental Crisis*, edited by C. A. Bowers and Frederique Apffel-Marglin, 83–100. Mahwah, NJ: Lawrence Erlbaum Associates, 2005.

Simon, Stephanie. "Special Report: Class Struggle—How Charter Schools Get the Students They Want." *Reuters*, February 17, 2013. http://www.reuters.com/article/2013/02/15/us-usa-charters-admissions-idUSBRE91E0HF20130215.

Sirin, Selcuk R. "Socioeconomic Status and Student Achievement: A Meta-Analytic Review of Research." *Review of Educational Research* 75, no. 3 (2005): 417–53.

Sleeter, Christine. "Ethnic Studies and the Struggle in Tucson." *Education Week* 31, no. 21 (2012). http://www.edweek.org/ew/articles/2012/02/15/21sleeter.h31.html?tkn=VRMFRGuUcYPvsaR7iQ0tSO0BuBkBdu8hRyIN&cmp=clp-edweek.

Smith, Steven B. "Althusser and the Overdetermined Self." *Review of Politics* 46, no. 4 (1984): 516–38.

———. "Althusser's Marxism without a Knowing Subject." *American Political Science Review* 79, no. 3 (1985): 641–55.

Solorzano, Daniel and Tara Yosso. "Maintaining Social Justice Hopes within Academic Realities: A Freirean Approach to Critical race/LatCrit Pedagogy." *Denver University Law Review* 78 (2001): 69–92.

Sommeiller, Estelle, Mark Price, and Ellis Wazeter. "Income Inequality in the U.S. by State, Metropolitan Area, and County." Economic Policy Institute, June 16, 2016. http://www.epi.org/files/pdf/107100.pdf.

Stefanos, Asgedet. "African Women and Revolutionary Change: A Freirian and Feminist Perspective." In *Mentoring the Mentor: A Critical Dialogue with Paulo Freire*, edited by Paulo Freire, with James W. Fraser, Donaldo Macedo, Tanya McKinnon, William T. Stokes, and Shirley Steinberg, 243–71. Studies in the Postmodern Theories of Education. New York: Peter Lang, 1997.

Stern, Sol. "Pedagogy of the Oppressor: Another Reason Why U.S. Ed Schools Are so Awful: The Ongoing Influence of Brazilian Marxist Paulo Freire." *City Journal*, 2009. https://www.city-journal.org/html/pedagogy-oppressor-13168.html.

Stith, Jonathan, Hiram Rivera, and Chinyere Tutashinda. "A Vision for Black Lives: Policy Demands for Black Power, Freedom, and Justice: An End to the Privatization of Education and Real Community Control by Parents, Students, and Community Members of Schools Including Democratic School Boards and Community Control of Curriculum, Hiring, Firing, and Discipline Policies." Movement for Black Lives, 2016. https://policy.m4bl.org/wp-content/uploads/2016/07/Community-Control-of-Schools-Policy-Brief.pdf.

Stovall, David. "Mayoral Control: Reform, Whiteness, and Critical Race Analysis of Neoliberal Educational Policy." In *What's Race Got to Do with It?: How Current School Reform Policy Maintains Racial and Economic Inequality*, edited by Bree Picower and Edwin Mayorga, 45–58. New York: Peter Lang, 2015.

Strauss, Valerie. "Bill Gates: 'It Would Be Great If Our Education Stuff Worked But . . . '" The Answer Sheet. *Washington Post*, September 27, 2013. http://www.washingtonpost.com/blogs/answer-sheet/wp/2013/09/27/bill-gates-it-would-be-great-if-our-education-stuff-worked-but/.

Suri, Jeremi. *The Global Revolutions of 1968*. New York: W.W. Norton & Company, 2007.

Tan, Xuan, and Rochelle Michel. "Why Do Standardized Testing Programs Report Scaled Scores?: Why Not Just Report the Raw or Percent-Correct Scores?" *ETS R&D Connections*, 2011. https://www.ets.org/Media/Research/pdf/RD_Connections16.pdf.

Tasaki, Ray. "New Dawn Rising: History and Summation of the Japan Town Collective." In *Legacy to Liberation: Politics and Culture of Revolutionary Asian Pacific America*, edited by Fred Ho, 53–58. San Francisco: Big Red Media and AK Press, 2000.

Taylor, Keeanga-Yamahtta. "Don't Shame the First Steps of a Resistance." *Socialist Worker*, January 24, 2017. https://socialistworker.org/2017/01/24/dont-shame-the-first-steps-of-a-resistance.

———. *From #Blacklivesmatter to Black Liberation*. Chicago: Haymarket Books, 2016.

———, ed. *How We Get Free: Black Feminism and the Combahee River Collective*. Chicago: Haymarket Books, 2017.

Tenayuca, Emma, and Homer Brooks. "The Mexican Question in the Southwest." *Communist* 18, no. 3 (1939): 157–68.

Terry, III, Albert L. "A Few Words on Marxism and Identity Politics." *Left Voice*, January 8, 2017. http://www.leftvoice.org/A-Few-Words-on-Marxism-and-Identity-Politics.

Tian, Chenshan. *Chinese Dialectics: From Yijing to Marxism*. New York: Lexington Books, 2005.

———. "Development of Dialectical Materialism in China." In *History of Chinese Philosophy*, edited by Bo Mou, 512–38. Routledge History of World Philosophies. New York: Routledge, 2009.

Tintiangco-Cubales, Allyson, Rita Kohli, Jocyl Sacramento, Nick Henning, Ruchi Agarwal-Rangnath, and Christine Sleeter. "Toward an Ethnic Studies Pedagogy: Implications for K–12 Schools from the Research." *Urban Review* 47, no. 1 (2015): 104–25. doi:10.1007/s11256-014-0280-y.

Toribio, Helen C. "Dare to Struggle: The KDP and Filipino American Politics." In *Legacy to Liberation: Politics and Culture of Revolutionary Asian Pacific America*, edited by Fred Ho, 31–46. San Francisco: Big Red Media and AK Press, 2000.

Toulmin, Stephen. "The Mozart of Psychology." *New York Review of Books*, September 28, 1978.

Tran, Dao X. "Forget Teaching to the Test–Castle Bridge Boycotts It!" In Hagopian, *More Than a Score: The New Uprising against High-Stakes Testing*, edited by Jesse Hagopian, 211–18. Chicago: Haymarket Books, 2014.

Trask, H. K. *From a Native Daughter: Colonialism and Sovereignty in Hawaii*. Rev. ed. Honolulu: University of Hawaii Press, 1999.

Tuck, Eve, and K. Wayne Yang. "Decolonization Is Not a Metaphor." *Decolonization: Indigeneity, Education, and Society* 1, no. 1 (2012): 1–40.

Valenzuela, Angela, ed. *Leaving Children Behind: How "Texas Style" Accountability Fails Latino Youth*. Social Context of Education. New York: State University of New York Press, 2005.

Vargas, Zaragosa. *Labor Rights Are Civil Rights: Mexican American Workers in Twentieth-Century America*. Princeton, NJ: Princeton University Press, 2005.

———. "Tejana Radical: Emma Tenayuca and the San Antonio Labor Movement during the Great Depression." *Pacific Historical Review* 66, no. 4 (1997): 553–80.

Vasquez, Grimaldo Rengifo. "Nurturance in the Andes." In *Rethinking Freire: Globalization and the Environmental Crisis*, edited by C. A. Bowers and Frederique Apffel-Marglin, 31–47. Mahwah, NJ: Lawrence Erlbaum Associates, 2005.

Vasquez Heilig, Julian, Jennifer Jellison Holme, Anthony V. LeClair, Lindsay D. Redd, and Derrick Ward. "The Problematic Segregation of Special Populations in Charter Schools Relative to Traditional Public Schools." *Stanford Law and Policy Review* 27 (2016): 251–94.

Vicens, A. J. "Bill Gates Spent More than $200 Million to Promote Common Core. Here's Where It Went: The Gates Foundation Has Bankrolled a Sprawling Network of Groups to Advance the Standards." *Mother Jones*, September 4, 2014. http://www.motherjones.

com/politics/2014/09/bill-melinda-gates-foundation-common-core/.

Villacana de Castro, Luis S. "A Critique of Vygotsky's Misapprehension of Marx's 'Phenomenal Forms.'" *Science and Society* 79, no. 1 (2015): 90–113.

Vinson, Kevin D., and E. Wayne Ross. "Controlling Images: The Power of High-Stakes Testing." In *Education as Enforcement: The Militarization and Corporatization of Schools*, edited by Kenneth J. Saltman and David A. Gabbard, 241–58. New York: RoutledgeFalmer, 2003.

Viola, Michael. "Toward a Filipino/a Critical (FilCrit) Pedagogy: A Study of United States Educational Exposure Programs to the Philippines." PhD diss. Proquest Dissertations & Theses, 2012. http://gradworks.umi.com/35/08/3508951.html.

Vygotsky, Lev S. "Development of Higher Mental Functions." In *Psychological Research in the U.S.S.R.*, edited by A. Leontyev, A. Luryia, and A. Smirnov, 11–45. Moscow: Progress Publishers, 1966.

———. "The Genesis of Higher Mental Functions." In *The Concept of Activity in Soviet Psychology*, edited and translated by James V. Wertsch, 144–88. Armonk, NY: M. E. Sharpe, 1981.

———. *Mind in Society.* In Vygotsky, *The Development of Higher Psychological Processes*, edited by M. Cole, V. John-Steiner, S. Scribner, and E. Souberman. Cambridge, MA: Harvard University Press, 1978.

———. "The Problem of the Cultural Development of the Child." *Journal of Genetic Psychology: Child Behavior, Animal Behavior, and Comparative Psychology* 36, no. 1 (1929): 415–34.

———. "Thinking and Speech." In *The Collected Works of L. S. Vygotsky: Problems of General Psychology Including the Volume Thinking and Speech*, edited by Robert W. Rieber and Aaron Carton, translated by Norris Minick. Vol. 1, 37–285. Cognition and Language. New York: Plenum Press, 1987.

———. *Thought and Language*. Translated by E. Hanfmann. Cambridge, MA: The MIT. Press, 1962.

———. *Thought and Language*. Translated by A. Kozulin. 1st ed. Cambridge, MA: The MIT Press, 1986.

Ware, J. Gabriel. "Ethnic Studies Courses Break down Barriers and Benefit Everyone—so Why the Resistance?" *Yes! Magazine*, March 23, 2017. http://www.yesmagazine.org/peace-justice/ethnic-studies-courses-break-down-barriers-and-benefit-everyone-so-why-the-resistance-20170323.

Weber, Mark. "Common Core Testing: Who's the Real 'Liar'?" *Jersey Jazzman*, September 25, 2015. http://jerseyjazzman.blogspot.com

/2015/09/common-core-testing-whos-real-liar.html.

———. "How Every Kid Could Go to Bill Gate's Private School." *Jersey Jazzman*, April 24, 2013. http://jerseyjazzman.blogspot.com/2013/04/how-every-kid-could-go-to-bill-gatess.html.

———. "Standardized Tests: Symptoms, Not Causes." *Jersey Jazzman*, May 24, 2015. http://jerseyjazzman.blogspot.com/2015/05/standardized-tests-symptoms-not-causes.html.

———. "Steve Perry: The Final Debunk." *Jersey Jazzman*, May 27, 2013. http://jerseyjazzman.blogspot.com/2013/05/dr-steve-perry-final-debunk.html.

Weiler, Kathleen. "Freire and a Feminist Pedagogy of Difference." *Harvard Educational Review* 61, no. 4 (1991): 449–74.

Weller, Christian E., and Jeffrey Thompson. *Wealth Inequality among Asian Americans Greater than among Whites*. Report. Center for American Progress, December 20, 2016. https://www.americanprogress.org/issues/race/reports/2016/12/20/295359/wealth-inequality-among-asian-americans-greater-than-among-whites/.

Welner, Kevin G. "The Dirty Dozen: How Charter Schools Influence Student Enrollment." *Teachers College Record*, May 5, 2013. http://www.tcrecord.org/Content.asp?ContentID=17104.

Wertsch, James V. *Vygotsky and the Social Formation of Mind*. Cambridge, MA: Harvard University Press, 1985.

Whelan, Luke. "Seattle Teacher Strike Is the Lates Front Line in America's Public School Wars: It's about Much More than a Wage Dispute." *Mother Jones*, September 15, 2015. http://www.motherjones.com/politics/2015/09/heres-why-seattle-teacheres-are-strike/.

Williams, Michelle. *The Roots of Participatory Democracy: Democratic Communists in South Africa and Kerala, India*. New York: Palgrave Macmillan, 2008.

Williams, R. *Marxism and Literature*. New York: Oxford University Press, 1977.

Willis, Paul. "Foot Soldiers of Modernity: The Dialectics of Cultural Consumption and the 21st-Century School." *Harvard Educational Review* 73, no. 3 (2003): 390–415.

———. *Learning to Labor: How Working-Class Kids Get Working-Class Jobs*. New York: Columbia University Press, 1977.

Wing, Nick. "When the Media Treats White Suspects and Killers Better than Black Victims." Black Voices, *Huffington Post*, August 14, 2014. http://www.huffingtonpost.com/2014/08/14/media-black-victims_n_5673291.html.

Wise, Tim. "With Friends like These, Who Needs Glenn Beck?: Racism and White Privilege on the Liberal-Left." Tim Wise, official website. August 17, 2010. http://www.timwise.org/2010/08/with-friends-like-these-who-needs-glenn-beck-racism-and-white-privilege-on-the-liberal-left/.

Wolff, Daniel. "Speculating on Education." *Counterpunch*, September 25, 2009. http://www.counterpunch.org/2009/09/25/speculating-on-education/.

Wong, Kenneth K., and Francis X. Shen. "When Mayors Lead Urban Schools: Assessing the Effects of Mayoral Takeovers." In *Besieged: School Boards and the Future of Education Politics*, edited by William G. Howell, 81–101. Washington, DC: Brookings Institutions Press, 2005.

Woods, Alan. "Chapter 2: The Early Dialecticians." *In Defence of Marxism*, July 9, 2006. Available at http://www.marxist.com/history-philosophy-dialectics-materialism/page-2.htm.

Woods, Alan, and Ted Grant. *Reason in Revolt: Dialectical Philosophy and Modern Science*. North American edition. Vol. 1. New York: Algora Publishing, 2002.

Wu, Huizhong. "The 'Model Minority' Myth: Why Asian-American Poverty Goes Unseen." *Mashable*, December 14, 2015. http://mashable.com/2015/12/14/asian-american-poverty/#_7xAoYLYigqs.

Yip, Steve. "Serve the People—Yesterday and Today: The Legacy of Wei Min She." In *Legacy to Liberation: Politics and Culture of Revolutionary Asian Pacific America*, edited by Fred Ho, 15–30. San Francisco: Big Red Media and AK Press, 2000.

Zeichner, Kenneth M., and Cesar Pena-Sandoval. "Venture Philanthropy and Teacher Education Policy in the U.S.: The Role of the New Schools Venture Fund." *Teachers College Record* 117, no. 6 (2015). http://www.tcrecord.org.

Zinn Education Project. "Zinn Education Project: Teaching a People's History." Zinn Education Project, 2017. https://zinnedproject.org.

Zinn, Howard. *A People's History of the United States: 1492–Present*. Rev. ed. New York: Harper Perennial, 1995.

Index

About the Author

Marc Studer

A former public high school teacher, Wayne Au is a Professor in the School of Educational Studies at the University of Washington Bothell, and he is an editor for the social justice teaching magazine and publisher, *Rethinking Schools*. His work focuses on critical education theory and practice, critical policy analysis, and teaching for social justice, where he has engaged in both academic and public scholarship about high-stakes testing, charter schools, and anti-racist education. A devoted father and partner, most recently Dr. Au has been working in the Seattle area to support Black Lives Matter in schools and the implementation of Ethnic Studies in the K-12 curriculum.

Dr. Au is also a widely published scholar whose works have appeared in *Teachers College Record*, the *Harvard Educational Review*, and *Educational Researcher*, among others. His recent books include *Mapping Corporate Education Reform* (coedited with Joseph J. Ferrare, Routledge 2015), *Reclaiming the Multicultural Roots of the U.S. Curriculum* (coauthored with Anthony Brown and Dolores Calderon, TC Press, 2016), and *Teaching for Black Lives* (co-edited with Dyan Watson and Jesse Hagopian, Rethinking Schools, 2018). In 2015 the Critical Educators for Social Justice group of American Educational Research Association recognized Dr. Au as a "distinguished scholar activist," and he won the William H. Watkins award for scholar activism from the Society of Professors of Education in 2017.